Master European Realists

of the Nineteenth Century

George J. Becker

FREDERICK UNGAR PUBLISHING CO.

NEW YORK

Copyright © 1982 by Frederick Ungar Publishing Co., Inc

Printed in the United States of America

Library of Congress Cataloging in Publication Data

Becker, George Joseph.
    Master European realists of the nineteenth century.

    Bibliography: p.
    Includes index.
    Contents: Precursors—Gustave Flaubert—Edmond
and Jules de Goncourt—[etc.]
    1. European literature—19th century—History and
criticism. 2. Realism in literature. I. Title.
PN761.B35   809'.912   81-70124
ISBN 0-8044-2046-7   AACR2

Contents

Clearly, then, it is no part of the storyteller's craft to describe only what is good or beautiful. Sometimes, of course, virtue will be his theme, but he may then make such play with it as he will. But he is just as likely to have been struck by numerous examples of vice and folly in the world around him, and about them he has exactly the same feelings as about the preeminently good deeds which he encounters: they are important and must all be garnered in. Thus anything whatsoever may become the subject of a novel, provided only that it happens in this mundane life and not in some fairyland beyond our human ken.

Lady Murasaki
The Tale of the Genji,
Modern Library, pp. 501–2

Foreword

Since I have had the temerity to offer an examination of seven major literary figures in one volume (not to mention a more casual glance at several others), I must attempt to blunt the protest that may be made. I do not deny for any of these writers the existence of other dimensions or the value of other approaches to their works. I have undertaken only to assess these authors as realists because I believe that needs to be done, inasmuch as, singly and together, they are major formulators of that mode in fiction. Though these writers belong to two different generations and to three different national cultures, I see each of them as learning by doing, as going through a process of experiment with new subject matter and new techniques under the impulsion of a body of ideas—a view of life—which was dominant in their time. To do this and stay within the bounds of what can be managed in a single volume I have had to take shortcuts, to omit aspects of a given author's works that provide no particular grist for this mill, to leave out in some instances a whole segment of a writer's *opus* because in it he had not yet come to the realistic mode or had already gone beyond it. I am not conscious of having rigged my demonstration by ignoring evidence inconvenient for my purpose, but that ultimately is for informed readers to decide.

Why these seven and no others as "master realists"? To a large extent, the final choice imposed itself. I was unable to agree with Harry Levin that Balzac and Stendhal belonged in this company, let alone Proust. Upon examination it became clear to me that Turgenev, whom I had expected to include in my collection, must also be placed in the category of incomplete or protorealists. To my surprise, Ibsen and Maupassant also had to be eliminated, the former because he was only incidentally a realist; the latter because he seems to me extremely limited, bound largely to a formula, shallow in his exploration of the human condition. The writers whom I regret having had to leave out are Eça de Queirós and Giovanni Verga. They are fresh and original writers, but it would do them a disservice to put them in this company.

It has seemed reasonable and necessary to assume that the reader will be familiar with the major works of most of these authors, which are part of the general literary heritage. Thus, I have avoided any summary of narrative content except in the cases of the Goncourts and of Galdós, where such an assumption is unfounded. The translations from French and Spanish of their works are my own. The translations from the Russian are the standard and generally accessible Constance Garnett versions unless otherwise indicated. There is a notable inconsistency in my handling of titles. I have left those of French and Spanish works in the original; fortunately most of them consist of proper names and present little difficulty. For Russian works I have used the English titles established long ago by Constance Garnett with a few minor exceptions. The transliteration of Russian names also presents some inconsistency. In general, I have followed the practice of the Library of Congress, but there are some deviations into established spelling that are more immediately intelligible phonetically than those used by the Library of Congress.

Special thanks are due to the Fulbright program for the grant that permitted me to study Spanish realism, particularly the novels of Galdós, in Madrid; to the staffs of the British Museum, the Bibliothèque Nationale, and the Biblioteca Nacional; and, of course, to the readers' services librarians of Swarthmore College and of Western Washington University.

George J. Becker

Bellingham, Washington
November, 1981

1

Precursors

Although the nineteenth century is the age of realism in European literature, it is also the century of romanticism and of nascent symbolism. As in any other era there exists a flux of literary movements and aspirations, a pointing forward and a looking back, a constant subjection to conflicting pressures of literary modes which, to a considerable degree, makes precise formulation of their principles and purposes difficult, if not impossible. When we look at this problem from the standpoint of the individual writer, we get a more immediate sense of the difficulty. For example, Flaubert, born in 1821, develops his literary sensibility under the luxuriant rays of the romantic sun; it is to be expected that he should first produce a work that can only be called romantic. When he turns away from this course, he cannot erase his intellectual nurture or recast his temperament by an act of will, though he can do much to keep these from interfering with achieving the new goals he has set. Similarly, to take a writer outside the argument of this book, a George Moore may for a while be caught up by the enthusiasms of a regnant naturalism, only after a time to desert that standard for a new one which is more congenial to his nature and more indicative of his aesthetic creed. How much Taine's *race* and *milieu* have to do with the development of

1

literary genius we must leave to the psychologists. That the *moment* is at least of equal importance is scarcely necessary of demonstration.

Thus we can see that it is most unlikely to find a complete realist, even at the flood tide of the movement, since a given writer is on the one hand pulled back by the literary allegiances of his youth and on the other may be drawn forward at the peak of his accomplishment into new ways, either because he finds these more congenial or because he desires to attempt something new. Since this is the case, it follows that even among those whom we may call the *master realists* there will be considerable irregularity of pattern. There will be broken allegiances. There will be, perhaps both before and after their realistic achievement, an emphasis that cannot properly be called by that name. Indeed, inasmuch as the idea of writing by formula is scarcely consonant with the ideal of literary innovation, we must expect irregularities, contradictions, and divagations even when an author is in full pursuit of realistic goals.

As I have argued elsewhere,[1] we can get a knowledge of what realism was only by induction, by an examination of the multitude of works that are called realistic. However, this induction must be carried out with caution, with a prudent regard for the statements of doctrine that have been made both by writers and critics. Otherwise, we may find ourselves in the unhappy position of having to base our generalization on a multitude of cases that are suspect; works, that out of ignorance, inertia, or embattled prejudice have been given that tag. We must, then, with whatever risk of being arbitrary and rigid is entailed, set up some criteria by which to judge the realism of a work. We must, however tentatively, sketch out a definition, or a description at least, of what realism in literature is. Such a definition, it has long seemed to me, must take into account three correlative elements, the subject matter presented, the manner in which that subject matter is handled, and the implicit or emergent (certainly rarely overt) philosophical position that is taken. All of these must be present in a truly realistic work, though their presence is not in itself a guarantee of complete or unflawed realism.

To begin with the most obvious element, that of subject matter, this is where realism began, in direct reaction to romantic fantasy and flight from everyday reality. The prevailing fiction of the early part of the century was set by preference in the far away and long ago. It sought the exotic for color, for heightened passion, for actions of magnitude. It avoided the observed and observable place precisely because honest observation would impede flights of the imagination by the weight of humdrum, sordid, and unidealized facts. The personages of such fiction were as exotic as their setting, simplified and inflated to an equal level of hyperbole. One result was that they were all very much alike underneath their various exotic costumes. After a while their adventures and trials began to pall, since all but the most benumbed addicts of this kind of fiction could recognize its basic monotony. The convention became empty and meaningless; there was no real point of attachment for readers of flesh and blood. It was at this point of satiation that Champfleury, the author of the first book on the subject, *Le Réalisme* (1857), called for a new direction for fiction, a fiction based on the choice of modern and popular subjects. A generation later Karl Bleibtreu, fighting the same kind of conventional anemia in Germany, put the goal in more provocative language, saying that by realism is to be understood "that direction of art which renounces all cloud-cuckoo-iands and does its best to keep to the ground of reality in its reflection of life."[2]

With a more sophisticated ambition than that summed up by Champfleury's simple formula, writers and critics came to see realism not merely as a coming down to earth from the clouds but as an acceptance of all the phenomena of earth as fit subjects for literature. What started as rebellion against monotony and narrowness took on the vigor of an aesthetic crusade. Hippolyte Taine espoused a comprehensive inquiry about human nature in all its variations and degenerations. Whereas such a program smacks of an all too evident scientism, its repercussions go beyond science and into the world of social laws and mores. As Zola put it, speaking specifically of naturalism, it is "equally the return to nature and to man; it is direct observation, exact anatomy, the acceptance of what is."[3]

Apposite to this formulation are two correlative elements. E. M. de Vogüé stated an obvious and important truth when he called realism "an art of observation rather than of imagination, one which boasts that it observes life as it is in its wholeness and complexity with the least possible prejudice on the part of the artist. It takes men under ordinary conditions, shows characters in the course of their everyday existence, average and changing."[4] More recently Mary Colum has stated this proposition in another way: ". . . realism may be described as the attempt to give a reproduction of life as actually lived by the average person, or by what, in the author's experience, is the average person. . . ."[5] These notions of the observed and the average are well summed up by William Dean Howells's phrase, "the realism of the commonplace," which led to Gamaliel Bradford's condescending summation of it as "the attempt to depict the world as the ordinary man sees it, the average, commonplace man."[6]

This, in turn, entails another new departure. To get at the average, the realistic writer tends to descend to the lower levels of society, to seek out the mode, the area of most frequent or widespread experience. Such a drift downward was inevitable because of the desire to counter vapid romantic idealizings with the realest real, with the greatest reality of the greatest number, based on the author's observation. For a time, middle-class material sufficed by contrast to that of a stereotyped aristocratic milieu. Zola, however, explored a lower level of experience at least half of the time, and this proletarian, or peasant stratum, having the additional advantage of novelty, was thoroughly exploited by late nineteenth-century writers. Gorky brought his readers to a still lower level, that of the classless and uprooted, an interest that has been picked up in the United States by such writers as Nelson Algren and Hubert Selby. However, since all societies provide some sort of social forms, such *déracinés,* though proper objects of realistic study, drop below the norm and risk becoming exotics in their own right. Statistically in the world at large the mode would fall in that human group who are continually on the verge of starvation, a condition characteristic of much of Asia, Africa, and Latin America. Since relatively little writing has sprung from those areas, in practice the mode for realists has lain at a somewhat higher level, one of economic insecurity but not starvation.

The main thing to bear in mind is that no area of human experience, esoteric or average, is closed to the realist, who has the right to depict that which he knows at first hand on the basis of careful and unbiased observation. Vast new domains have been appropriated to literature, not always to its advantage, since much of the writing has been pedestrian and scarcely above the level of inept sociological reports. Still, the gain in freshness and variety has been immeasurable. We might set a useful, if ultimately false, antithesis by suggesting that the older novel was mainly about love, whereas the realistic novel is about money. This at least suggests the descent from the rarefied to the down to earth, from aspiration to actuality. Average experience is bound up in millions of little niggling situations that grow out of material considerations running all the way from sluggishness of the bowels to preoccupation with how to pay the next installment on the television set. Certainly more of a man's experience is occupied by his job, the spending of money, and the pursuit of simple satisfactions than is devoted to intense, single-minded passion. To leave love, or venereal excitement, out of account would be to falsify in the opposite direction, but to diminish its importance, to deny it the role of chief energizing force in fiction has been surely to make a giant stride in the direction of truth.

It is when we come to the second main aspect of realism, the techniques by which these new materials are to be presented and the goal of truthful representation to be achieved, that the problem becomes complex. Here the doctrine of objectivity is all-important. Not only is realism an art of observation on the part of the author; it demands a similar stance from the reader. In other words, it seeks to have the data speak for themselves with a minimum of direction or interference. Much has been written to prove the impossibility of complete authorial objectivity. This, however, is largely beside the point. An early American critic's description, made without caviling, still stands as an excellent statement of this goal: ". . . realism stands without, not within; describes without evidence of personal sympathy; seldom indulges in exclamations, reflections, or sermons based upon the narratives which it offers; leaves the reader to draw his own conclusions concerning right and wrong; describes by implication, or minute rather than large characterization; is fond of petty details. . . ."⁷ The formula for realistic art is to see men and things exactly and dispassionately and to present them in that way. As Joseph Warren Beach puts it, the effort is "to present human nature objectively, to label it scientifically."⁸ Or in W. L. Courtney's succinct formula: "Realism means above all else a devotion to the bare and explicit truth of human life and human character, and the avoidance of all romantic or poetic devices for obscuring the main issues."⁹

As we shall see when we examine individual authors, a primary consideration is the stance that the narrator takes, what is technically called point of view. The ideal position for the realist is that of the completely withdrawn third-person narrator, one who may be unobtrusively omniscient or who may confine himself only to that which a ubiquitous observer might see. The main thing is for the narrative voice, a necessary evil, to refine itself to such impersonality as almost to cease to exist, with the result that the events of the narrative appear to be playing themselves out without the mediation of an observer. This is avowedly an illusion, but it is one that can be maintained if authorial withdrawal is truly practiced. Any self-consciousness, for example, about how fictional events can be known and attested, will disturb the air of objectivity by reminding the reader that there is an authorial voice after all.

A related problem is the kind of action and the kind of

characters the novelist chooses. Traditional fabulation is emphatic; it heightens by a variety of means. Realistic writing, on the other hand, by its choice of material alone achieves some deemphasis. Such underplaying must be supported by appropriate techniques; otherwise there will be a gigantism or sensationalism of the commonplace. We may first consider the use of a single life as subject, remembering that it will have been chosen not because of its singularity but because it is representative. Honest observation will preclude selection of only the peaks of existence; in fact, it will preclude finding much in the way of peaks. Seismic upheavals, catastrophic consequences are not for the realist. He is tied to the humdrum and repetitive, to a slow erosion of body and soul rather than to dramatic loss of fortune and change of direction.

All this leads one to the conclusion that it is dangerous to rest a case on the single instance, even though virtually all realists have done so at one time or another. When there is a single figure it is easy for readers to seize upon some aspects of the portrait and ignore others, thereby wresting the statement from its representative base. The way around this problem is not far to seek and was early discovered. It lies in the use of the cross section, which is partly implied by the term "slice of life," though it takes in more than that phrase covers. The cross section has two important uses that are interrelated. It provides a gamut of personalities and situations that, to the extent that they are subject to the same causal influences, give the illusion of an adequate induction. Moreover, by a spread of emphasis, such an approach reduces the importance of the single protagonist, who by definition is too salient a figure for a realistic work. Perhaps the most convincing gamuts are those to be found in works that really present a *group* or *mass* protagonist. A well-known example is John Steinbeck's novel *The Grapes of Wrath,* about which there have been some interesting differences of opinion because of uncertainty as to who the protagonist is. The answer is that it is the Joad family, representing the great mass of the dispossessed, expanded, however, to include such a special figure as Casy the preacher. War novels frequently make use of a natural but miscellaneous, and therefore representative, unit such as a squad or platoon, which is certainly more acceptable than John Dos Passos' titular three soldiers.

An important technical step is a deliberate lack of resolution as the novel or play ends. It is not enough to invoke T. S. Eliot's "not with a bang but a whimper" as apposite here, though the whimper, the unaccented beat, is certainly preferable to a fully orchestrated coda of recapitulative completeness. What logical stopping place is there for a realistic action? When boy gets girl? When scientist wins the Nobel Prize? When political aspirant is elected to office? Such a success-story-ending format implies completion, finality, and this is what a realistic reading of experience generally denies—except for the finality of death. Thus, the realist is increasingly wary of beginnings and endings. What he wants is middle, a representative portion of an action carried out long enough for it to convey its own nature, its own truth. There is no need in final chapter or epilogue to project forward in time, winding up the actions that have been followed. The outcomes of such actions are best inferred from them, and a forward-looking tableau at the end is so much sentimental superfluity.

The tendency of realistic works toward dramatic form is one that we examine with a good deal of interest and with varying conclusions as we discuss the writers singled out for study in this volume. Diminished narrative framework is one part of this tendency toward dramatic form; density and frequency of dialogue is another. However, to let a narrative be carried by dialogue alone is to commit oneself to *longueurs* at which even the most convinced realist must balk. The solution is usually a compromise, a mixture of narrative and of dramatic scene, moving as time goes on to a preponderance of the latter, as writers and readers alike accept the idea that a work can speak for itself with a minimum of explanation. This tendency automatically entails an effort toward accurate representation of speech. Phonography is linked to photography as part of realistic method. What the realist needs to do is to convey the flavor of vernacular speech, of the repetitive banality of much of human utterance, without becoming unintelligible to most readers or drowning them in a bath of verbal stupidity.

Finally the realist must avoid the vast armory of rhetorical means for tipping the scales of the reader's judgment. An obvious minor device is the tag name. It is too contrived to have characters named Jack Burden or Joanna Burden in novels about guilt. The same problem exists with symbolic situations, though these are harder to avoid. At least a realistic writer can avoid having as a character a sacrificial victim who is thirty-three years old and has a foster father, or a young girl who out of piety toward the dead defies her uncle and refuses to adhere to patterns of conventional behavior. The pitfalls of rhetoric are many and subtle. Irony and burlesque are obvious interventions, as is fine writing generally. The whole area of style was one of the most difficult for the realist to handle, especially in an age that had inherited the idea that flowery, impassioned language was the necessary vesture of literature. Stendhal's ideal of the "court record" style sums up the new stylistic goal, though not necessarily the means by which to reach it.

When we turn to the third major aspect of realism, its philosophical basis, we become involved in paradox. It is a fundamental tenet that the realist is one who depicts human experience without an *a priori* position. How then can the realist be said to have a philosophical position? No doubt the answer must be that his view of the world does rest on certain broad assumptions without which he would not be a realist. He believes in a general way in the primacy of the material data of life and the causality that they exercise. He sees men as very much a part of the physical universe, more complex than others of its creatures but not essentially different from them, above all subject to the same laws as they. His is a world of observed data; he tends to ignore those constructs that are called supernatural, because to be *above nature* is to be *outside nature,* and therefore not to be at all. Such beliefs in the realist's opinion are the product of either ignorance or folly, and he will have none of them.

The annals of nineteenth-century literature are very instructive on this point. Again and again we encounter an opposition of the *ideal* and the *real*. This becomes a metaphysical as well as an aesthetic controversy, and in the long run it is the metaphysical considerations that are basic. Realists have long been assailed for their lack of metaphysical subtlety; they are what the philosophers call "naive realists." Whereas the term is decidedly derogatory, and is intended to be so, to use it does not dispose of the problem. If the realist does not know exactly what reality is, he certainly has a conviction about what it is not. It is not some absolute essence or perfection that has existed for all time in crystalline purity beneath or beyond or above the crude and deceptive vesture of phenomena. In summary, the realist denies the whole idealistic metaphysic of the romantic age (as well as the Platonic *idea)* and places his belief in something more immediately apprehensible by the senses. The realist believes that the physical properties of things have existence and continuity outside of perception, and he believes, making allowance for certain abnormalities, that all perceivers will perceive pretty much the same thing.

In general, it is on this common-sense view that our attitudes and values have been based for over a century, even though in fact it no longer jibes with the formulations of modern physics. Certainly, philosophical realism and literary realism are parallel, and the latter is ultimately dependent on the former. In short, we may say that the realists have in common a vigorous faith in the findings of the natural sciences and a disposition to ignore or discount traditional beliefs that are at odds with those findings. Some realists are more explicit than others about their beliefs; the clearest test of their position is not so much what they *say* about it as in the conditions and forces that they *show* controlling human destiny. Emphasis on causality may vary with the shifting emphasis of doctrine, but the causes must be natural causes if the work is to be realistic.

Realists are not necessarily naturalists, though they must share in the basic tenets of the latter school. The difference is largely one of emphasis and explicitness. Realists must share in the materialistic determinism of naturalism, but they may give more latitude to causality, especially as psychological forces come to be recognized. They are also less rigid in defining the animality of man, feeling no obligation to present him metaphorically in terms of "lower" species. Probably the most important difference is that realists do not insist as absolutely on pessimism as do their naturalist brethren. They do recognize that like all organisms the human organism does go downhill to physical decline and death. That is incontrovertible fact. Since it is fact, there is little point in qualifying it as failure, yet that is the tone of the naturalist demonstrations, in which all too often the prospect of a sorry end is allowed to overshadow the incidental joys of being alive.

Another way of looking at the philosophical orientation is to consider the mind-body problem. Because the idealists made excessive claims for the power of mind or spirit, the realists in their reaction inevitably attempted to redress the balance by a strong bias toward the primacy of physical process, often to the virtual exclusion of mind as a meaningful part of experience. However, in the long run the realist must ultimately fall back on the findings of science, rather than his own predilections, in this disputed area. He cannot deny the existence of mind merely because it suits his prejudice to do so. In general, it can be said that many early realists, under the dominance of a strict materialism, eliminated mind to as great an extent as possible, but that fairly soon, caught up by the evidence of their own untruthfulness, they were led to portray the effect, if not the efficacy, of the mental process. To the extent, however, that some writers went to the opposite extreme and concentrated on mind to the exclusion of matter, they failed in their aim as realists. Proust, though no realist in any basic sense, did not commit this error. His novel is grounded in physical and social fact to a degree that his adulators have not always been willing to concede.

All three of these broad areas of realistic interest and emphasis are simultaneously present in the work of the great realists, though in varying degrees. It is clearly not enough to use realistic materials, for without realistic technique those materials may be badly bowdlerized. Conversely, if such techniques are applied to nonrealistic materials we will get only a specious simulacrum of reality. Finally, neither such materials nor such techniques can be used effectively in a philosophical climate of supernaturalism, mysticism, or wishful thinking, one that is not soundly based on observation and therefore tightly controlled by dispassionate analysis and understanding of the causal patterns of the natural world. Above all we must bear in mind that the realistic work teaches more than it delights. But it is not a forum for special pleading. It shows and stops there. The reader—the experienced reader—must do the rest.

With these observations in mind we can now turn to several of the chief novelists of the early part of the nineteenth century who have often been called realistic and try to determine the extent of their participation in the movement. The useful figures for this purpose are four, chosen partly because of their reputation, and partly because of their influence. Balzac, Stendhal, Gogol, and Turgenev were certainly in varying degrees looking and working forward to what the later realists succeeded in doing in fiction. These men were important novelists in their own right; their works stand on their own feet. It is conceivable that to some they are more aesthetically acceptable than those of their orthodoxly realistic successors. But these writers were not full-fledged realists, and that is what matters in this context. In what follows I have no intention of criticizing them for their failure to measure up to an arbitrary standard, but a demonstration of where they fell short of, or departed from, the major canons of realistic writing as described and substantiated at length hereafter will illustrate the mode in a concrete way.

To begin, it is necessary to point out that all of these writers were installed as ancestors by their successors. This is less an act of natural piety than it is one of self-legitimatization. Whatever the hostility or indifference these early writers may have encountered, it was as nothing compared with the outcry that greeted the later realists. Moreover, these predecessors may be said ultimately to have won acceptance because of those elements that in one way or another attentuated their realism. Thus it is not surprising that Zola and Dostoevsky in particular, since they were the most embattled innovators in the second half of the century, should invoke the partially canonized shades of Balzac and Gogol as having already done what they were setting out to do. This was not a conscious dishonesty; rather it was an effort to create a realistic tradition, a sense of continuity, which would make their own works more acceptable because they were less revolutionary. Such an attitude is not without its internal contradictions, since both Zola and Dostoevsky prided themselves on their originality. Still, in the lonely position of trailblazers, it is likely that on occasion they sought comfort in lineage and respectability by linking themselves with putative ancestors who had achieved respectability.

The figure who loomed largest among these early novelists, and who still looms very large today (though the *cognoscenti* have now for a couple of generations given the palm to Stendhal), was the legendary Balzac, who died in 1850. The high reputation as a realist that Balzac still holds almost a century and a half after his death may owe more to the repetition of critical commonplaces than to informed reexamination of his work. In particular it is the famous preface to *La Comédie Humaine* that has been taken as a realistic pronunciamento; however, even if it were, the novels would not substantiate this claim for realism.

The first point that Balzac makes in his preface is a comparison between humanity and animality, stating that "There is but one Animal," since the Creator used a single pattern for all organized beings. This basic animal takes its variations in form from the environment in which it is obliged to develop. By an extension of this comparison, society is to be seen as resembling nature, producing social species comparable to zoological species. There is, however, one important difference. Society is more varied than nature and has freaks that nature does not allow herself. In other words, society is actually a more varied and complex matrix than nature. This statement is evidence of a decided scientism and is thus allied with the attitudes of the later realists.

To seek out and illuminate the great variety of social species is not enough for Balzac. He seeks to be a social historian, pointing out with some justice that the most famous novelists previously had spent their talent in producing a few typical figures, in describing a limited part of life. He seeks to be "only the secretary" who will set down the lineaments of French society in the hope of writing a true social history, a documentary work that will reveal the true nature of the times. Balzac is not, however, content to be merely "an archeologist of social furniture, a cataloguer of professions, a registrar of good and evil." He wants to seek out the causes of these phenomena, reflecting on first principles and seeking to discover in what particulars societies approach or deviate from "the eternal laws of truth and beauty." Balzac has already committed himself to the principles of Catholicism and Monarchy, which he extols as the most conducive to social order. In short, his approach is not really empirical, since he comes to an examination of society with a body of firmly established values.

As a novelist Balzac also leaves something to be desired. In spite of the impact that his various *character-types* made on his and succeeding generations, we must question whether character drawing and analysis was really his forte. Balzac's characters are on the whole static, puppets controlled by a single string. They are very classical in their being, though they are set against a new and minutely observed background. Whatever its deficiencies, however, this characterization is in line with new currents of thought. As Dargan and Weinberg say, "At the basis of his scheme lies a deterministic, scientific view founded on his theory that environment, trades, and professions divide men, so to speak, into social species comparable to the classifications of the zoological world."[10]

Where Balzac is great, and unique for his time, is in the completeness and solidity of his setting, of the topographical and social background. Perhaps there is a bit of nostalgia operative here. In a changing Paris (and France), where physical landmarks were going down day by day, Balzac manifests a passionate desire to fix forever the location and appearance of every street and every building. The cumulative effect of this solid and detailed depiction is almost overpowering. Paris receives the bulk of this topographical documentation and is re-created with stunning exactitude as we move through the many novels by Balzac that have their setting there, but we get the same effect in little for Tours, Saumur, Issoudun, and other provincial towns that provide the background for other major novels.

Having said this much in praise of Balzac's realism—which surely made an impression on his successors and provided a sound foundation for the nineteenth-century realistic novel—we must look at his weaknesses and outright incapacities, which stem from two sources. One is a choice of the sensational and spectacular for his actions; the other is a constant and vivacious authorial presence. These two tendencies work against the realistic power of the details and force us, even as we become immersed in the novels, to withdraw and look upon them as highly personal artifice. To put the case more strongly, we can say that although Balzac is brilliant in his insistence on using new material, he does not know what to do with this material when it comes to conducting narrative action. Balzac seems fated after his long, rich expositions to undermine their veracity by the use of trite and exaggerated plots. His helplessness in the conduct of narrative action is frequently made evident by his return at intervals to more exposition, description of a new setting, or an account of the antecedents of a new character. Where there is an elaborated action, it almost always develops in the direction of melodrama. This is the most salient feature of Balzac's irrealism. In spite of his phenomenal grasp of many of the data of everyday life, in spite of his insistence on money and power as the mainsprings of his society, in spite of his emphasis on venality as the normal state of the human soul, Balzac insists on showing these elements writ large, in the form of sensational headlines, so to speak.

Yet we must not be too severe with Balzac. He is impressed by the fact of changing social forms, by the unleashing of energies on the part of the previously subordinated and docile lower class. Perhaps more than any of the other figures presented in this volume Balzac is aware of social process and seeks to set forth its dynamics. This accounts for the remarkable contemporaneity of even those novels whose events occurred early in the century. But Balzac is not a detached observer. He is partisan, a vehement antagonist, not so much of change, which he cannot arrest, as of the values and attitudes that change brings. It is abundantly evident that Balzac is Catholic and royalist, that he believes in the superiority of the social stratification that preceded the convulsions of political and industrial revolution, that he condemns, if not repudiates, the new emerging society.

Yet this is not the whole story; there is a subtle ambivalence in Balzac. Even though he examines the present in order to praise the past, he does a kind of homage to the present by his absorbed charting of the dynamic process that contradicts the static ideal to which he gives formal adherence. Balzac is fascinated by *arrivistes,* even though he is repelled by them. It is into them that he pours his greatest creative energies. What he shows us is not far from a Darwinian struggle for survival; his characters at best win only a temporary surcease from, or staying of, inevitable decline. Thus, there is considerable continuity from Balzac's characters to those of Zola—the members of the Rougon-Macquart family in particular—as they pit themselves against the adverse forces of their physical and social environment. It is not at all certain that Zola's overall depiction probes any deeper than Balzac's, but he does handle his actions more successfully and avoids at least some of Balzac's gigantism. He achieves a cannier sense of the interplay of material circumstance and individual situation, and he keeps out of the way of his demonstration, thanks no doubt to the intervening examples of Flaubert and the Goncourts.

We need make no such extensive commentary on the achievement and influence of Stendhal, who died in 1842 and whose fame had to wait until the twentieth century. His great achievement was a deflation of romantic notions of character and behavior, and to a degree of rhetoric. There is something recognizably modern about Stendhal's chief exhibits, Julien Sorel, Lucien Leuwen, and Fabrice del Dongo, in their expenditure of energy and in their failure as they butt their heads against the stone walls of adverse causality. Yet the approach of this author is basically deductive. He begins with a premise about the impossibility of achieving happiness and proceeds in the major novels to substantiate this belief by exhibiting a peasant, a member of the middle class, and an aristocrat learning through their failures that egoism rules the world and that human effort is futile.

One consequence of this single-track demonstration is that Stendhal does not depend greatly on documentation, on *les petits faits vrais* that he extols. The pattern of events is the important thing. In an incomplete work like *Lucien Leuwen* one feels a certain irritation over the lack of substantiation by means of detail. For example, there is virtually none of Balzac's topographical particularity. Besançon in *Le Rouge et le Noir* is like Nancy in *Lucien Leuwen,* and both are indistinguishable from Stendhal's native Grenoble. *La Chartreuse de Parme* has more abundant detail because of the demands of the action, but it is clearly not Parma or any other place in particular, the court and castle-prison being generic, not individualized. Even the famous Waterloo episode is vague and imprecise. It is easy to see that Stendhal has moved his action from the physically particularized locale to the generalized arena of social intercourse, that he has universalized rather than made concrete, that he is not interested in specifically individual actions and situations.

The actions of these novels are hyperbolic. The most nearly down to earth is that of Julien Sorel, but his translation from peasant household to tutor to invaluable assistant for a nobleman would tax credulity if the reader saw it as more than a device on which to hang the moral of the tale. There is in *Lucien Leuwen* a good representation of the fatuity of life in a garrison town, but we get a much less credible or restrained account of how politics works in Lucien's forays into grass-roots politics or in his father's intrigues in the Chamber of Deputies and among the ministers. *La Chartreuse de Parme* is charming in its absurdity. More cerebral than Graustark or Zenda, it is still a comic-opera world in which the most bizarre events take place, where alarums and excursions are commonplace. (This, oddly enough, in spite of the fact that Stendhal patterned the action of the novel after the events of one of the *chroniques italiennes* he had found in Rome. This account from the fifteenth century, called *Origine delle Grandezze della Famiglia Farnese,* even provides the name of Clelia for Fabrice's loved one. To transplant a fifteenth-century tale into the nineteenth century is certainly to show little concern for specific actuality and to demonstrate a taste not merely for the universal but for the picturesque.)

Yet there were things to be learned from Stendhal by the later realists—if they read him. Already we find a hatred of the bourgeois world for the barriers it puts in the way of the superior man and for the tawdriness of its ideals, an attitude closely allied with the vision of later writers like Flaubert. There is a sense of the illogical complexity of human emotions, of the simultaneous presence of antithetical elements, of baseness and sublimity, not unlike what Dostoevsky would show, though much less penetrating. Above all, there is a new soberness of language, in the narration itself though not in the dialogue. It is clearly the beginning of a reportorial language. It is this innovation that has been of particular impact on twentieth-century realists.

The presence of Gogol among the protorealists seems to be a case of misapprehension. Anyone coming to him today, in the perspective of more than a century of realistic writing, will find it impossible to place Gogol in the movement. It was apparently the critic Belinsky, who, needing an example of literature based on the common people, cited Gogol as fulfilling that need. Though Dostoevsky's oft-quoted statement: "We all came out from under Gogol's Overcoat," is probably apocryphal, it attests again to the need felt for respectable ancestors. In fact, in Russia a better ancestor would have been Pushkin, who, in spite of his adaptation of many of the strains of Western European romanticism, had also a sober, detached capacity for observation.

Gogol's works did provide certain popular objects of observation raised to the level of the grotesque and therefore skewed away from realistic accuracy. He turned in *The Overcoat, The Inspector General,* and *Dead Souls* to contemporary, humdrum life. Gogol looked at people and situations from a skeptical, matter-of-fact point of view and broke stereotypes. But his effect in all three cases is one of caricature, an application to realistic materials of the technique employed in such an obviously absurd piece as "The Nose." The line to be drawn between satire or caricature and careful documentary, which by its accuracy and weight produces a condemnation of social situations, is not always an easy one to discover if the critic is more concerned about social criticism than he is about realistic accuracy. It is here that critical confusion about Gogol has its source, a confusion between strictly realistic depiction, which is sometimes allied to social criticism, and the direct assault through satire. *Dead Souls,* for example, is not a documented examination of the condition of serfdom; it is a work that by its zany, incredible devices points up the absurdity, if not the horror, of such a condition. The grotesquerie of Gogol is uniquely his own; his literary purposes are, however, traditional. To call him a realist because he uses ordinary materials from everyday life is to ignore completely the vital part that technique has to play in ensuring the accuracy of the depiction.

The reputation of Ivan Turgenev as a realist, and generally as a novelist, was much greater eighty or ninety years ago than it is today. In his pioneer study of the Russian novel, Count de Vogüé saw Turgenev as equal in power to Tolstoy and Dostoevsky. Henry James considered him one of the most important novelists of the century. Yet in his *Introduction to Russian Realism* (1965), Ernest J. Simmons does not even consider Turgenev, though he does include Gogol. This subsidence in reputation is important for our discussion, providing at least superficial evidence that Turgenev shared in the impetus of the developing realistic movement without seeking or achieving a full-fledged realism.

Of his Russian contemporaries it was Tolstoy whom Turgenev revered the most, in spite of a prolonged personal estrangement. As early as October 1852, Turgenev recognized Tolstoy's talent from reading *Childhood,* and in 1855, he was rapturous over *Sevastopol.* Years later he said of *The Cossacks* that the more he read it the more convinced he was that it was Tolstoy's masterpiece and the masterpiece of all Russian literature. However, Turgenev was candidly critical of another side of Tolstoy, his didactic side. Turgenev did not like *Anna Karenina* because Tolstoy had crawled into "the Moscow swamp" of "orthodoxy, nobles, Slavophilism . . . sour cabbage soup, and the absence of soap—in a word, chaos."[11] It would seem that Turgenev was undoubtedly objecting less to the novel than to the Russia which it portrayed, but clearly the darker tone of *Anna Karenina* was less acceptable to him than the sunlight of Tolstoy's earlier works. Turgenev's attitude toward Dostoevsky was much more hostile; he wrote of the latter's *A Raw Youth:* "God, what a taste of sourness and what a hospital stench it has—and also mumblings and ignorant psychological tinkering which no one needs!"[12]

The limits to what Turgenev would accept for representation in fiction are even more evident in his response to the writings of his French contemporaries. Loyal to them as a friend, Turgenev had serious misgivings about their art, though this did not deter him from attempting to make them known abroad. He was able, for example, to speak of Zola's fairly mediocre *Son Excellence Eugène Rougon* as "a wonderful book," and to go all out in praise of the nonrealistic *La Faute de l'Abbé Mouret,* but when it came to *L'Assommoir,* the first novel in which Zola showed the full force of his realism, Turgenev called it "a completely confused book," protesting among other things against the use of the word *merde* "en toutes lettres." Yet he was able to take Maupassant in stride, a few months before his death calling Maupassant "undoubtedly the most talented of all contemporary French writers." "Nothing like it *[Une Vie]* has appeared since *Madame Bovary.*"[13]

These critical responses help us to define Turgenev's own attitudes and practice. His was a diminishing involvement in realism in spite of his twenty-year-old association with the major French writers and his close, if embattled, relations with his Russian contemporaries. All of these novelists speedily went beyond what Turgenev was willing to provide as a mirror of reality, so that he soon came to appear limited and old-fashioned to the new generation.

Authorial withdrawal is Turgenev's greatest virtue and the source of his influence on other novelists. He did strive for objective representation; he did write about what he knew; and he was not notional or personal in his narration. He made no concession to the idea that the good should be triumphant, though it must be conceded that he did idealize the Russian gentlewoman. His one distinctive quality was a sensibility that responds lyrically to natural beauty, but this lyrical strain was confined to the setting; no attempt was made to extend it to human beings or to use it in ironic contrast with the debased condition of human beings.

In developing his novels Turgenev found it impossible to get away from a love story, and a rather anemic one at that. Such actions are used as a means of showing important characteristics of the Russian mentality, but they are not equal to that burden and amount to a faded stereotype of sentimental cast. The reader finds it hard to believe that even in the unenergetic, boring atmosphere of the country estate love is all that occupies the minds of men and women. It is for this reason that *Fathers and Sons* is more effective than Turgenev's other novels. Its love intrigues are not stereotyped; the love affair between Bazarov and Madame Odintsov helps to define one side of his nature; and even Arkady's speedy succumbing to Katya's charms is a means of indicating the conventionality that underlies his conventional revolt. On the whole, however, we are bound to conclude that Turgenev did not have much narrative range, that he did not see a story in the mundane events that became grist for the realistic mill.

Another serious fault is the tendency of Turgenev's later novels to subordinate narrative to program or thesis, which in turn compounds the inadequacy of the love story as narrative vehicle. During the years in which Turgenev was writing there was a disposition in Russia to use fiction as a means to raise and explore political questions. Two late novels, *Smoke* (1867) and *Virgin Soil* (1876), are proof of this tendency. In the former the author uses a foreign setting to show the inadequacy of the Russians and their need to learn from the West. In defense of the latter novel, which was strongly attacked, Turgenev said in a letter that his purpose was "to take young people who, for the most part, are good and honest and show that despite their honesty their very cause is so false and impractical that it cannot fail to lead them to complete fiasco."[14] This defense and the criticism that provoked it are evidence that Turgenev turned his later works into tracts for the times, only thinly disguised and thinly developed as narrative.

By reason of its relative objectivity, *Fathers and Sons* (1861) is the most successful of Turgenev's novels, though it too provoked a storm of criticism. It is a close study of a new type, the emergent man of science who has cut loose from traditional values, as is necessary, but has not found much in the way of clearly defined new values to sustain him in his independence. In contrast are the traditional attitudes of the old regime represented by Pavel Petrovich and of simple desire for bourgeois creature comfort represented by Nikolai Petrovich, the father of Bazarov's friend Arkady. What is remarkable about this presentation is that no one comes off very well, that there is a considerable recognition of good and enduring qualities in the incompetent, just as there is recognition of the blind spots and incapacities of the generally competent Bazarov. Turgenev's objectivity here functions at its best, except for the authorial intrusion in the half-comforting final passage, which is so out of key with the rest of the novel.

When all is said and done, of all Turgenev's writings it is *A*

Sportsman's Sketches that comes the closest to a realistic goal. But this work is not a novel. It contains no narrative framework other than the presence of a peripatetic sportsman. Even the individual sketches are descriptive rather than narrative–reportorial, if one can stretch the term that far. Here collectively we have what Turgenev denies us in his novels: a rich cross section of country types who are individuals first and are not stretched thin to become universals. The balance of social levels is beautifully maintained. The rulers are shown in their slothfulness, their rustic boredom, their financial incapacity, and their insensitiveness to the suffering of others. The lowly beings, serfs or others, are presented with equal justice. Some of them manage an adequate adaptation to their disadvantaged situation; some rail against it; some sink like stones without a cry. Without undue emphasis, absolutely without intrusive commentary, the author here achieves what it should be the goal of any realistic writer to provide: a clear, honest, undistorted picture that will produce its own effect without schematic pressure or overt authorial direction. Of all Turgenev's works this is the one that pointed most surely toward the future.

It is of importance to note that none of these four protorealists was overtly committed to the materialist vision of developing nineteenth-century science, although Balzac seemed at times to be carrying on a flirtation with it. This may ultimately be the reason why they did not, or could not, go the whole distance as realists. Certainly they had in common an interest in modern subjects and came much closer than most of their predecessors in holding up a mirror to the actual situations in which people lived. They were less uniform in their interest in popular subjects, though all of them except Stendhal made some effort in that direction. Where they were retrograde was in the choice of actions that did not reflect ordinary life and in an approach that fell short of dispassionate examination of contemporary life. Balzac went overboard in the direction of melodrama. Stendhal was deductive in his approach. Gogol inclined to the traditional forms of satire and the grotesque. Turgenev was in too much of his work a presenter and defender of theses. And to add one name that often received enthusiastic mention by novelists later in the century, Dickens, though definitely using the modern and the popular, skewed them in the interest of sentiment. To cite these limitations, to indicate the pitfalls in the way of writing true as the later realists understood it, is not to condemn these writers unduly, but merely to put them in their proper place in the continuum of nineteenth-century literature. Realism certainly developed faster because of their pioneer efforts and, on the whole, cannot be said to have suffered from the imperfection of their examples.

2

Gustave Flaubert

The two worlds of Gustave Flaubert's literary creation are as much a critical commonplace as are the two personalities that are asserted to have been at war within his being. This double ambivalence has contributed heavily to the confusion as to what, precisely, was realistic about his writing, and it has led to some extravagant conclusions: Since *Madame Bovary* is a realistic work, the succeeding novel, *Salammbô,* though a novel of historical reconstruction, must be realistic also, and once that leap is made, it is only a step to the assertion that *La Tentation de Saint Antoine* must somehow exhibit realistic qualities as well. Contrariwise, since these latter works are lyrical, it is tempting to assert that *Madame Bovary* and *l'Education Sentimentale* are also *cris de coeur* and that the case for Flaubert's realism is untenable. Since the author has told us that he was inhabited by two personalities, one which loved to dig and wallow in the dirt, another which sought to wing aloft on the plane of the Ideal, it is perhaps inevitable that some critics have not scrupled to give full preference to whichever personality suits their literary predilections as the essential Flaubert.

The way out of this confusion is relatively straightforward

and is, in addition, instructive for the study of literary realism. The first step is, if possible, to avoid the temptation to discuss works of literature primarily as biography—though this is not to deny the interest of such an effort as a nonliterary and speculative activity. The formation of an author is necessarily the result of his experience, and his works inevitably draw upon that experience in some way. But it seems unimportant that the life of Frédéric Moreau contains many points of similarity with that of the author, just as the outburst, "Madame Bovary, c'est moi!" can by no means be taken as a literal key to the novel in question. Faithfulness to the facts of experience does not preclude a certain complexity of representation of character and scene in which many specifically observed elements are merged into a single depiction. If this were not so, realistic writing could never rise above the level of authenticated anecdote.

At the appropriate point we pay some attention to Flaubert's statements about his works and his intentions, about his literary principles and practice, but the definitive evidence lies in the works themselves, about which there may be disagreement and controversy, but beyond which there is no court of appeal. The facts in Flaubert's case are simple. He wrote four works that have to do with observable, everyday life; he wrote four others that are evocations of the far away and long ago. We may lament the one achievement or the other, but we have no choice but to accept it, making the obvious comment that an author born in France in 1821 was likely in his youth to have accepted romantic models and might easily be expected on occasion to revert to that way of writing. What is surprising, and proof of Flaubert's powerful originality, is that he should have attempted to break away from the models of his youth and that by his success in doing so he should have become, to whatever extent we may determine, one of the great innovators in a new kind of fiction. To ignore works that belong to the romantic category of fiction is not unduly to disparage them. But our task here is to consider Flaubert's realistic works in terms of subject matter, method, and implicit philosophy so as to determine what is to be found there as an example for later writers and as a challenge forcing the reeducation of readers.

Flaubert's formula, "Yvetot donc vaut Constantinople," is our springboard into his world. The meaning of the first term is as plain as that of the second: Yvetot stands for the ordinary, humdrum, everyday life lived by most people (with a bow to the author's native Normandy). It also stands for that which is accessible to observation. Superficially, Flaubert was precipitated into this world by accident when his friends Bouilhet and Du Camp rejected the first version of *La Tentation de Saint Antoine,* urging Flaubert to take "a down-to-earth subject, one of those incidents of which bourgeois life is full, something like Balzac's *La Cousine Bette* or *Le Cousin Pons."* Whether joyfully or not, Flaubert came to recognize the novelty and challenge of such new material, writing to Louise Colet on February 8, 1852: "I am in a completely different world now, that of attentive observation of the dullest details. My eyes are fixed on the spores of mildew growing on the soul. It is a long way from there to the mythological and theological pyrotechnics of *Saint Antoine.* And just as the subject is different, so do I write in an entirely different manner. In my book I do not want there to be a *single* movement, or a *single* reflection of the author." In a letter of November 6, 1853, Flaubert writes Colet in hortatory tone: "Let us absorb the objective; let it circulate in us, until it is externalized in such a way that no one can understand that marvelous chemistry. . . . Let us be magnifying mirrors of external truth." After completing *Madame Bovary,* however, he recants, or at least qualifies his enthusiasm for this kind of material, writing to Laurent-Pichat on October 2, 1856 (the first installment of the novel had appeared in *La Revue de Paris* the previous day):

> Don't you believe that this ignoble reality, the depiction of which disgusts you, also sickens my heart to an equal extent? If you knew me better, you would know that I execrate ordinary life. I have

always withdrawn from it as much as I could. But aesthetically I
wanted, this time, and only this time, to get hold of it to the very
bottom. Thus I have undertaken it in an heroic manner—by that I
mean minute, meticulous—accepting everything, saying everything, depicting everything—a most ambitious statement.

Whatever his misgivings or repugnance, Flaubert came back to
such material periodically throughout his life after his excursions to "Constantinople," which he failed to make worth as
much as "Yvetot."

Of the major realists, Flaubert probably has the narrowest
range of subject matter (Ibsen and Maupassant are his chief
rivals in this respect). He confines himself with one exception to
a very limited area of provincial life, mostly in Normandy.
Madame Bovary shows the two small towns of Tostes and
Yonville-l'Abbaye, with an opening on the horizon to Rouen,
which is not different from them in any significant respect. *Un
Coeur Simple* is laid in the small town of Pont-l'Evêque,
whereas *Bouvard et Pécuchet*, after preliminaries in Paris, uses a
Norman farming community as its scene. *L'Education Sentimentale* reproduces a similar milieu in that part of the action
that takes place at Nogent (southeast of Paris), but it does for
the most part deal with the provincial in Paris, in the manner of
Balzac. This latter novel definitely widens the social spectrum
by giving us the world of business, of polite society, and of
bohemian arts and politics. This is by no means the limits of the
world Flaubert knew (after all he was invited to Compiègne by
the emperor), but in his fiction he is content to show the
bourgeoisie and rarely drops into the world of the laboring
class. Félicité in *Un Coeur Simple* is an integral part of the
eminently bourgeois Aubain household and takes her being
from it.

More important than these social and geographical boundaries are the moral and intellectual ones. His characters are
tightly enclosed in a circle of "received ideas"; they live and die
on a diet of the commonplace. Of all Flaubert's works *Madame*

Bovary is the one that is most clearly characterized by this prevailing mediocrity, a fact which provoked Sainte-Beuve's complaint that "the good is too much absent," by which he meant that no one is raised above the dead level of the commonplace.[1] It is true that some of the characters *aspire,* but we cannot ignore the hackneyed nature of their aspiration. It is absurd where it is not sinister, as in the case of Homais, or self-deluding, as in the case of Emma.

Just as the characters in a realistic work must remain within the range of the ordinary, the events recounted cannot have exceptional color or significance. Heroic achievement, tragic loss, rescue from the brink of disaster, all the hyperbolic tropes of fiction must be given up if the commonplace world of the mediocre man is to be truthfully presented. Indeed, the very idea of *plot* goes by the boards. Flaubert's statement: "This book is a biography rather than a developed plot. Drama has little place in it . . ." leads to the recognition that a new body of subject matter may, in turn, necessitate a new approach to materials. It is on this subject that the novelist has the most to say. In a letter to Louise Colet on February 1, 1852, he says: "I think you can have no idea of the kind of book I am writing. In my other books I was slovenly; in this I am trying to be impeccable and to follow a geometrically straight line. No lyricism, no comments. The author's personality is absent." He makes frequent reference to the need to curb his propensity for metaphor, to the need to squash comparisons like lice. It is evident that his struggle to find *le mot juste* is more than a finicky concern for a polished style. It indicates rather the need for a new style, one that is precise, unassertive, and even-flowing.

Flaubert's great discovery, and the doctrine most associated with his name, is the idea of complete authorial withdrawal, of narrative objectivity. In a letter to Mlle Leroyer de Chantepie on December 12, 1857, he remarks that previously "The novel has been nothing but the exposition of the personality of the author, and indeed I would say this of all literature in general, with the exception of two or three men perhaps. However, the moral sciences must take a new path and proceed, as do the physical sciences, in an atmosphere of impartiality"—a statement that is anticipatory of Zola's later doctrines about science and literature. In Flaubert this passion for objectivity springs from something deeper than pseudoscientism. It expresses a whole new conception of how literature should achieve its results:

> The same thing is true in art. Passion does not make poetry, and the more personal you are, the more feeble you will be. I have always sinned in that direction myself; that's because I have always put myself into everything I have written. For example, it was I who was there in place of Saint Anthony; the Temptation was for me and not for the reader. *The less you feel a thing the more you are likely to express it as it is* (as it is *always* in itself, in its essence, freed of all ephemeral contingent elements). But you have to have the ability *to make yourself feel it.* (To Louise Colet, July 6, 1852)

The frequency with which Flaubert brings up these ideas gives us reason to believe that they were firmly held. In another letter to Louise Colet (November 16, 1852), he inveighs against "amusing the public with ourselves, which I find horrible and too naive." He reports to her with satisfaction on March 19, 1854, that "in this book there is not one *movement* in my name, and the personality of the author is *completely* absent." There is a very important statement on this subject to Mlle Leroyer de Chantepie on March 18, 1857:

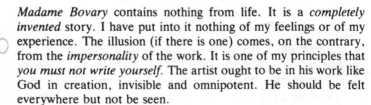

> *Madame Bovary* contains nothing from life. It is a *completely invented* story. I have put into it nothing of my feelings or of my experience. The illusion (if there is one) comes, on the contrary, from the *impersonality* of the work. It is one of my principles that *you must not write yourself.* The artist ought to be in his work like God in creation, invisible and omnipotent. He should be felt everywhere but not be seen.
> Art ought, moreover, to rise above personal feelings and

nervous susceptibilities! It is time to give it the precision of the
physical sciences, by means of a pitiless method!

Flaubert preaches this gospel to George Sand, a practitioner
of the emotional school, writing of his abhorrence at putting
any of his feelings down on paper and declaring that "Great Art
is scientific and impersonal." (December 16, 1866) In another
letter to Sand on February 6, 1876, he is even more emphatic:
"As for revealing my personal opinion about the people whom I
introduce on scene, no, no, a thousand times no! I do not feel I
have that right. If the reader is not able to draw from a book the
morality which is to be found there, it is because the reader is an
imbecile or because the book is *false* from the standpoint of
exactness."

The most common instrument of objectivity, a rigidly
impersonal third-person narrative, automatically inhibits the
emotional wallowing of the romantic hero as narrator or of the
romantic novelist as harp to the wind. It is possible certainly for
the author to intrude into this kind of narrative or for him to tip
the scales away from objectivity by surreptitious means, but
Flaubert adheres scrupulously to his doctrine so far as any
direct intervention is concerned. *Madame Bovary* begins vaguely in the first person with an unspecified "we" invoking memories of Charles Bovary at school, but this stance ends on page 6
with the admission that "none of us" can now recall anything
about Charles because he was so ordinary. From that point on
the narrative becomes strictly impersonal, indicating that the
pseudo-first person was used briefly to give a sense of verisimilitude and was dropped once it had fulfilled that function.

No such introductory device is used in Flaubert's other
works. *L'Education Sentimentale* begins with a scene on a
departing river boat, focusing eventually on Frédéric Moreau,
"a young man of eighteen, who had long hair and held an album
under his arm," who was standing motionless by the tiller. *Un
Coeur Simple* opens with the general statement that for fifty
years the good ladies of Pont-l'Evêque had been envious of
Madame Aubain because of her servant Félicité, and keeps

consistently to this removed tone. *Bouvard et Pécuchet* begins with a scene: "As the temperature was 91 degrees, the Boulevard Bourbon was absolutely deserted"; then the two men who are to be the protagonists come on stage. Even *Salammbô* opens with what amounts to a stage direction: "It was at Megara, a suburb of Carthage, in Hamilcar's gardens," and continues with five pages of objective description before a line of dialogue is uttered. Already at Flaubert's hands the tendency of the novel to approach the self-sustaining quality of the drama begins to be evident. He compensates for the visual advantage of the stage by a mass of objective detail that drama cannot incorporate (except through setting and stage directions). However, whereas Flaubert's objectivity preserves the distancing of the drama, he does not come as close to that form as many of his successors. Indeed, it is somewhat paradoxical that all the versions of *La Tentation de Saint Antoine* should have been cast in at least partial dramatic form whereas his realistic works recede from such immediacy.

A serious problem is the relation of the objective narrator to external and internal data. By the distancing that is implicit in the third-person stance he is logically denied access to the minds of his characters. There are, however, degrees in that removal. We can ignore what the characters think and feel and merely witness their actions and hear their remarks as we would in the theater, or we can on occasion be told what they feel and think in some form of summary narrative that does not give the immediacy of mental and emotional states, thus diminishing their power to convince. Certainly it is not necessary to argue that a realistic presentation must be external. In fact, the opposite is the more tenable position, as we see in discussing later writers. But care must be exercised in the selection of inner events. The selection is likely to be on a purely logical basis; that is, of all the possible thoughts and feelings only those are chosen which have a logical connection with the external demonstration—logical in terms of direct consonance, or logical in terms of ironic deflation. What is left out under such circumstances is most of what inhabits the human being and gives him life. Under these conditions the strictly external depiction is preferable, since what it leaves out is not necessarily denied, whereas the limited selection of the logically connected internal data seems to deny the existence or relevance of anything else.

These remarks have a bearing on all of Flaubert's realistic novels. They do not ignore what goes on in the characters' minds, but they limit such depiction to the logically relevant. *Un Coeur Simple* is an excellent case in point. The external demonstration is unexceptionable: a devoted servant whose existence has meaning only in terms of those whom she serves, whose range of communication narrows to the vanishing point as she grows older, being eventually confined to conversations with a stuffed parrot that, for good measure, she confuses with the Holy Ghost. As demonstration this is brilliant, economical, arresting, and neat. The only trouble is that it does not ring true. Flaubert has not gotten inside Félicité's head; rather he has put something there of his own invention, which is better than anything he might have found there because it is direct and unencumbered with irrelevancies. For artistic completeness Flaubert has moved from the area of external depiction to the realm of the internal, but he has contradicted everything his external representation has prepared us for by introducing an element of the bizarre for the sake of its striking (and terminal) effect. In other words, in the interest of art he has here improved upon reality and therefore falsified it. In what is otherwise a masterpiece of realism Flaubert has, in fact, gone beyond realism—or fallen short of it—by violating one aspect of the doctrine of objectivity.

A last problem growing out of authorial withdrawal is the relation of the particular to the universal. There is nothing to prevent the realist from giving the reader a strictly individual portrait; in fact, his reliance on particulars leads him to do so in the first instance. The realist's work carries no conviction unless it has the authentic stamp of the individual case. At the same time the realist does not want to deal with exceptions; he wants his characters and situations to be representative. How else can he avoid the charge that he has chosen on a bias? It is in an effort to meet his problem that the most interesting technical innovations of the realistic novel were made, that what we may call the art of the cross section was developed. Since Flaubert was considered by his contemporaries and those who came after him to be the high priest of objectivity, it is therefore important to see how he handled these related problems in his major works.

Madame Bovary is, by common consent, one of the truly great novels of the nineteenth century, not the least of its greatness being that it points two ways: to realism and to something that goes beyond realism, to the new literary mode of the age and to a way out of the impasse that that mode would produce. Without wishing to discredit the latter aspect of the work, it is here important to examine *Madame Bovary* primarily as a realistic novel, to find out what it offered in the way of innovation and example to those who later undertook to write in the new mode.

The subject of the work is indicated by the subtitle, "Moeurs de Province," which may be rendered somewhat flippantly as "What it is like to live in the provinces." Although Flaubert apparently never considered calling the novel anything but *Madame Bovary*, that title by itself is misleading. The book is not exclusively about Emma in the way that *Germinie Lacerteux* by the Goncourts, for example, is about the title character. With all these authors, the single-life portrait is a frequent approach, but Flaubert does not use it here any more than Tolstoy uses it in *Anna Karenina*. Emma, though important and consistently interesting, is only a part of a larger whole. Because the book is complicated in structure and essentially new in strategy, it does provide an immediate challenge to the reader to cast off his or her traditional expectations so that the reader may meet the novel on its own terms. The reader has to find his way on the basis of what is given with no direct aid from the author—and with perhaps a degree of deception because of the author's choice of title.

What we have here is a sort of social-norm induction, though there are those who claim that it is far from being an exhaustive one. In the foreground under close scrutiny are three major characters, each of whom meets life with his or her characteristic approach. It is significant that the novel begins and ends with Charles Bovary; this should be enough to warn the reader away from concentrating on Emma as *the* protagonist. But in addition, beginning with Part Two and the removal from Tostes to Yonville, there is the ubiquity of Homais, who is irritatingly present in every major scene and who is given the very last word in the novel by receiving the Legion of Honor. Thus we have three major characters meeting life in different ways, all of them held up to attentive and fairly equal examination. Once we have reached this conclusion on the basis of quantity, emphasis, and position, we can see the novel as trilinear, though not tripartite, since the various strands are continually intermingled. In short, the novel has meaning only as we contemplate these three lives simultaneously.

If we accept this triple object of examination, then we must conclude that to reduce or remove any one of these elements would be to alter the novel as it exists, for it is the interplay of these elements that constitutes its statement, bounded and qualified naturally by the other elements also present in the work. For the sake of simplicity of analysis it is best to begin only with the three life histories, which we soon learn represent distinct life strategies. Charles is passive; things happen to him and he is powerless against them. In his way he is a good man, patient, undemanding, essentially kindly, but more than a bit obtuse. He is pushed into medicine and his first marriage by his mother. Emma removes him from the relative security of Tostes to Yonville, where Homais becomes the malign manipulator of Charles's life through his efforts to maintain his own primacy as a man of medicine of the community and through the specific trap of the clubfoot operation (urged by Emma as well).

The main area of Charles's incompetence is in his domestic life. He does not directly resist Emma's efforts to make him over, but his common clay is not capable of much reshaping. He is easily duped by her efforts to achieve gentility and pseudo-grandeur; he lends himself unwittingly to her infidelities, and when after her death he discovers that she has not been faithful, his response is the passive "C'est la faute de la fatalité." By reason of the opening scene of the novel, in which Charles is exhibited as something of a fool, it becomes impossible either to admire or pity him. He simply cannot be raised out of the rut of plodding mediocrity; only the most arrant sentimentality can make him into saint or martyr. In short, by the accumulation of significant detail and characteristic action we are bound to see that the particular way in which he faces life is a failure.

Homais, though he appears fairly late in the novel, quickly takes on a leading role as the kind of man who is alert to every opportunity, quick to manipulate events to his own advantage. His most salient trait is his scientism. A century before C. P. Snow used the term, Homais is the "new man." He believes in progress, so-called, and is a vulgar and undiscriminating mouthpiece for new doctrines that spring from an insufficiently based positivism, a stereotyped anticlericalism, and a pseudoliberalism. He wins every trick, including the Legion of Honor, yet by doing so he is discredited. We conclude the novel with the observation that if this is what it takes to succeed we will have none of it, an attitude which is largely induced by the pervasive irony of the work.

Though Emma is initially and consistently depreciated, she is by reason of her association with Charles and Homais actually raised somewhat in the end. This is not to deny that her way of approaching life is also an egregious failure that is analyzed in the most careful detail. She represents a principle of energy without direction and without control. She never adequately defines her goals and she has no idea of the means necessary to attain them. She wants something more and better than the stale life in which she is stifled, but like Charles and Homais she too lives by clichés, romantic clichés in her case. Her vision is blurred; she confuses tinsel and gold, merges amatory and sartorial visions into one delusive whole, and in her undiscriminating yearning for whatever is chic, from wolfhounds to lovers, digs her own pit and falls into it, suffering a harrowing destruction as the result of her last, but characteristic, greedy gesture.

As the novel presents itself to us, each of these three efforts to live, to adapt somehow to the limiting terms of human experience, is a failure, each of which is reinforced and at the same time qualified by the presence of the others. This is not an either-or sort of novel. One way of life is not denigrated in order to extol another, as Tolstoy comes close to doing in *Anna Karenina*. Flaubert's much quoted phrase, "Ils sont dans le vrai," has no relevance here. None of the three leading characters is on the right track; none of them can be valued, or disdained, beyond a certain point, for, in the case of Emma, her aspiration, however tawdry and cheap, takes on a certain virtue when compared with the calculating opportunism of Homais or the abject passivity of Charles, just as Charles's passivity becomes a kind of residual sweetness when we see it in contrast with the egoistic agitation of the other two, and Homais' success, however nauseating, is at least an efficient application of means to ends.

The place of Léon in a position of middle emphasis merely reinforces this negative conclusion. Essentially a reflection of Emma in his vague discontent, in his sensual longings, in his flight from actuality, Léon nonetheless pulls himself up short when adultery comes to have all the boredom of marriage. He extricates himself coldly from Emma's grasp before he has made a complete fool of himself and joins the majority in a marriage of convenience and superficial propriety to the all too pointedly named Mlle Leboeuf. This is clearly not the way out. Again Emma takes on some vigor and legitimacy by comparison. However confused her aspiration, it is genuine, more than a titillation of the senses. However vulgar her adulteries, they spring from a genuine passion when compared with Léon's egotistical satisfaction over having a mistress or cutting a figure before the girls in a house of prostitution.

As a setting there is the consistently drab human landscape of the provincial town, a carefully assembled cross section of the inhabitants of Yonville, whose function is to verify and extend the statement of the major characters. The importance of this cross section is evident in the scenic presentation of these personalities at the Lion d'Or on the evening of the Bovarys' arrival. Through obvious symbolic means Binet, the tax collector, stands out as the most important of these people. He makes wooden napkin rings in his spare time; the endless flow of these banal objects by their repetitious circularity stands for humdrum human existence. The others are cut from the same cloth. They are earthbound, egoistic, preoccupied with money and advantage, contributors to Emma's downfall or echoing it in their own lives. Bournisien, the parish priest, more gross farmer than shepherd of souls, is incapable of understanding Emma's need for spiritual guidance. Lheureux, the shopkeeper, seeks to enmesh her in a web of debt. Guillaumin, the notary, is willing to buy her tarnished body on her last frenzied day. Rodolphe, the conventional sensualist, carries on an affair with her as long as it suits his convenience, foreseeing its termination before it even begins. Mère Rolet levies discreet blackmail. And so it goes. Flaubert's skill is sharply in evidence in the presentation of these background figures. Each is clearly though succinctly individualized; none of them is allowed to step into the foreground. Together they form the desolate community that is the provincial milieu and so reinforce the desolation of the major lives being examined. There is an intricate connection between "moeurs de province" as established by this ensemble and the full-length portraits of the major figures.

We can see the almost reflex nature of Sainte-Beuve's complaint that the good is too much absent. The drab grayness of the human landscape is not broken by any rays of light. True,

Justin is devoted to Emma and weeps at her funeral, but this is not an indication that he will rise above the spiritual level of Yonville. True, old Père Rouault assures Charles that he will continue to send a Christmas turkey. True, Dr. Larivière (presumably modeled on Flaubert's doctor father), a god in a whirlwind arriving from outside this futile world, suggests that there are other ways of being. Yet though he snubs Dr. Canivet and Homais successfully, his presence avails nothing at the moment and does nothing to undermine the forces that Homais represents. Old Catherine Leroux at the agricultural fair is an appealing figure of lifelong devotion, but devotion is curiously like servitude and she is placed on a level with the beasts at the fair.

Has Flaubert then tipped the scales by his bias? Has he shown only the types of human beings that he wishes to find in a provincial town, thereby stacking the cards against human goodness and sensitivity? Only the reader can check what is represented in this milieu against his or her own observation of similar social settings. The reader may decide that in principle there must be some people in Yonville who rise above the level shown, but may also argue that they would be so few that to show even one of them would be to distort the picture. It is odd that at this point in the argument it is necessary for the defender of realism to desert the normally held correspondence theory of truth and resort to some extent to the coherence theory, by which the exception, the abnormal for a given norm, must be left out as destructive of the veracity of representation.

The events in the novel are relatively unimportant. Perhaps the overall pattern for Emma and Charles is rather more of a precipitate downhill slide than would be observed under ordinary circumstances. However, on the whole incidents are presented for their representative quality and none of them is endowed with undue dramatic intensity, with one or two exceptions. The incident that is probably most open to question is the famous closed cab scene in Rouen: Picturesque, overemphatic, ultimately part of a symbolic pattern, it is scarcely consonant with either Léon's or Emma's nature and native caution. It smacks of invention. Then there is Emma's suicide. Is it part of the logical continuum of a life such as hers, or is it a dramatic contrivance to give a powerful resolution to this series of drab events? Certainly later realistic practice is against Flaubert. Perhaps, however, it is best not to quarrel with the decision here. [Emma is a hysterical woman; she is driven to frenzy on the last day of her life; her choice of arsenic is not a calculated one (though unfortunately it is carefully prepared for earlier in the novel).] There is some fine writing on the occasion of the last sacraments, but this is balanced by the banal behavior of Homais and Bournisien during the deathwatch. Nonetheless later realists would probably have avoided death as the termination of this life, and without question they would have avoided the neat tying up of the action even to telling the fate of little Berthe.

Idealism

We may conclude, in spite of the questions raised, that in general the continuum of events is kept on a fairly even level and that there is consistency in the handling of character and incident. Charles has no miraculous successes. Emma does not fly away on the wings of love and she finds no way to dissolve the net she has woven about herself. Homais does not get his comeuppance but consolidates himself in his malignant success. All of this represents a destruction of the conventional romantic pattern and of individual romantic stereotypes. It provides a detailed and convincing replica of life for those who do not reject it on *a priori* grounds. Because of the tightness of construction the novel is somewhere between schematic organization and photograph, but there is nothing in its schematic organization that would contradict what a photograph would show. The critical point of analysis comes when we consider the additional means used to shape and qualify the essential representation, the highlighting and angle shots in which the impersonal photographer has indulged in order to raise and sharpen his photograph.

The major and pervasive shaping device used in the novel is

irony. It is here that most critics charge Flaubert with a clear departure from objectivity. It is here that, at its very beginning, modern realism bears the seeds of its own destruction, or transformation. There is, to be sure, an irony of events as we all observe and reflect upon them, a basic disparity between perception and actuality, between expectation and what occurs, between overt statements of motive and covert springs of action. Yet this disparity is not a steady and undeviating fact of experience, or, even if it is, we perceive it gradually and discontinuously, coming to see it as a dimension of our lives only through the accumulation of experience. Flaubert, and here it is proper to speak of the author's manipulations in personal terms, never lets us escape this vision of irony—*his* vision of irony, for he gives us no chance to achieve our own.

The great scenes of the novel are hammer blows of irony. Emma would have liked a wedding at midnight with torches; what she gets is a vulgar peasant celebration at which grossness of appetite is the dominant note. The ball at Vaubyessard is viewed by Cinderella Emma as something out of fairyland, but we have a contrast of perception. Charles's rigid boredom is in contrast with Emma's fainting ecstasy, an ecstasy that is punctured for us also by the presence of the old duke, an ugly senile figure in whom Emma, however, sees the noble visage of one who has slept in the bed of a queen. Similarly, the renowned *Comices Agricoles* scene, over which the author labored so long in the hope of making it "bien symphonique," has as its raison d'être a consummate exercise in ironical juxtaposition. On the balcony Rodolphe exhales amorous platitudes, while on the platform below the prefect's representative utters the platitudes of politics, and the word *manure* rises up from the crowd to provide a devastating commentary on both. Equally contrived is the irony at Emma's deathbed and the deathwatch that follows. In court Flaubert was able to defend himself against the charge of impiety by showing that he had taken the words from the office for the dying. But he cannot defend himself against the charge of manipulating these materials for ironic effect. The anointing of the "mouth which had opened to utter lies, which complained in pride, and cried out in sensual pleasure," and of "the feet, once so swift to fly to the satisfaction of her desire, and which now would never run again," etc., is an artistic heightening, an outspoken statement of what the reader is capable of inferring from the novel as a whole. This is not meant to imply that Flaubert necessarily falsifies by this means, though he does overstate. The facts are not really allowed to speak for themselves. There is an unnecessary pointing up of plain statement, a driving home of a view of life which, if valid, should be emergent and not imposed. These constant hammer blows of irony give the reader no option but to adopt a particular view.

Irony is not the only means by which basic data are given pattern and emphasis. There is a close texture of imagery that, admirable and poetic as it may be in itself, goes beyond realism. It is here in particular that we can see Flaubert reaching toward symbolism, in fact to have already arrived there. This first realist was nothing if not a stylist, but on occasion style, as exhibited in his work, implies contrivance. From the rich and intricate verbal and imagistic patterns of this novel only two examples of such arbitrary pointing up are cited. One is the motif of death and dissolution. In James T. Farrell's study of Studs Lonigan, also a realistic novel, this theme seems to be legitimately present. It is part of the pattern of emotional response of the Irish enclave to which Studs belongs, and it is a consequence of the life of excess that he and his gang lead. In Flaubert's novel the theme seems to be dragged in as a poignant reminder of the folly of spending the one life we have as rashly as Emma spends hers, or as blindly as the other characters spend theirs. Although death is implicit in all human experience, it is not a major preoccupation of the people of Yonville as we are allowed to see them. We might say that it is what they should be thinking about. The *memento mori* motif first appears with the crumbling wedding bouquet of Charles's first wife, a likely enough datum. It is picked up with insistence on the duke's being a death's head at the Vaubyessard ball. The narrative actually pauses while we receive a rather full description of the graveyard at Yonville and the growing of potatoes in that fertile soil by Lestiboudois, the verger. With the clubfoot operation there is added the literal corruption of the flesh. The physical agonies of Emma's death are capped by the image of the black bile issuing from her mouth (a detail that Zola copied in *L'Assommoir* with Mother Coupeau's "emptying" and that became a kind of convention for realistic writing of the "stark" variety).

Another instance of poetic manipulation is somewhat less flagrant, perhaps because the reader comes to assimilate it through a fairly slow inductive process. The novel abounds in images of whirling, fainting, and running around in circles. As she dances at Vaubyessard, Emma almost faints, both from the heat of the waltz and from her happiness. When she receives Rodolphe's letter of farewell, Emma flees to the attic and there, to the hum of Binet's lathe, the world dissolves into motion and she does faint. The random ride with Léon in the closed cab provides another use of this image, this time both humorous and erotic. By now we begin to see the whole novel in terms of motion, especially on the part of Emma as she strives vaguely and erratically for something she considers to be happiness. This comes to a tremendous climax when, on her last day, she runs frantically from one person to another in an almost insane effort somehow to save herself from disaster, a motion that culminates in her blindly grabbing up of a handful of arsenic, which, though it does ultimately bring rest, does so only after the most violent writhing. This metaphor of blind, grasping, whirling motion characterizes Emma's whole life. It is one we cannot escape. It is an artistic intervention that shortcuts the demonstration by the data, though it does not contradict them. By its emphasis, moreover, the metaphor probably gives Emma a more salient place in the novel than impartial handling of triple focus should allow.

An obvious authorial intervention that needs only passing

mention is the use of tag names. As indicated earlier, this is an old device that is inappropriate to the new literature. This device is offensive to most readers, whether the character be called Christopher Newman or J. Alfred Prufrock, because most readers dislike having conclusions forced upon them in advance of the facts. Flaubert uses this device in two ways: ironically when he calls the stagecoach on which Emma makes her weekly trips to amorous dalliance with Léon in Rouen *l'Hirondelle,* that is the swallow, harbinger of happiness— further complicated by calling the coachman Hivert, suggestive of winter and the end of happiness. He also uses tag names in a more direct way. Few readers can ignore the bovine implications of the name Bovary or the pejorative tone of Homais, which is a gross derivation from *homme.* It is likely that Bournisien, the name of the curé, will suggest the idea of *borné,* that is, *limited.* Such associations may, to be sure, turn out to be accidental, since all names have associations for somebody. Here, however, the impact is direct and repeated, though fortunately not general, and we must conclude that the scales are being weighted toward particular judgments.

These strictures do not diminish *Madame Bovary* as a work of art. They merely indicate that Flaubert in some respects fell short of the absolute objectivity that he set himself and which is central to a realistic depiction. (Possibly it would be more accurate to say that even at the beginning he went *beyond* realism out of impatience with its self-denying ordinances.) When we turn to his second major novel, *L'Education Sentimentale,* published more than ten years later, we have a chance to consider whether Flaubert has consolidated or diminished his realistic position.

One important thing to observe about this work is that structurally it is not a repetition of *Madame Bovary.* Here there is a single figure consistently in the foreground: the experience of Frédéric Moreau is the novel. With one unfortunate exception we do not shift away from Frédéric or become privy to the emotions of others except as they are revealed in conversation in Frédéric's presence. The problem here is how to give this particular figure amplitude and representativeness. As in the first novel, Flaubert allows himself a broad time span in which to demonstrate the nature of the life he sets before us. For the novel proper there is a period of eleven years, from 1840 to Louis Napoleon's coup d'état in December 1851, from Frédéric's entry into adult life until *l'an trentième de son âge*. There are also a few pages of what amounts to an epilogue in 1867, but this is not an essential part of the novel. The period covered is sufficient for Frédéric's development, or lack of it, for repetition of responses to give support for the conclusions reached. Erosion is a function of time, and time here eats insensibly away at hope and romantic expectation.

What happens to Frédéric Moreau is subtly supported by what happens to a considerable number of youthful figures. As in Tolstoy's *War and Peace* we see a band of young men starting out together, providing if not a cross section, at least a sheaf of parallel experiences. Closest to Frédéric is Deslauriers, so close as to be a foil, but definitely not sharing the central position as was the case in a youthful version of this work called *Novembre*. With less detail we follow Hussonnet, Dussardier, Pellerin, Cisy, Martinon, and Sénécal, not an unmanageable group by any means, but a sufficiently varied one to generalize Frédéric's experience. By a particularly happy stroke we have in Arnoux and Regimbart two older and perennially hopeful figures who follow the same path. A number of key scenes bring these various men together, both to demonstrate in conversation the emptiness of their ambitions and to remind the reader of the similarity of their experiences.

This technique takes on particular resonance by being tied to historical events. What happened to Frédéric could have happened anywhere at any time. This novel, however, locates his experience in a given time and place. The moral and emotional setting is the tag end of romantic idealism as it manifested itself in the 1840s, was shattered by the abortive Revolution of 1848, and received its coup de grâce on December 2, 1851. The observation made by the editor of the *Pléiade* edition that the second hero of the novel is the people of Paris is a sentimental overstatement. But as Frédéric drowns in his languorous emotions of love, so do others drown in their perfervid dream of a perfect society. In other words, it is not one kind of dream but all kinds that collapse under the pressure of actuality.

The novel early presents evidence of political unrest in the demonstration by university students where Dussardier, a clerk in laces and ribbons, first appears. This strand is never allowed to drop for long, for if the Left is not shown in action, members of the Right are seen reacting. In the course of the narrative we have detailed scenes of the Revolution of 1848, though overorganized and presented largely for their elements of the picturesque. The novel ends with a contrived ironical shock: The good Dussardier is cut down by the forces of reaction after December 2 by none other than the former revolutionary Sénécal, who has joined the forces of repression. Particularly pointed and contrived is the dovetailing of incidents in Frédéric's life with public events. It is during the February uprising that Madame Arnoux fails their first rendezvous and he, out of spite, takes Rosanette to the apartment he has prepared for the other woman, and it is on the eve of the coup d'état that he renounces marriage with Madame Dambreuse.

The skein of narrative events as they involve Frédéric is not tightly bound. He lives through a series of typical experiences, none of which leads anywhere in particular. He flees from his home town as soon as he inherits money. Home stands for a mediocre, earthbound existence, as does the projected marriage with Louise. (There is no effort to represent a life with her as being *"dans le vrai,"* although for a time that polarity seems possible. However, such a contrast is denied at the end when we discover that Louise, having married Deslauriers, has run off with a singer.) We see Frédéric as an intimate of the Dambreuse connection of wealth and social position, but incapable of the single-minded pursuit characteristic of Martinon, who is courting the niece. Frédéric cannot even take advantage of this entrée to make money, letting the opportunities first offered by the financier slip away and later being unwilling to sell himself to the widow. He seeks to enter the bohemian world of art and letters, where he has fugitive ambitions but no talent or perseverance. He is also caught up by the political enthusiasm of his contemporaries, but he misses the important conspiratorial rendezvous in February 1848 because of his assignation with Madame Arnoux.

At the age of eighteen Frédéric has fallen in love with Madame Arnoux and his existence thereafter is dominated by a romantic and hopeless passion. The affair has its ups and downs; he frequently disengages himself for long intervals, only to become enmeshed again, using this as justification for his nonaction in other areas. This love affair is not altogether convincing because it has too dominant a position in the novel. And it is sheer bathos to have Madame Arnoux reappear white-haired sixteen years later and tell Frédéric that she had loved him all the time. There is also a trite countertheme of Frédéric's profane love, which is likewise raised to an intensity that goes beyond realistic measure. He divides his energies between Rosanette and Madame Dambreuse, who are merely two aspects of the same gluttony of the senses, of the same abstraction of *la vie libertine.*

Indeed when we look at the novel in terms of the young man's attachment to abstractions, to forms that have no meaning, nearly everything falls into place. Under such a reading what the novel does not need is elements of tight intrigue. Frédéric provides his own motive force for misadventure; he is certain to stumble because his feet are never firmly on the ground. Thus introduction of intrigue in the last part is a mistake. The manipulation by Rosanette and Madame Dambreuse of debts against Arnoux as revenge on the wife's ineffable figure of virtue is so much Balzacian balderdash, as is the role of Mlle Vatnaz, an importation from *La Cousine Bette* through the agency of a poltergeist.

Certain other elements of narrative content are open to question. The novel seems to be more static than *Madame Bovary,* containing a number of set pieces that are relevant but not really necessary. The inclusion or exclusion of one of these scenes seems to make absolutely no difference to the development of the novel. To cite only three cases, there is the masked ball, the pillaging of the Tuileries during the Revolution of 1848, and the period spent at Fontainebleau. The first is acceptable as showing a milieu, a moral ambiance useful to our understanding of the novel, though rather too disengaged from its action. The second seems to be there because the Revolution is part of the background, but by its prominence it tends to discredit the Revolution unduly. There is no true justification for the Fontainebleau episode, which apparently exists for the ten pages of fine writing it contains.

In this work there is no emphatic use of irony. This does not mean that it is absent, for the whole conceptual basis of the work is the disparity between expectation and what happens, between desire and actuality, but that is not harped upon with insistence. What the novel does have is a consistent tone of melancholy and boredom. This note is struck on the third page when we are told that at each turn of the river the boat encountered the same curtain of pale poplars. The countryside was completely empty, "and boredom, vaguely diffused, seemed to retard the movement of the boat and make the travelers appear even more insignificant." Likewise on his return to Paris with his inheritance Frédéric is struck by the ugliness of the banlieue and is overcome by disappointment. When Madame Arnoux fails to come to their rendezvous, he hears the rain fall. The long passage about Fontainebleau is the culmination of this strain, echoed with real substance by the mood of resignation in the final pages.

Without subscribing to the fallacy of imitative form, we can suggest that the novel is at its best when it is most boring and that it deviates dangerously from its purpose when it strikes an emphatic note. The reality that it mirrors is that of a man and an era floating on a sea of insubstantial dreams, hearkening to the siren strains of an empty idealism, until they are wrecked on the reefs of reality. The wreckage is not the result of evil personal machinations, and the novel is false whenever it invokes such mechanisms. It is rather the result of feckless spontaneity of reaction, and it is hardly necessary for Frédéric to confirm this at the end when he speaks of his "failure to go in a straight line," a conclusion promptly beclouded by Deslauriers' assertion that his own failure is the result of "excess of rectitude." The novel ends with a recollection of schoolboy days when Frédéric, drawn by curiosity to the local brothel, is laughed out of countenance and runs away, an amusing, if vulgar, instance of his inability to proceed with determination.

Un Coeur Simple is a work that has often been considered as a perfect exemplar of realistic art. It represents one of the major realistic goals, the summing up of a representative life, as is also seen in the writings of the Goncourts (and Guy de Maupassant). It necessarily gives an external view: the characteristic facts in the life of a simple, devoted peasant woman, which by addition are what her life amounts to. The statement of the work is orderly, almost analytical; in its course subtraction is the main operation. Félicité loses her normal points of human contact one after another. Her lover marries someone else; her sister exploits her; her nephew dies in a foreign land; her parrot Loulou dies; and finally Madame Aubain dies, leaving Félicité to finish out her days in poverty with only the stuffed parrot to talk to.

This tale takes on a certain extension because the servant's life is echoed by that of her mistress. Madame Aubain loses her husband, daughter, son, and part of her slender fortune, and dies resigned since she has been cut off from all that she holds dear. In both cases "the narrow circle of her ideas" becomes increasingly restricted. In both cases external events such as the July Revolution (of 1830) scarcely ripple the pool of the provincial backwater of Pont-l'Evêque. Both lives are a dismal diminution. They are not made up of a balance sheet but run to a single page headed "loss." For economy and rightness of detail, for measured meaninglessness of time, for unemphatic language, this work is a masterpiece. Nothing jars; there is nothing in excess except for the fantasy of the parrot at the end. There is no recourse to heavy irony: This is just the way such lives are in capsule demonstration.

Strangely enough, this very perfection arouses some misgivings. The reader who can disengage himself from the apparent logic of the demonstration begins to wonder if it is after all accurate. Certainly these are the events central to and symptomatic of these two lives. But there is too much left out: the whole area of affective experience is ignored or foreshortened. We scarcely hear a human voice speaking, and when we do it is carefully pitched in the most banal and uncommunicative tones:

> "But, Madame, I have had no news for six months . . !"
> "From whom do you mean?"
> "Why, from my nephew!"
> "Oh, your nephew!"

Vicomte de Vogüé's strictures are certainly apposite here: We do not get the breath of a human soul. There is almost painful irony in the fact that this perfect application of method should raise the deepest misgivings about the efficacy of that method.

The last of Flaubert's works, *Bouvard et Pécuchet,* which was incomplete at his death, is not realistic, is in fact scarcely a novel. Its limitations are useful in helping to define the mode and Flaubert's relations to it. Here, if anywhere, the observation made by Emilia Pardo Bazán that "the Zola school employs a method of abstraction and accumulation, brings together on a single stage and in a single character all the torpidity, abominations, and evils of which a group of lost souls is capable" is justified. This work is another *Candide,* rewritten this time by a realist, with the inescapable difference that in Voltaire's work the conclusion that one should cultivate one's garden is productive and minimally hopeful, whereas the projected return of Flaubert's heroes to a life of copying is the

negation of negations. It is idle to try to see in this work any of
the warmth of humanity. The tour of all areas of human
knowledge is so synthetic as to be ridiculous. It corresponds to
no actuality of human experience and, lacking that correspondence, fails to generate a human response. The approach here
is forthrightly deductive. The author begins with a thesis of the
impossibility of knowledge and the impregnable stupidity of
received ideas, and proceeds to illustrate this by means of
contrived situations that exist only for the sake of the demonstration. An inductive approach would have taken two representative men and put them in recognizably human situations in
which they would succeed or fail in terms of their natures and
the forces of their environment.

This is not to deny that this work has flashes of novelistic
brilliance. In handling details Flaubert is here at his best:
economical, direct, unadorned, humorous. He re-creates the
Norman countryside and social milieu, the very mud in which
people are stuck. His recurring minor characters are unforgettable: Gorju, Madame Bordin, the curé, and others. The resistance to change by entrenched interest or stupidity is well
rendered; the sullen suspicion of neighbors, the wildfire current
of superstition, all are well done. In Chapter 6, which deals with
the happenings of 1848, there is an excellent fusion of private
and public events. *Bouvard et Pécuchet* contains passages
showing great novelistic skill, as good as anything the author
ever did. Flaubert can no longer complain that he is like a man
trying to play the piano with lead balls on his fingers. He has
mastered his technique: He is impeccable in his impersonality,
but he is using these skills for satiric or doctrinal ends. He has
not here dipped into the stream of life and brought up a
representative sample. Instead he has arranged and catalogued
in logical, analytical fashion. This is his *Summa,* and it is no less
doctrinal than that of St. Thomas Aquinas.

Although it is a much earlier novel, *Salammbô* is best
considered here as a contrast to the whole body of Flaubert's
realistic work. How can a novel set in ancient Carthage

undertake to be realistic? What can we say of Flaubert's impassioned defense of its veracity? In default of observation the realistic historical novel must be built on documents, and in this case there are no documents, or virtually none, and few artifacts. Under such circumstances the outcome will be at best an intuitive reconstruction conveying the essence of ancient life through the invention of supporting data. Flaubert complained as usual in his letters about the difficulty of writing this book and about the paucity of material from which to make his reconstruction. After a quick visit to modern Tunis he offered a prayer to "the powers of plastic emotion" for aid, and admitted that it was only by way of the Beautiful that he could make his work "living and true." What he produced is a succession of colorful and cadenced set pieces, in which harmony of the ensemble is the dominant goal, so that the eye and ear in sensory delight will deter the mind from analysis and judgment. The most glowing defense of this work came, suitably, from Théophile Gautier, who was himself a colorist in literature. He declared: "No doubt the study of current reality has its merit. . . . But is it not a fine dream, one made to tempt an artist, to isolate himself from his own time and to reconstruct through the veil of centuries a vanished civilization, a world that has disappeared?" Gautier was convinced that *Salammbô* would be considered one of the great literary monuments of the century, and with precision passed judgment that "it is not a work of history, it is not a novel, it is an *epic poem!*"[2]

In spite of his complaints about the lack of data on which to base the work, Flaubert reacted with anguish against criticisms that raised doubts about the novel's accuracy. He wrote long answers to two of his most important critics in an attempt to refute such a charge, and he included these answers in an appendix to the second edition of the work. One of those critics was Guillaume Froehner, a distinguished Orientalist, who took exception to a multitude of linguistic and factual details in the book and called into question Flaubert's acquaintance with such basic texts that did exist. The other critic was Sainte-Beuve, who, after a distressingly long silence, finally in December 1862 gave over three of his *Lundis* to a discussion of the book. A matter of immediate irritation to Flaubert was this critic's comparison of his work with Chateaubriand's *Les Martyrs.* (To compare any realist with Chateaubriand was to wave a red flag.) In his reply to Sainte-Beuve Flaubert asserted that "Chateaubriand's system seems to me to be diametrically opposed to mine. He took the ideal as his starting point; he dreamed of *typical* martyrs. For my part, I wished to set up a mirage by applying the methods of the modern novel to antiquity, and I have tried to be simple."[3] After going on to refute a number of charges of inverisimilitude, Flaubert came to an interesting admission: Perhaps Sainte-Beuve was right in his doubts about the possibility of a historical novel that draws on antiquity, but Flaubert holds fast to the belief that he has made "something which resembles Carthage. But that is not the question. I don't care a hoot for archeology! If the color is not even, if the details are dissonant, if manners and morals do not spring from religion and action from passion, if the characters are not consistent, the costumes not appropriate to their function and the architecture to the climate, if, in short, there is no harmony, then I am wrong. If not, I am not wrong and everything hangs together."[4]

To reach this position of justification is to desert the very ground on which realism stands. As mentioned earlier, the test of a realistic work is that it *corresponds* in all important elements to that which can be seen and experienced in reality. But now Flaubert has taken refuge in an idealist view of truth that holds that *coherence,* a logical hanging together, is the test. To push such an argument to an extreme, although his Carthage may in all respects be false with regard to what actually existed in the time and place portrayed, it is still true—and real—by reason of its inner coherence. By a further extension, there could be as many real Carthages as there were minds with the skill and power to create harmonious ensembles, and it would be beside the point to indicate a disparity between these creations and that which, in fact, existed. This Truth-Beauty, Beauty-Truth conception need not surprise us. It was clearly implicit in Flaubert's early statements about using mediocre materials to create a thing of beauty. But the fact remains that in this statement he reveals an aesthetic that is closer to that of Proust than it is to that of the orthodox realists.

One other criticism of *Salammbô* is important, though Flaubert never knew about it. There is a long entry in the Goncourt *Journal* for May 6, 1861 (written after the Goncourt brothers had heard the work read at a marathon sitting), in which they raise two objections. One is that the characterizations do not bring into play the feelings of a specifically Carthaginian humanity but present only the banal and general sentiments of humanity at large. This, and other lapses from the specific, leads the Goncourts to the conclusion that the world of the novel is a world of Flaubert's invention. Their own objection is a curious one. They insist that "the personality of the author, so well concealed in *Madame Bovary,* pierces through here, inflated, declamatory, melodramatic, in love with strong colors, addicted to high illumination." They also object to the syntax of the novel as being tired and phlegmatic like that of a university don. What they are apparently pointing to is a personal style that they find unsuited to the subject, for with respect to direct authorial intrusion Flaubert conducts himself irreproachably. The narrative voice is withdrawn and magisterial, contributing mightily to the illusion of a self-subsistent account by its distancing effect.

The most obvious liability in writing a work like *Salammbô* is the impossibility of providing a sense of tight causality. If the data are conjectural, then the causal pattern lacks conviction and is best ignored. This is no doubt the reason for Flaubert's recourse to a method which is pictorial rather than logical. The whole question of the philosophical underpinning of his novels is a vexing one, however, and is not easily resolved by his fugitive and impromptu remarks in his letters. We may recall an early one to Mlle Leroyer de Chantepie invoking for the novel "the precision of the physical sciences by means of a pitiless method!" Flaubert insists on several occasions that he has made it a point of honor to conceal as completely as possible the scientific spade work that was necessary for his description of pathological states. On the one hand, this reliance on the scientific method does not necessarily connote determinism. On the other, even though the authorial voice never comments on the inevitability of a certain outcome, on the impact of material causality, there is an inevitability about the fates of his characters that is relentless, even implacable, though it is on a moral plane that this is demonstrated. We are not called upon, in the manner of Zola, to contemplate the force exercised by heredity and environment. They are givens, and the important exhibition is the limited nature of human response by reason of whatever determinism is relevant. Thus it is in its effects rather than in precedent theorizing that Flaubert's world is deterministic. Without straining too much we can see it as a jungle world in which its inhabitants exhaust their slender force in a struggle for survival and in the course of living are diminished in stature by this necessity. Moreover, Flaubert shows no escape from this harsh mesh of circumstance. Emma and Frédéric both proceed on a straight and inescapable path to destruction or nonentity. By extension, the inhabitants of Yonville follow much the same path, and by a more grandiose extension the people of France produce and suffer from the follies of 1848 and 1851.

What is notable about this reading of experience is its pessimism. If the materialism and determinism are covert, the pessimism is open to all eyes. Thus, in contrast with Zola, where the former elements are articles of pugnacious faith over which a kind of optimism can triumph, with Flaubert there is no insistence on a deterministic thesis, but the pessimism is deep and abiding. All paths fail in *Madame Bovary*. The story of a young man's education toward disillusionment is also the story of an era in *L'Education Sentimentale*. Progressive contraction of being is the experience of Madame Aubain and Félicité alike in *Un Coeur Simple*. The folly of Bouvard and Pécuchet is exceeded only by that of the human windmills at whom they tilt. Holding such a judgment of human worth and human possibility, it is logical enough that Flaubert in his last book should desert the area of objective representation for overt satire. The wonder is that he maintained his objective stance so long. His is a savage indignation directed not merely at the middle class. When in an early letter he signed himself "bourgeoisophobus," Flaubert would have been better advised to write it "anthropophobus."

Since he held this position, it is also not surprising that he looked upon art as an escape. We should not forget the letter to Laurent-Pichat the day after the first installment of *Madame Bovary* appeared, in which Flaubert speaks of "this ignoble reality," and of his execration of ordinary life. Even earlier at the very beginning of his struggle to compose that novel, he wrote to Louise Colet on January 16, 1852: "What strikes me as beautiful, what I should like to do, is a book about nothing, a book without external attachments, which would hold together by itself through the internal force of its style . . . a book which would have virtually no subject, or one in which the subject would be almost invisible, if that is possible." *La Tentation de Sainte Antoine, Hérodias, La Légende de Saint Julien l'Hospitalier,* and *Salammbô* are not works about nothing, but they are escapes from the externality that their author execrated, and they do hold together by the internal force of style. They are a reprieve from the labors of innovation that the realistic works demanded, but they are unoriginal in comparison with those other works, which attempt to engage with the ugly and repugnant elements of external attachments.

Thus in his later years, Gustave Flaubert, the friend and associate and mentor of the major realists in France—Zola, Edmond de Goncourt, Daudet, Maupassant, and Turgenev—could with something like consistency write to George Sand: "But note that I hate what is conventionally called *realism,* although people regard me as one of its high priests. Try to figure that out!" (February 6, 1876). And to Turgenev: "Reality, as I see it, should only be a springboard. Our friends [Daudet and Zola] are convinced that by itself it is the whole State. Such materialism makes me angry . . ." (November, 8, 1877).

3

Edmond and Jules de Goncourt

Of all the major realists of the nineteenth century the Goncourt brothers, Edmond and Jules, have had the least success in maintaining their renown as novelists. Today it is the Académie Goncourt and its annual prize that keep their name alive. Some twenty years ago there was a brief flurry over the publication of the integral text of their *Journal*, an event that had been delayed for forty years. But the excitement quickly subsided when it became apparent that nothing of importance had been suppressed in the incomplete edition, and this monument, interesting as it is, has not led to widespread fame for the Goncourts. Among connoisseurs Edmond Goncourt has a certain reputation for his part in introducing Japanese art to Western eyes, and both brothers are known in such circles for their lively interest in the art, life, and manners of eighteenth-century France. Although there is in the world of letters a vague awareness that the Goncourts wrote, together or singly, some eleven novels, it is rare to find a general reader who is acquainted with these works, and outside of libraries it is difficult even to find the works themselves in French, let alone in English.

Diminished literary reputations must usually be left to their fate. In this case, however, since the Goncourt brothers were a major force in the development of French realism, their contribution to that literary current must be assessed. *Germinie Lacerteux* and its famous manifesto-preface published in 1865 are of primary importance, bridging the span between *Madame Bovary* and Zola's Rougon-Macquart series. To this work should be added at least *Renée Mauperin, Manette Salomon,* and Edmond's *La Fille Elisa* as important examples of realism in fiction. Beyond what these of their works offered as examples is the fact of the brothers' *literary presence* in Paris at the very center of critical discussion and novelistic and dramatic experimentation from the early 1850s until Edmond's death in July 1896—a period of artistic and literary ferment faithfully, if chaotically, chronicled in the famous *Journal.* None of the other realists, major or minor, has as much to say about their art as did the Goncourts. Even the vociferous Zola confined his critical utterances to a relatively short period of time.

Finally, though this is a matter of less importance, the Goncourts were acquainted with all the French realists as well as with writers from other countries. Through the various regular dinners—Brébant, Magny, and others—in which they participated, and later through Edmond's Sunday gatherings in his *Grenier,* there came within range of the Goncourt talk, and the Goncourt recording pen, such intimates as Flaubert, Zola, Daudet, and Turgenev; such intellectual leaders as Taine, Renan, and Berthelot; and a whole host of lesser writers and writers who would become famous but were then still in formation, among them Henry James, George Moore, J.-K. Huysmans, and Guy de Maupassant, to mention only those with an obvious affiliation with the realist-naturalist school. There was, in short, some truth in Edmond's irritating reiteration in his later years that he and his brother had been the chief catalytic agent in the creation of the new literature.

A belated formal recognition of this role was accorded to Edmond by his literary brethren on March 1, 1895, at a dinner attended by 310 persons at which eulogies were read from such foreigners as Georg Brandes, who wrote: "All Scandinavian writers will join with me today as I shout: *'Glory to the innovating master!'* " Raymond Poincaré, at that time Minister of Public Instruction, gave an address in which he conferred on Edmond the grade of officer of the Legion of Honor. There was also a toast by J. M. Hérédia, a discourse by Georges Clemenceau, and tributes by Henri Céard, Henri de Regnier, Zola, and Daudet. Many of those in attendance must have recalled the memories of Flaubert, dead in 1880, of Turgenev, dead in 1883, and of Maupassant, dead in 1893, who in sympathy and brotherhood belonged to that living assembly.

Before we examine the works of the two Goncourt brothers for what they contained that was new to the novel, it will be useful to follow in some detail the critical utterances they made *seriatim* over the years in the prefaces and entries in the *Journal*. What we discern from these entries after the inception of the *Journal* on December 2, 1851, is that these brothers did not begin as realists. Their dreams were typical: They offered a play, *La Nuit de Saint-Sylvestre,* to the Comédie Française because Jules Janin had told them that the way to achieve success was to conquer the theater. When the play was refused, they wrote in the *Journal* on December 21, 1851: "That was the end of that. Our soap bubble had burst. And actually our little piece was no more than that. That's the way of first dreams in literature." Their next enthusiasm was the publication *Paris,* which they called "the first literary daily paper since the beginning of the world." For some years they were typical young men enamored of literature, seeking fame rather than any specific literary accomplishment, modeling themselves after writers who were then in vogue.

As it turned out, the Goncourts' way to realism came not through literary efforts but through research for, and writing of, a kind of social history. Their interest in objets d'art of the eighteenth century led them from collector's mania to study of the period and a resultant cultivation of a talent for observation. The *Journal* for June 9, 1856, records the brothers' visit to Montalembert, who praised their *Histoire de la Société Fran-*

çaise pendant le Directoire for its catalogue of Paris sights and buildings (the first chapter was a hundred-page promenade through the Paris of sixty years before). The brothers have left us abundant evidence of their avidity for research, telling of the thousands of drawings, prints, paintings—*documents* in short— that they had examined before writing their various social histories and intimate biographies. Like Stendhal they became enamored of *le petit fait vrai,* though they did seek in it an element of color and the picturesque. Of their originality in this kind of writing Pierre Sabatier says: "They brought to history a conception completely different from that of the writers who before them had attempted this genre. If to them, in Michelet's words, history was to be 'a resurrection,' that resurrection was to be brought about above all by the most exact and most documented evocation of milieu and décor in which the human beings of the past had lived."[1] This critic suggests that such a taste led the Goncourts straight to the novel, i.e., "history that might have been," since their desire to make historical charac- ters live in an authentic background would be one of the necessary elements of the modern novel.

A subsidiary enthusiasm also led the brothers in this direc- tion. They were for many years closely allied by friendship and interests with Gavarni, an important artist whose forte was subjects from everyday life. On November 25, 1856, they wrote in the *Journal:* "To think that, except for Gavarni, there is absolutely nobody who has made himself the painter of nineteenth-century life and costume. A whole world is there, and the brush has not touched it." A month before (October 30) they had commented "Realism is born and breaks out at the time when the daguerreotype and photograph show how much art differs from reality"—so far as I have been able to discover, their first use of the term *realism* in print. A few years later (November 12, 1861) they recede a bit from a realistic position: "The future of modern art, will it not be in a combination of Gavarni and Rembrandt, the reality of man and his costume transfigured by the magic of shadows and light, by the sun, a poetry of the colors that fall from the hand of the painter?"

There is early recognition by the brothers of the importance of *Madame Bovary* and of Sainte-Beuve's famous article in *Lundi* about it. Also in the September 3–21, 1857, entry they make an interesting contrast between Balzac's *Les Paysans* and George Sand's *La Mare au Diable,* assailing the false tradition of the latter that bedecks peasants with ribbons, a convention that has come down from *Paul et Virginie.* Yet on October 6, 1861, the brothers express reservations about Balzac, who is "perhaps less a great physiological anatomist than a great painter of interiors. It seems to me sometimes that he has observed furniture much more than people." A notation on October 24, 1864, brings Diderot and Balzac together in a way that helps to define the Goncourts' emerging conception of the novel: "Dramatic movement, gesture, and life did not begin in the novel until Diderot. Up to then there were dialogues but no novels. The novel, since Balzac, no longer has anything in common with what our ancestors understood by a novel. The novel of today is made from *documents,* recounted or copied from nature, as history is made from written documents." Given this position, it is not surprising that the Goncourts think that the best education for a writer would be, from the time he leaves school until he is twenty-five or thirty, to set down without action all that he sees and feels, at the same time forgetting what he has read as completely as possible.

The critical comments made by Edmond during the quarter century after Jules' death are less spontaneous and often seem to be motivated by fraternal piety, by a desire to see justice done to the memory of Jules and therefore to the living Edmond, and also by a gnawing jealousy of Zola's preeminence. During those years Edmond thought of himself increasingly as *chef d'école,* and conceived of that school in terms much less dogmatic and restrictive than did the militant naturalists. He came to see realism, as some modern critics do, more as an extension of the renovating force of romanticism than as the product of scientific thought. He wrote on January 25, 1876, that "the literature inaugurated by Flaubert and the Goncourts could, I think, be defined as follows: a rigorous study of nature in a prose speaking the language of poetry." He did concede, however, that the value of romanticism was to infuse blood and color into the French language, which was dying of anemia; as for the human beings it created, they were not of this world (April 13, 1879).

The outspoken, and often niggling, depreciation of Zola is the least happy part of Edmond de Goncourt's critical writing. As early as 1876, months before the success of *L'Assommoir*, Edmond was proclaiming that he and his brother were the great literary revolutionists of the century, something that had not been noticed because they did not shout it to the heavens. A couple of months later, in a better mood, Edmond complacently recorded a dinner at which "the young people of realist-naturalist letters" officially consecrated Flaubert, Zola, and himself as "the three masters of the present hour." Yet again a few days later Edmond denied Zola's right to an equal place, asking what Zola had written before Edmond's *Germinie Lacerteux*, which came to Zola as a revelation and on which he immediately modeled *Thérèse Raquin*.

The culmination of jealousy and charges of plagiarism came in October 1885 over similarities that Goncourt saw in Zola's *L'Oeuvre* to his own *Manette Salomon*. He burst out against Zola's "thefts, his plagiarisms, his piracies, his scarcely honest behavior toward me in leading people to believe that the phrase *human documents* and many other expressions and ideas came from him and, in his critical statements, pretending a benevolent attitude, even representing my literature as a small chapel which the young should refrain from entering." A few months later Edmond accused Zola's play *Renée* (drawn from the novel *La Curée)* of being a plagiarism of the Goncourts' *Renée Mauperin.*

On June 1, 1891, commenting on the interview he had given Jules Huret for the latter's *Enquête sur l'Evolution Littéraire,* Edmond pointed out that he might have said to the reporter: "I provided the complete formula for naturalism in *Germinie Lacerteux,* and *L'Assommoir* was made absolutely according to the method shown in the former. Now I have been the first one to emerge from naturalism—and not the way Zola did it in servile imitation, when the success of *L'Abbé Constantin* caused him to write *Le Rêve*—but because I found the genre in its original form worn out. Yes, I was the first to move out of it by using the new materials with which the young of today wish to replace it—by *dreams, symbolism, satanism,* etc., etc.—by writing *Les Frères Zemganno* and *La Faustin,* I, the inventor of naturalism, sought to dematerialize it before anyone else thought of doing so."

Whereas Edmond de Goncourt declared himself on the side of the moderns on many occasions, his acceptance of the new literature was nonetheless considerably qualified, and rather temperamentally so. He expressed agreement with Daudet in depreciating psychological novels in the manner of Stendhal, works in which thought is more important than action. He was generally hostile to the new writing in Russia and Scandinavia, largely because of the growing reputation of foreign writers. The vogue for the Russians in the 1880s he saw as a reaction of right-thinking people who were looking for something with which to counter the success of the French "naturist" novel: "For incontestably it is the same kind of literature: the reality of things human seen from the sad human side, not the poetic. And neither Tolstoy nor Dosteovsky nor the others invented this literature! They took it from Flaubert, from me, from Zola, at the same time crossing it strongly with a strain of Poe" *(Journal,* October 1887). In 1895 Edmond gave an interview to *Le Rappel* in which he inveighed against the Russians and Scandinavians, who, he said, owed everything to the French school and particularly to the Goncourts: "Strindberg admitted to me the other day that he was aware that he owed me the secret of his analytical theater; and Ibsen and the others have also had to recognize that they derived from me."

From these sporadic and often biased outbursts, and from the more carefully considered prefaces, we can discern certain more or less firmly held positions:

The Goncourts considered themselves *realists,* though they often used the term *naturiste.* On many occasions Edmond equated realism and naturalism; on others he shrank from the sordidness and vulgarity often ascribed to naturalism.

They preached the right and the necessity of the novelist to open up the subject of the poor and the outcast in a "spirit of intellectual curiosity and out of pity for human misery." However, this was not normally their chosen subject matter and they insisted that for those who were well acquainted with higher social levels a realism of the drawing room was equally possible.

They placed great emphasis on the use of *human documents*.

Although they did not make a cult of authorial objectivity, they practiced it with fair consistency.

They saw themselves as using an analytical method in fiction.

They placed great stress on the use of a natural language, not a literary one; yet at the same time they were exponents of what they called *l'écriture artiste*.

The Goncourts' claims to innovation in doctrine and technique are sometimes overstressed for polemic purposes. They must yield primacy to Flaubert's *Madame Bovary* in showing the way to a new prose fiction, but it cannot be denied that after Flaubert they are the next in line among the innovators of the French novel. Moreover, the Goncourts developed a type of realistic novel that is different from that produced by either Flaubert or Zola, a type that had some influence on those two writers as well as on the younger members of the realist-naturalist group. Writing in collaboration, the brothers published seven novels before Jules's death on June 20, 1870: *En 18..* (1851), *Charles Demailly* (made over from a play, *Les Hommes de Lettres*) (1860), *Soeur Philomène* (1861), *Renée Mauperin* (1864), *Germinie Lacerteux* (1865), *Manette Salomon* (1867), and *Madame Gervaisais* (1869). Edmond, the surviving brother, published four more novels: *La Fille Elisa* (1877), *Les Frères Zemganno* (1879), *La Faustin* (1882), and *Chérie* (1884). In addition, there was the early play *Henriette Maréchal*, not to mention the dramatic vehicles drawn from the novels in later years.

When we ask ourselves what world these novels depict, what new territory is opened up by the Goncourts, we get a somewhat ambiguous answer. The world which they appropriated to themselves is less definitive than that of their rivals and contemporaries. The reason for this is simple enough. The Goncourts were actually less interested in details of physical and social setting than they were in analysis of character. The range of milieus in their novels is therefore as wide and as varied as their works: the lower levels of society for *Germinie Lacerteux* and *La Fille Elisa;* the world of the arts in *Charles Demailly, Manette Salomon,* and *La Faustin;* the upper levels of society in *Renée Mauperin* and *Chérie;* and three very special milieus in *Les Frères Zemganno, Madame Gervaisais,* and *Soeur Philomène.* Even where the general background is the same, as in *Renée Mauperin* and *Chérie,* the individuals and the specific environment studied are distinct. Whatever the merits of the Goncourt novels, they have as catholic a range as Zola provided in the Rougon-Macquart, and the milieus are consistently well studied. The Goncourts' claim that there could and should be a realism of the drawing room, of the Faubourg St. Germain, was put to the test in some of the novels, though for the time in which they wrote, their most original investigations were of the lower world of servants and prostitutes.

The preface to *Germinie Lacerteux* is deservedly famous for its scorn of "alcove confessions," "vapid and consolatory reading," and for its insistence that the novel should be "the great, serious, impassioned, living form of literary study and social examination," that it should become a form of social history. This position is restated thirteen years later in the preface to *La Fille Elisa,* which the author said was "written with the same feeling of intellectual curiosity and pity for human misery" as the earlier book and which he had consciously made "austere and chaste," seeking to do nothing more than move the reader to a sad meditation. "But it has been impossible for me at times not to speak as a doctor, as a scientist, as an historian. It would be truly harmful to us, the young and serious school of the modern novel, to forbid us to think, to analyze, to describe all that it is permitted to others to put in a volume which on its cover is inscribed STUDY or some such serious title. At this point in time it is not possible to condemn the genre to be the amusement of young ladies on railway journeys."

The great innovation of the Goncourts is less in the precise corner of reality chosen than in the idea of the case study, of the psychological analysis of a single character, usually a woman. Even in their genesis these works bear the mark of the case study. *La Fille Elisa* had its beginning as early as 1855, when a note appeared in the *Journal* about a dinner at a brothel and an inmate who is enamored of a traveling salesman, to which a number of years later is added a statement about the outrage felt on a visit to a women's penitentiary because of the imposition of the rule of silence on the prisoners. *Germinie Lacerteux* grew out of the shocking discovery of the debauched life led for many years by their own servant Rose, revelations that shook the brothers to the roots of their moral being but which they speedily translated into literature. *Madame Gervaisais* was patterned closely on the life of an aunt who became a *dévotée* and died in Rome. In only one novel, *Manette Salomon,* might it be said that these authors began with a world into which characters gradually found their way.

What we have here, considerably before Zola thought of the term, is a series of *experiments,* where an individual is placed in a situation and his or her actions are traced to their logical end. In nearly every instance we have a case of breakdown brought about by nervosity (with the clear exception of *Les Frères Zemganno,* where the breakdown is physical and for the most part by reason of external causes). If it were not for the fact that seven of the Goncourts' novels were written before the illness and death of Jules, we might look upon them as a repeated morbid statement of his fate. At any rate, the brothers seize upon a basic fact of their observation, the tendency of the human organism to run off the track, not necessarily by reason of some exceptional or overwhelming strain.[2] They observe this nervosity chiefly in women, and for the most part in women who occupy a physically comfortable place in the world, though the two representatives of *le bas monde,* Germinie and Elisa, degenerate the most dramatically. These, however, are not psychological novels as we understand the term today. There is virtually no effort to probe the mind or to represent its interior states. These novelists are generally content to look on from the outside, to chronicle the process of degeneration without attempting to explain it in any but general terms. These case histories are perhaps too simplified, too monolithic for our contemporary taste, but they are written with authority, and in their way are as portentous for the future of fiction as are Dostovesky's studies of driven personalities.

Balzacian prolixity of detail is not for the Goncourts. As they were working on *Manette Salomon,* the most dense of their novels in background, they declared: "Material description of things and places is not, in the novel as we understand it, description for description's sake." Their insistence on the relative unimportance of detail does not imply that they scanted their research. Rather they performed it faithfully, though complainingly, and attempted, like Flaubert, to keep their spadework from showing. *Soeur Philomène* was preceded by a careful examinaton of the hospital milieu. They read books of medicine in profusion to get exact information on the maladies from which their characters suffered.[3] As they prepared to write *Madame Gervaisais* the Goncourts shuffled through their notes on Rome, and they hung a plan of that city on their door so as to be almost physically there and able to pass their eyes over it as they wrote their novel. They went to trials at the Cour d'Assises to gather material for *La Fille Elisa,* and when Edmond took that book up again six years later, his immediate complaint was against his need to be a "conscientious policeman" as he, now alone, went on the prowl for human documents in the area around the Ecole Militaire.

When we turn to the technical devices and innovations of the Goncourts, we are on ground that is of great interest today, because, as has been suggested, they stand for a procedure somewhat counter to the massive, saturated cross section of society which we generally associate with the realist-naturalists. If *Soeur Philomène,* their first real novel, is slight, scarcely more than a suggestive, tantalizing anecdote, *Renée Mauperin* is a work of substance and must be examined carefully. Pierre Sabatier states that the brothers wrote this novel "with the idea of showing the faults of the young bourgeoisie, its egoism, its hypocrisy, its conventions, the web of ordinary intrigues which make up its life, and its thirst for honor and riches and its scorn for the individual aspirations of the soul."[4] It is hard to see this novel as so overtly programmatic, but it does provide a broad cross section of the bourgeoisie: M. Mauperin, a former officer and now a successful manufacturer, who is very indulgent to Renée, his third child; Madame Mauperin, the usual mother eager for advantageous marriage and worldly success for her children, conveniently forgetful of her own ordinary origins but caustic about those of others; Henri Mauperin, the essence of calculation, seeking the most advantageous marriage possible while sowing his wild oats with what he considers distinction; a daughter older than Renée who is exactly like all other right-thinking young matrons; a suitor who is like all other young men of his class, and who succeeds in being "mediocre with éclat." There is also the Bourjot family representing a higher level of the middle class and able to offer a dowry of a million francs for their daughter Noémi, who is an anemic contrast with the vital Renée. They are a family of *arrivistes* on a superior scale, the father a turncoat from liberalism who worries about the threat of new ideas to his property and money; the mother achieving a calculated social success of chill grandeur, dominated by a passion for Henri Mauperin, whose mistress she is, and going mad after his death. Finally, there is a peripheral figure, Denoisel, a friend of the Mauperin family, who contrives on a limited income to play the game of bourgeois values without believing in them.

Whereas this collection of middle-class figures is drawn carefully from life, the action of the novel is not, for it abounds in excessively romanesque elements: Henri's liaison and Noémi's knowledge of her mother's guilt; the fatal duel with its ironic significance; the surprise revelation that Renée has alerted Villacourt as to her brother's assumption of his family name. There is also a difficulty in the handling of exposition. Biographical information about the various characters is introduced at intervals in an evident effort to avoid the dense expository beginning of the typical Balzac novel, but sporadic introduction is also awkward, particularly when as late as Chapter 35 we encounter eight pages of history of the Villacourt family from 1803 to the present.

What is most arresting about this novel is its reliance on dramatic scene—to an extent not equalled in the later works of the Goncourts. There is an opening conversation between Renée and her current suitor as they swim lazily in the Seine. This is continued by a scene in the Mauperin salon that evening in which Renée, by her outrageous behavior, disposes of the suitor permanently. In all some fifty pages are almost entirely in dialogue, interrupted only by a block of biographical information about M. Mauperin. These scenes are followed by a dialogue between Madame Mauperin and the Abbé Blampoix, a society priest, which is perfect in its urbanity and unction, then by one between Renée and her father alone at lunch. In short, the first hundred pages of the novel are devoted to events of two days in a scenic manner that is vivid and dramatic.

The remainder of the work is not so tight-knit in organization or so direct in presentation, though there are excellent scenes, such as the call the Mauperins make on the Bourjots, or the at home given by the elder Mauperin daughter, which is presented in eight pages of dialogue. It is this kind of scene plus a considerable amount of narrated material that gives us the substance of the bourgeois world of Paris. The rest of the novel suffers from having to exist in time so as to permit a series of plot developments to take place. The Mauperin son receives consent to his marriage with Noémi on condition that he provide her with a noble name. Over a year must elapse before he can bring this about, and the sudden irruption of the farouche Villacourt on scene to provoke a duel is a radical change of tone. Similarly, Renée's fatal illness is prepared for in the most perfunctory way, by a brief indication of faintness and palpitation early in the novel. Her collapse after her brother's death and her inescapable decline seem out of key with the other events. The ending of the work is flawed by a page of sentimental writing showing the Mauperin parents wandering disconsolately over Europe in a kind of shadow existence during their last years, for we suddenly learn that not only have they lost Renée and Henri but also their other daughter has catastrophically died in childbirth.

We find, then, in this work a somewhat dubious success, in that manner and expedients are not all of a piece. If the novel is to be basically scenic in treatment, as it promises in the beginning, then it must give up a good deal of narrated material and move more closely toward a dramatic presentation. If it is to be a picture of a young woman in revolt against the conventions and values of her society and who therefore shows a certain recalcitrance of social behavior, then it would be better not to bring in physiological decline. If the tone is to be one of clinical detachment in the presentation of characters and mores, then we cannot tolerate the descent into sentimentality at the end. In spite of these qualifications, however, it is a fresh and lively work; above all it has a wonderful vigor of language, especially in the dialogue. This does not strike today's reader as in any way unusual, but the authors themselves were aware of their audacity, writing in the *Journal* for April 13, 1864: "People are protesting a good deal right now against the language of our *Renée Mauperin*—especially the men of the world of the brasserie. Yet the tonality we gave it was far short of actuality."

Whether Sabatier is correct in seeing *Germinie Lacerteux* as the high point in the Goncourts' career, as *Madame Bovary* was for Flaubert and *L'Assommoir* was for Zola, we must agree that this is an important work: "Whether one considers the subject treated, or the way in which they treated it, bearing in mind the date when it was written, one is obliged to salute *Germinie Lacerteux* as the arrival of naturalism."[5] What strikes Sabatier as particularly original about the work is its clinical detachment:

> The Goncourts renewed in literature the experiment of Vesalius in the field of medicine when he decided to plunge his scalpel into a corpse in order to seek there a lesson of life. Certainly above everything else the authors of *Germinie Lacerteux* were interested in explaining physiologically the reactions of their characters. They were drawn by the clinical "side" of their subjects; that is why, in spite of their repugnance, they forced themselves to visits to the hospital, forced themselves to look at the sick, to have cases explained to them by technicians and even to be present at operations. No novelist before them had felt such scruples and such desire for scientific documentation.[6]

Structurally this novel marks an advance over its predecessor in certain respects, and a retrogression so far as dramatic presentation is concerned. A whole life is to be summed up and illuminated here; thus dramatic scene may well have struck the authors as uneconomical. Although there are bits of dialogue, there are only two main occasions when it strikes the reader's attention. The first occurs in Chapter 14, where there is a conversation in argot with Adèle, the servant of a kept woman. It is not until Chapter 48 that speech again comes to the fore in a conversation between Adèle and Gautruche, whom Germinie meets at a picnic in the Bois de Vincennes. Otherwise this work uses dialogue sparingly, at most giving it as a culmination to a narrative passage.

The initial expository information is presented with some ingenuity. The novel begins with a conversation between Germinie and her ailing employer, Mlle de Varandeuil, which quickly becomes a monologue account by Germinie of her past life. Then there are thirty pages of summary narrative of the life of the listener, who is not paying much attention to her servant. After this there are ten more pages of narration of Germinie's experiences after her arrival in Paris. Thereafter the novel proceeds in short chapters, rarely given any dramatic organization, in which we follow Germinie in the ups and downs of her life in the capital. We learn that she has gone through a period of intense religious devotion, which is followed by an equally intense devotion to a niece until that is brought to an end by the removal of the niece's family to Algeria. A new phase begins with her acquaintance with Madame Jupillon, the proprietor of a neighborhood creamery. Germinie takes the latter's school-boy son under her wing, visiting him at his pension with his mother and then alone when the mother is ill, generally coming to treat him as if he were her own child.

After several years Germinie finds that she is in love with the rapidly developing adolescent, though she is able to contain her passion for a time: "That happy and unsatisfied love produced in Germinie's physical being a singular physiological phenomenon. One would have said that the passion that flowed in her renewed and transformed her lymphatic personality. . . . A marvelous animation had come to her." She now gives herself completely to the life of the creamery, spending every spare moment from her service there. We are flatly told by the narrator that "In all this by-play the creamery proprietor wanted only one thing, to attach and keep a servant who cost her nothing." We are even told that young Jupillon is no good: "This man, emerging from childhood, brought to his first liaison as his entire ardor and flame the cold instincts of swinishness that are awakened in childhood by bad books, by the whisper-ings of comrades, by conversations at boarding school—the first breath of impurity which deflowers desire." This is editorializ-ing of a very overt sort, a sin of which the Goncourts were, fortunately, not often guilty.

The central portion, a graphic account of Germinie's besot-ted passion for Jupillon, by its tone and subject makes an important contribution to the vividness of the novel. We see her humiliated at a dance hall. We are told that she has lost the respect of the inhabitants of the quartier as soon as her relations with the young man are known. She takes all her savings and even borrows money in order to set him up in a glove shop. She becomes pregnant by him, and in one of the most moving scenes of the novel manages to prepare and serve Mlle de Varandeuil's annual Twelfth Night dinner for the children of relatives and friends in spite of the onset of labor. As she leaves the building to take a taxi to the hospital, Germinie is accosted by Jupillon, who succeeds in extorting from her forty francs that she needs for her accouchement. The daughter is born and put with a wet nurse in the country. Germinie is ecstatic over being a mother and makes regular visits to see the child on her days off. Her joy is destroyed when the child suddenly dies, and she undergoes a severe crisis that is described in close physical detail. This is followed by months of "brutish sorrow." She takes to drink with Adèle and others as she is increasingly neglected by Jupillon, whose mother casts her off in a burst of virtuous indignation when she learns, or pretends to learn, for the first time that Germinie has had a child. However, after some months when Jupillon finds that he has drawn an unlucky number in the draft lottery, he and his mother play up to Germinie and she is cajoled into finding the twenty-three hundred francs needed to buy a substitute. By this time she is so deeply in debt that she can never recover; her debts are her master and will possess her forever.

Though she has no illusions about her lover, Germinie is devoured by jealousy. She spies on him; she becomes a solitary drinker; she steals from her mistress when Jupillon demands money. Her whole demeanor changes; she seems to become again the stupid peasant who arrived in Paris years before. Sexual need torments her, though she resists the frightful temptation for months before giving in. Then comes the picnic at Vincennes and an affair with Gautruche, whose indignities she suffers without complaint. She beats the pavement when he is not available and finds her lovers "between a hospital, a slaughterhouse, and a cemetery." (Compare the boundaries in Zola's *L'Assommoir.*) When Gautruche, like the Jupillons, thinks of acquiring a servant by marriage, she turns on him, particularly outraged at the suggestion that she desert Mlle de Varandeuil. At last, having spent a whole night night in the rain spying on Jupillon, Germinie is attacked by pleurisy, refuses to go to bed, and soon reaches the point where tuberculosis has destroyed one lung and is making inroads on the other. Her peasant stubbornness finally gives way, and she consents to go to Lariboisière Hospital, where she dies at the age of forty-one. The novel ends with the discovery by Mlle de Varandeuil of her servant's hidden debauched life in a powerful scene with the concierge. Mlle de Varandeuil's revulsion and rejection—she says a common grave is good enough for Germinie—is followed by repentance. She goes to the cemetery, looks for the grave, and we leave her kneeling in the snow at the approximate place where Germinie lies. Again the authors mar the ending by two or three pages of sentimental effusion: "Oh, Paris, thou art the heart of the world, the great humane city, the great city of love and brotherhood. . . . The poor are thy citizens like the rich."

The details of this work, which probes to the very center of human depravity, are handled with restraint. The novel manages to convey an atmosphere of debauchery in terms that are nonspecific. Perhaps such modesty in approach was a necessity: We learn from the *Journal* for October 12, 1864, that the publisher, Charpentier, objected to a passage at the end of Chapter 1 in which Germinie recounts that upon her arrival in Paris she was covered with lice. The publisher thought that "vermin" was as far as the authors could be allowed to go in affronting the public. They burst out against that public, asking why they should conceal the existence of lice on the bodies of the poor and be forced to "lie to the public and conceal all the ugly side of life."

Whereas *Germinie Lacerteux* is one of those novels that concentrates on the life of a single individual, it has a framework that goes beyond limited scope. It is built from beginning to end, though with somewhat uneven emphasis, on a contrast between the peasant woman and her aristocratic mistress. The stoic, austere rectitude of the latter is established at the beginning, and her shocked rejection and ultimate acceptance of Germinie provide the dramatic ending. Though in the body of the novel there is little about Mlle de Varandeuil, she is always present, and Germinie's varying modes of behavior take on meaning and proportion as they are set beside the unvarying goodness, simplicity, and naive blindness of her employer. Yet at the same time devotion is the one constant in Germinie's life. She is ennobled by this stubborn adherence to duty, even though she steals, just as her mistress is ennobled by affection, trust, and final acceptance of her erring servant. This device of contrast works exceptionally well, for it helps us to keep the protagonist in perspective without depreciating her.

Though much less famous than the article about *Madame Bovary,* Sainte-Beuve's letter about *Germinie Lacerteux* shows a strong sense of the originality of this work: ". . . already I have been struck by one thing, that to judge this work properly and talk about it, we need a poetics quite different from the old, a poetics suited to the production of a nervous art and a new kind of research. And that in itself is great praise for a work: that it should raise a question of this importance forces one out of the old attitudes and onto new tracks. I hope your daring will be understood; I should like to find means to help bring this about."[7] There is considerable irony in the fact that when Flaubert came to write *Un Coeur Simple* some years later, he drew on *Germinie Lacerteux* both for the relationship of servant and mistress and for the psychological pattern of Félicité's life, though he reduced the erotic element to a minimum. On the other hand, Zola, who confessed that his direction was changed by reading this book, immediately conceived *Thérèse Raquin,* in which the erotic content and sensationalism in general dominate the work.

The next Goncourt novel, *Manette Salomon,* is quite different from the other works of these writers, both for its scope and for its detail. The title is a misnomer, for Manette Salomon figures almost incidentally (except by obvious contrivance at the end), and the proper title is the one which the authors discarded, *L'Atelier Langibout.* This is an unusually long novel for the Goncourts, running to 472 pages, which attests to the density of description. Only in this work do they attempt to present a milieu extensively, perhaps because here the background is primary and the characters emerge naturally from it in a manner not unlike that of Zola as he developed the Rougon-Macquart.

Manette Salomon contains a good deal of authorial commentary about the development of the arts, which is interesting in itself and necessary to the statement of the work, though it is presented somewhat less than spontaneously. For example, as early as Chapter 3 there is a discussion of the cultural climate, of the fall of romanticism, and of the disastrous effect of literature on painting, which is polarized between Ingres and Delacroix: "One saw nowhere any attempt, any effort, any audacity which sought truth, which came to grips with modern life, which showed to the ambitious young on their way up that great despised side of art, contemporaneity." Such commentaries frequently come from the characters themselves, as when Chassagnol suggests: "It may be that the Beautiful today is enveloped, interred, concentrated. Perhaps in order to find it there must be analysis, a microscope, myopic eyes, the methods of the new psychology. . . . Did not Balzac find greatness in money, housekeeping, and the dirtiness of modern things, in a heap of things in which past centuries did not see two cents' worth of art?" In spite of numerous statements of this sort the novel does not preach to any disconcerting extent. Rather it exhibits the awkwardness and self-consciousness frequently found among realists when they need to supply special technical backgrounds to make their actions intelligible.

The work opens with a dramatic scene of a very mixed crowd going into the Botanical Gardens and with a highly impressionistic description of the view down on Paris from that slight elevation. This leads to several pages of dialogue, pretty much in argot, introducing various young painters who are to figure later in the novel. A bit later we have a detailed description of the Langibout studio, of the artists, and of their workaday routine, a scene that is summed up in conventional literary terms as "atelier of misery and of youth, a real garret of hope." Numerous other artistic interiors are rather briefly sketched, and there are accounts of the Salons of various years, the intrigues involved in the acceptance of paintings for the

Salons, and the philistine reactions of the public. The most impressive part of the novel from the standpoint of documentation is an eighty-page passage beginning with Chapter 71 that describes, without any particular narrative continuity except what the presence of Coriolis and his mistress provides, the life of the artists of the so-called Barbizon group at a time when Barbizon represented Bohemia and not the sacred groves of hallowed genius.

This general background is supported, perhaps too mechanically, by a developed cross section. The artist whom we follow most closely is Naz de Coriolis, a Creole from Mauritius, who has a real ability to see in a new way. He is contrasted with Garnotelle, a canny opportunist without a shred of originality who nonetheless wins all the prizes, from the Prix de Rome to riches and popular acclaim. On the sidelines is Chassagnol, a kind of self-taught theoretician of art, who becomes a useful, if obvious, mouthpiece for opinions about art. Finally, there is Anatole, essentially an adventurer in life, who never gives much continuous application to his modest talents as artist, but whose presence in the novel does endow it with a lively reality. Through his precarious existence we get a sense of the poverty and gaiety traditional among artists, and also a sense of the waste that comes from their hit-or-miss effort to see and create in an original way. For a time Anatole seems to be the central figure, but once he is rescued from destitution in Marseilles by Coriolis, who is returning from the Middle East, his position becomes secondary as he provides a kind of foil to both Garnotelle's conventionality and Coriolis' nervewracking attempts at originality. Manette Salomon also has a place in this cross section as model and inevitable mistress of painters, until an intrusive critical note is struck by the narrative voice and she is made the target of ungracious antifeminine, anti-Semitic attack.

About a third of the way through the novel Coriolis becomes the central figure and the major action seems to be his attempts to break through into a new kind of painting. From his sojourn in the Orient he has gained a new feeling for color, but the three pictures accepted by the 1852 Salon are not well received, partly because of the machinations of Garnotelle. At the 1853 Salon his *Bain Turc* is a success, but two pictures in the 1855 Salon, *A Draft Board* and *A Church Wedding*—done in the manner of Courbet—are failures because of the public's firm antipathy to the modern in painting, an attitude encouraged by the scandals attending Courbet's efforts. Not willing to accept the "new realism which he brought, a realism outside the stupidity of the daguerreotype and the charlatanism of the ugly," the public blocks Coriolis' development. His worldly failure causes his mistress, Manette, to ally herself with Garnotelle. In time her lover finds her so tyrannical that he attempts to escape, but he fails as the novel ends with a return to the Botanical Gardens where it began. There is a vision of nature, of animals, of vibrant life in a lyrical vein as "the former bohemian revisited the joys of Eden, and there arose in him, in almost heavenly fashion, a bit of the happiness of the first man before virgin nature."

In spite of the misleading title this novel is only incidentally a study of the breakdown of a single individual. Critics customarily speak of it as a demonstration of the havoc brought about by women, by domesticity, and by fixed affections in the domain of artistic creation. It is true that Coriolis does go down hill, that he is tamed by Manette's implacable desire for security and respectability. Yet the reader, though irritated by the occasional repetition of this theme, is not convinced and feels that there is a fatal weakness in Coriolis himself which is never uncovered. Because of this incomplete analysis, as well as the overt argument, the novel errs in placing too much emphasis upon Coriolis. It is with actual relief that we come back with Anatole to the normal life of artists, for we feel that the novel has at last returned to its true subject, a general picture of artist life. In short, this is a case where the materials of the novel do not permit the typical Goncourt analysis; the milieu is more important than the individuals, though the authors do not realize it.

The last of the Goncourt works under joint authorship is *Madame Gervaisais,* published in 1868. The brothers' trip to Rome in 1867 had as part of its purpose a study of the milieu in which the action of their novel would take place, a careful preparation that Edmond, with biting scorn, later compared to the quick way in which Zola worked up his massive *Rome.* The Goncourt novel is based on events that occurred in the life of an aunt, Nephtalie de Courmont, an account of which is given in *La Maison d'un Artiste,* and is repeated in the *Journal* for August 30, 1890. This is by far the most specialized of the Goncourt studies, one best described in Zola's words in an article in *Le Gaulois* for March 9, 1869: "I am going to consider this book as a simple psychological problem: How did Madame Gervaisais, taking the negations of philosophy as her starting point, arrive at the ecstasy of Saint Teresa? That is what I want to study with the Goncourts step by step. Enough of the critics will speak of the exquisite art of these authors. It will be a good thing also to show that these artists know where they are going and that a supreme logic presides over their delicately worked compositions." Armand de Pontmartin in *La Gazette de France* for March 14 of the same year gives a parallel description: "It is purely and simply (even though it be neither pure nor simple) a pathological study, applied this time to the effects of religious devotion—a moral or physical illness which is to be ranged alongside those of Renée Mauperin and Germinie Lacerteux."

In no other novel of the Goncourts do we get a better demonstration of the strength and weakness of the Goncourt approach. *Madame Gervaisais* is conducted on a line of absolute and incontrovertible logic in a style that is lucid and completely unmannered, yet evocative where evocation is needed. We see the protagonist first on her arrival in Rome, a woman somewhat ailing, somewhat ill at ease in a foreign city, chiefly concerned for the well-being of her beautiful son, who is not quite right. Her withdrawal from the world seems normal for the circumstances. Then as she gets better and becomes accustomed to Rome, she gives herself to the city, enjoys its special qualities, shares it in a simple way with her child, Pierre-Charles, and condones the thefts and incivilities of her Roman servant.

We learn that the special circumstances of her childhood association with her father and her withdrawal into herself during an unhappy marriage have made her into a bluestocking for whom the banal content of Catholicism has no attraction. At first her residence in Rome only strengthens this antipathy, for the sight of "certain gross idolatries had wounded the natural and delicate religiosity of her spiritual nature." Yet as she is drawn, almost in self-protection, to the beauty of pagan art and monuments, she at the same time finds them inadequate, and so "pagan art drew her back toward the beliefs rejected by the vigorous masculine reflections of her youth, beliefs to which the woman thought herself completely dead." The precipitant to change, however, comes through her situation as mother. Her son is near death when, at the suggestion of her landladies, she prays at San Agostino and a miracle occurs. A little later, at Castel Gandolfo, she meets a Polish countess who scorns her free-thinking and gives her the name of a Jesuit confessor. From the moment she enters the Gesù to confess to this priest, she is lost. Her decline is a descent that is almost a paradigm of saintly renunciation of the world: "Covertly a metamorphosis was taking place within Madame Gervaisais. The pride of her intelligence, her spirit of analysis, of research, of criticism; her personality based on judgment and energy, rare in her sex; her own ideas seemed bit by bit to decline in her through a revolution in her moral being, a sort of reversal of her nature." Finding the Jesuit confessor too mild, too indulgent, she has recourse to Father Sibilla, a kind of spiritual brute, whose sole design is to reduce her to absolute denial of the world, even including her child, with the result that finally "in her the earthly being ceased to exist," and she sinks to a perfect imitation of death in life. This spiritual denuding is accompanied by a rapid development of tuberculosis, so that even though she is roused to the world for a moment by the visit of her brother and to a realization of what she has done to herself and others, she dies, actually at the moment when she is about to be received in audience by the Pope.

This downward progress is logical, relentless, and completely comprehensible. But the weakness of the novel is that it is too geometrical and proceeds almost as an abstraction. It yields very little of revelatory action, even though there are brief dialogue passages that have the breath of life in them. Moreover, since other people, including the unfortunate Pierre-Charles, are of little importance in the novel, we must rely on what we are told about the protagonist, whose situation we do not come to feel because of the paucity of life-giving circumstances. At any rate, the novel is pure: it does not sentimentalize; it does not approve or condemn. It merely places before our eyes a case of intense religious disintegration. It is a preliminary sketch, a scenario, from which another novelist might have built a work filled with the substance of actuality. It is the essence of realism, with too little of its existential content, of the close engagement with actuality that gives life to other works in this mode.

Of the novels written by Edmond alone only two need more than casual examination. *Les Frères Zemganno* has a kind of sweetness because of its nostalgic tone. Except for some elements describing the milieu of the traveling circus it cannot be said to be realistic or to aim at being so. *La Faustin* can be considered to be a complete failure. Granted the trite subject of life in the theater, one might still expect from the author an accurate examination of that life. Instead the book is intensely, almost grotesquely, romantic, and it is hard to conceive of an action further removed from ordinary reality than it provides. Of the other two works *La Fille Elisa* is the one to which Edmond turned four years after his brother's death, since the brothers had had this work in mind for years and had done some preparation for it—going to the Cour d'Assises in March 1869 to get the background for the court scenes. The publication of this novel was preceded by the appearance of Huysmans' *Marthe; l'Histoire d'une Fille*, which immediately fell afoul of censorship. Edmond in the *Journal* professed to be worried over the fate of his novel, stating on December 30, 1876:

> I had planned to go farther in it and to spice up the manuscript with a lot of little discoveries that I could make in the worlds of prostitution and prison; but perhaps that would have been going too far. Also the thought that the book might be brought into court makes me lazy about doing anything more. I don't have the courage to do any more work on a book that is in danger of being suppressed.

As things turned out, this was the most successful of the Goncourt books, no doubt because of its subject, with a first printing of six thousand copies being sold out immediately, followed by a second printing of four thousand.

This work is more intricate in structure than those that preceded it. Like *Germinie Lacerteux,* to which it is closely related in subject, it gives a full-length treatment of the protagonist's life, but since the portions of that life which are under examination are of two sharply different kinds, a new approach is used. The opening scene is in a courtroom where the spectators are waiting for the jury to bring in a verdict after Elisa's trial for the murder of a young soldier. She is found guilty, and the emotion of the reader is heightened by the reading from the penal code of the requirement that all persons condemned to death be decapitated.

The first part of the novel then recapitulates in detail Elisa's life up to this point in a running narrative rather than by dramatic presentation of the life of a prostitute. There is no development, only a dipping into the events of her life from time to time for significant samples. Of all the Goncourt works this is the one with the most insistence on physiological and psychological causality. As Robert Ricatte says of it: "Edmond never enjoyed playing the realistic game so clearly."[8] We get a picture of Elisa's childhood with her mother, a midwife of brutal and uncertain temper. The child, who has typhoid twice in six years, is also given to violent outbursts of anger: "A refractory character, a disordered being with whom nothing could be done, whom there was no way of controlling. At the same time a flighty and changeable nature. . . ." From the clients whom her mother kept in the house Elisa learned "almost from the cradle everything that children do not know about love." In her early teens this obstinate creature ran away from her mother to a brothel in Lorraine, not out of desire for sensual pleasure but because she thought she would have an easy life. "She gave herself to the firstcomer. Elisa became a prostitute simply, naturally, almost without a tremor of consciousness . . . she had come to consider the sale and provision of love as a profession, a little less laborious than others, a profession where there was no off-season." "There was in Elisa neither erotic ardor nor desire for debauchery, nor turbulence of the senses." We follow her all over France with a traveling salesman lover. When she tires of his exploitation, she takes up the life of a Paris prostitute, frequently changing houses for the sake of variety. We learn about the brothels that serve the soldiers of the Ecole Militaire. For the first time we get an extended account of the interior of one of these establishments during working hours and a fair amount of information about Elisa's colleagues, though a quick cross sectioning of this kind was also done for the brothel in Lorraine. A very exceptional circumstance occurs when Elisa falls in love with a young soldier and has the joy of walking out with him on her days off.

The narrative continuity breaks off here, and we return to Elisa's later life, watching her arrival at the prison (the death sentence has been commuted), an arrival curiously similar to her arrival at the brothel years before. There is a vivid account of the prison regime of silence and its deleterious effects as well as of the general routine of the prison, symbolically called *Noirlieu*. Elisa's recalcitrant nature is aroused; she goes on a kind of strike against authority and is subjected to harsh punishment, but she cannot bend her will even though she would like to do so. At last the prison doctor intervenes, insisting that she has no normal sense of guilt or of free will.

Thereafter she is kept in special wards but in a deepening condition of hebetude as she regresses to childhood and its recollections. At the very end she receives permission to speak to a visitor, but it is too late. She is dead.

This section is interspersed with sentimental elements. Elisa has kept a letter from the little soldier, and it is from her ruminations over it that we belatedly get an account of how she murdered him in the Bois de Boulogne when she thought he was treating her merely as a sex object. Her mother and sister come to visit her, and she is terribly let down to discover that their motive is money, not affection. To make the death scene more poignant and the point of the book more explicit, there is a drastic shift in point of view in the final chapters. The narrator now becomes a person and recounts his visit to the prison, his horror at the regime of silence, and his attempt to give Elisa a chance to speak—which comes too late.

It is difficult to find a basis for unity in the two sections of the novel; their being yoked together is a kind of tour de force. However, the work is direct, precise, and balanced in the choice of detail. There is no inclination toward the picturesque, though there is a limited use of argot, which is printed in italics. There is careful attention to motivation and behavior patterns, even if this errs in the direction of generality. All of this is admirable for the kind of work it is. Yet most readers will conclude that the dramatic dislocation that comes from giving primacy to the trial warps the novel out of its desired focus of impersonal observation. From the very start it can be read as a plea, not as an analysis.

Chérie recalls *Renée Mauperin* written some twenty years before, and is a more convincing, more clinically presented book than the earlier one. In the preface to *La Faustin* in 1881, Goncourt alerted his readers that he wanted to write a novel that would simply be a psychological and physiological study of a young girl "reared and educated in the hot-house of the capital, a novel built on *human documents.*" (In a footnote Edmond defended the phrase as one that "most meaningfully defines the new method of the school which followed

romanticism. . . .") Edmond went on to solicit the collaboration of women to write him details about the life of little girls,
about the awakening of their minds and coquetry, about the
essential qualities of "the new being created at adolescence."
The preface to *Chérie* characterizes the novel as "a monograph
on the young girl, observed in the elegant setting of Riches,
Power, and the best people, a study of the young girl in the
official circles of the Second Empire." For this work, the author
tells us, he has done research to a depth that might be expected
for a work of history. His aim is to render "the pretty and
distinguished aspects of my subject, and I have worked to
recreate the reality of elegance . . . I could not bring myself to
make my young girl the nonhuman individual, the sexless,
abstract, and lyingly ideal creature of the *chic* novels of today
and yesterday."

> It will certainly be found that the narration of *Chérie* lacks indent,
> peripeties, intrigue. For my part, I find that there is still too much
> of this. If I might become younger by a few years, I would like to
> write novels with no more complication than exists in most of the
> intimate dramas of existence, with love affairs ending without any
> more suicides than the affairs through which we have all passed;
> and as for death, death which I employ deliberately as the
> denouement of my novels, of this one as well as the others,
> although it is a little more *comme il faut* than marriage, I would
> reject it also from my books as a theatrical means that should be
> scorned in serious literature. . . . I believe that adventure, *bookish*
> machination, has been worn out by Soulié and Sue and the great
> imaginative writers of the beginning of the century, and my idea is
> that the final evolution of the novel, in order for it to succeed
> completely in becoming the great vehicle of modern times, is to
> make it a work of pure analysis.

For this kind of writing Edmond believes that some other label
than *novel* will have to be found. He makes an interesting
protest against those who do not believe in making an effort to
write well, asserting the necessity of "a personal language, a
language that bears our signature." He expresses approval of

neologisms and presumably of vernacular and slang as well. Language must be well handled, for a failure to write well would allow vulgar reportage to take over.

Considering the preface to this, his last book, as "a sort of literary testament," Edmond recalls a statement made by Jules on a walk in the Bois de Boulogne a few months before his death: "Some day people will have to recognize that we wrote *Germinie Lacerteux* . . . and that *Germinie Lacerteux* is the paradigm of all that has been written since under the name of realism, naturalism, etc." This is a somewhat portentous preface for what J. H. Rosny called a minor work, but it does reflect the "temperament, the tastes, and the doctrines of Edmond de Goncourt." Certainly the novel proceeds in a straight line, never losing sight of its intention to present the development of a young girl of the upper classes. The heroine is the granddaughter of a Marshal of France, who has been recalled to public life as Minister of War. Her mother had become mad with grief after the death of her soldier husband at Sevastopol. The child is serious, usually sad, extraordinarily impressionable, and subject to disquieting outbursts of anger, examples of which are given in the form of a case study.

Nothing happens in the novel, which begins pictorially with a scene in which Chérie presides over a dinner party for eight little friends on her ninth birthday. There is an elaborate account of her preparation for her First Communion, which is accompanied by a temporary state of religious exaltation. This religious enthusiasm subsides; she goes through puberty torn between a sense of pride and a feeling of disgust over menstruation. We learn of her crushes and her first love by means of eleven pages of a diary covering a year. There is a ten-page disquisition on her friends, one of whom is described rather too emphatically by the narrator as *une possédée, une détraquée*, a perfect example of the moral illness of the nineteenth century as embodied in some of the women of the official world of the Second Empire. A chapter describes a visit to the office of Siesmeyer, a famous horticulturist at Versailles, which consists of a detailed inventory and no action whatever. Another chapter is given over to fourteen pages about taking tea in the salon; the next is about balls that Chérie attends, though in less detail. Thus we have a fairly complete picture of the young woman as she reaches adulthood.

Given her background, it is not surprising that Chérie may be psychologically unbalanced, but the novel gives little evidence of this and we are not prepared for the sudden and spectacular change of personality that she undergoes. A doctor comments that "ovulation demands fecundation" and says that in the exciting atmosphere of Paris young women sometimes die as a result of this nervous state. Chérie at any rate does die. Instead of death agonies we are given a powerful account of her erratic behavior toward the end of her life. The novel concludes documentarily with a *faire-part* announcing her death at the age of nineteen on June 20, 1870 (an unwarranted indulgence in private sentiment on the part of the author, since it is the day of Jules' death). What is remarkable about this last novel is that the author is still trying out new techniques. He abandons sustained action completely and tries to fill out his subject by means of literal documentation. It is not a successful experiment, but it does indicate one of the main lines of development that realists have tried to follow in this century, toward a fusion of factual data and fictional framework.

We cannot conclude an examination of the *opus* of the Goncourt brothers without recognizing their addiction to the theater. Their joint disappointment was the failure of a very mediocre play, *Henriette Maréchal,* which was staged in December 1865. The performance created such a tumult that virtually nothing of the play could be heard, and the diarist wrote on the morning after with a certain pride: "The head of the claque told me this morning that the theater has not seen such an uproar since [Victor Hugo's] *Hernani* and *Les Burgraves."* Interest in the theater continued to be one of Edmond's chief preoccupations in his later years, partly in deference to his brother's memory but also out of rivalry with the more successful Daudet and Zola. All of the Goncourt novels were dramatized during Edmond's last years, but none of them achieved any great success on the stage. The great event for Edmond was the reprise of *Henriette Maréchal* in March 1885. Only *Le Figaro* did it justice; the rest of the press was rather niggling. The critics did not recognize the play's originality in language and depiction of humanity. A few months later, on December 19, 1885, still smarting from critical condescension, Edmond declares: "When you get right down to it, up to now I know of only two plays which belong to the modern theater: *Henriette Maréchal,* which has the misfortune to be a forerunner, *Henriette Maréchal* and *Saphô.* You can't count the *Busnached* plays of Zola, and as for *Thérèse Raquin,* the play does indeed contain the novel but it does not have the least scenic modernity."[9]

In November 1886, *Renée Mauperin* was put on. As usual, Edmond had high expectations and hoped for a run of 100 performances. Though these hopes were not realized, he was consoled when the play was bought for American production. In October 1887, it was the turn of *Soeur Philomène,* which had its premiere at Antoine's Théâtre-Libre. During the next season Antoine undertook to do Goncourt's original play, *La Patrie en Danger,* without any overwhelming success. In December 1888, Edmond confided to his *Journal* that war had been declared on *Germinie Lacerteux* while the play was still in rehearsal by means of the canard that the leading actress, Réjane, had been forced against her will to utter the word *putain* (whore). The first performance is described on December 19 as "a real battle." *Le Figaro* for December 25, in an article entitled "Le Mot Sale" ("Dirty Words"), attacked the crudities of language in the novel, which, it said, were compounded in the play. (During this time the author took what comfort he could from the news that *Henriette Maréchal* had been performed with success in St. Petersburg.) Two years later, in December 1890, it was the turn of *La Fille Elisa,* and finally on February 29, 1896, *Manette Salomon* was put on and panned as usual. Edmond could not contain his amazement when two months later he went to pick up his share of the receipts from this play and found that it came to 7600 francs.

These various attempts, by Zola and even by Daudet as well, show the difficulty with which the citadel of conventional drama was to be reduced, and the deep-seated antagonism that existed on the part of theatergoers toward anything that sought to do more than entertain. But the obdurate response of the public should not lead us to overlook the inadequacies of these plays. They were essentially static; they lacked any sort of forward motion. Their power, if they had any, was the power of a real-life situation to speak for itself in language that rang true. Scenically, the plays seem to have been little more than a series of tableaus, like the children's party in *Germinie Lacerteux,* the brothel scene in *La Fille Elisa,* or, indeed, the fight at the washhouse in Zola's *L'Assommoir.* For the most respectful audience in the world these would still have failed to be absorbing dramas.

Although Edmond de Goncourt frequently spoke in the scientific idiom of Taine, Flaubert, and Zola, it is hard to believe that he had any particular grounding in the new materialistic science and philosophy. Indeed, his role of aristocrat and conservative militated against his assimilation of the new currents of thought. The *Journal* for April 7, 1869, contains an entry that is typical of his attitude (in this case of both brothers, since Jules was still alive):

> They were saying that Berthelot had predicted that in a hundred years of science man would know the secret of the atom and would be able at will to extinguish or relight the sun; that Claude Bernard for his part was asserting that after a hundred years of physiological science it would be possible to know the laws of organic life, of human creation. We raised no objections, but we firmly believe that at that point in the history of the world the good Lord with his white beard will arrive on earth with his bundle of keys and say to humankind, as they say at the Salon: "Gentlemen, it's closing time!"

Edmond clearly does not believe that the millennium will come through science, and he does not share in Zola's messianism for the novel as a branch of science. Yet it is equally clear that for the most part the characters whose lives he studies in his novels are subject to the unwavering force of determinism. He associates himself with this current of thought almost casually in a footnote to a *Journal* entry of May 24, 1885: "It is true that Taine marked Zola's thought rather early and readily: Taine's literary determinism, which was received with reticence in 1864, was accepted by Zola by September 1866. But determination of character by milieus is something that Zola verified among the novelists who influenced him directly, in Balzac and in a novel like *Germinie Lacerteux,* which he saluted as a revelation in 1865 twelve years before *L'Assommoir* and one year before his adherence to Taine." Sabatier says of the brothers that "They too were determinists, or rather fatalists, and in their pessimism and their distaste for surrounding vulgarity we must discover, as in Flaubert, the principal motive for their retreat into art."[10]

Retreat it no doubt was, but a retreat remarkable for its forward-looking aesthetic outlook. The Goncourts, especially Edmond, did accept the power of materiality and were disdainful of efforts to seek refuge in daydreams masquerading as novels. They methodically presented a gallery of modern characters, showing lives that they attempted to make authentic by massive research and cumulative observation. In a late *Journal* entry for August 30, 1893, Edmond wrote with disdain of the unwillingness of younger writers to do studies after nature and their penchant for creating what he called *metaphysical beings.* On the other hand, he had some reservations lest the prevailing materiality of the novel stifle the characters, lest milieu stand in such high relief around the feelings and passions that it almost stifle them. On July 24, 1885, Edmond set down the observation that "Perfection in art is the mixing in proper proportion of the real and *the imagined.* At the beginning of my literary career I had a predilection for the imagined. Later I became enamored exclusively of reality and that which is studied after nature. Now I remain faithful to reality but sometimes present it under a special light, which modifies it, poetizes it, tints it with fantasy."

This remark is not an accurate statement of Edmond's

general practice, though it is applicable to the two offbeat last works. It represents the path that he might well have been expected to take in view of his repugnance for vulgarity, his connoisseurship of eighteenth-century and Japanese art, and in the years after Jules's death his stoic acceptance of an emotionally empty existence. Instead Edmond remained faithful to reality and to realism as he understood it and was able to embody it in his own works of fiction. The presence of the Goncourts' clinically examined and presented case studies was a valuable addition to French realism, which might otherwise have been smothered in the accessory. It is with justice that Paul Bourget said that no one since Balzac had modified the art of the novel to as great an extent as the Goncourts.[11]

4

Emile Zola

In the history of the realistic movement it was Zola's fate to become the lightning rod that drew all the coruscating wrath and outrage of a disturbed literary universe. For the last twenty-five years of his life, at home and abroad, Zola was the scapegoat on whom was poured the accumulation of hatred and abuse that the new literature aroused among the idealists, the conservatives, and the prudish. By his writings and by his acts Zola alienated nearly every segment of the right-thinking public: The literary establishment refused to recognize him; the Church placed his works on the Index; to the great public his name became synonymous with filth; the publication of *La Terre* in England brought about the prosecution and humiliation of E. A. Vizetelly, the publisher; Zola was attacked personally by word and cartoon; there is even the possibility that his death in 1902 was by assasination.[1]

It is hard to say how much Zola actually sought the continuous public commotion that was evoked by his name. Certainly he did not shrink from it. He gave as good as he got and developed a talent for self-advertisement that caused the sales of his later works to rise to heights phenomenal for that day. Of the French writers of the nineteenth century only Victor Hugo imposed himself with equal power on the popular imagination. Of all the great realists only Tolstoy commanded equal public attention—though largely for extraliterary reasons. To the man in the street Zola was naturalism—a combative form of realism—and the outlines of man and doctrine were expanded and blurred beyond recognition as the heat of controversy inflated both to the dimensions of myth. After his death Zola's fame was eclipsed for several decades, but his example continued to work quietly. Today we must agree with Armand Lamoux that "Zola is indeed at the source . . . of a flourishing international literature, which is not esoteric or surrealistic or introspective, at the source of the novel which *accepts the existence of the external world and is willing* to take its themes from it."[2]

All the public fanfare belongs to literary history and, though still entertaining, takes us away from the central question of what Zola brought to the novel that impressed his contemporaries and was significant to the development of realism. One thing that it is easy to forget is that Zola belongs to the second generation of realistic writers, that a significant part of his formation was provided by the works of Flaubert and the Goncourts. Though he too had to struggle out of the morass of romantic sentiment and extravagance, his sense of direction was quickly established and readily maintained. He got his bearings as he read Taine and Darwin and Claude Bernard and as he pondered the implications of the works of Balzac and the Goncourts' *Germinie Lacerteux*. In a letter to his friend Antony Valabrègue sometime in 1864 Zola declared an only slightly qualified allegiance to realism. By an elaborate metaphor he equates a work of art to looking through a window opening on creation in which there is "a sort of transparent screen through which one sees things with more or less deformation." There are three kinds of screen, classic, romantic, and realistic. The latter is a simple piece of window glass "so perfectly transparent that images pass through it and are reproduced in all their reality." The result is that there is no change in line or color; the reproduction is exact and naive. However, though the realistic screen in effect denies its own existence, that is too proud a claim. It does tint and refract like any other glass; there is "a fine grey dust" that disturbs its limpidity. "Every object in passing through this medium loses some of its brightness, or rather is slightly darkened. . . . In short, the realistic screen, the last to have been produced by contemporary art, is a uniform pane that is very transparent without being altogether limpid and gives images as faithful as any screen can give." His sympathies are all for the realistic screen because it gives "immense beauties of solidity and truth. Only, I repeat, I cannot accept it on its own terms; I cannot admit that it gives us true images; and I assert that it ought to have some particular properties that deform the images and so make works of art out of these images. However, I fully accept its procedure, which is to place oneself in all openness before nature, to render it in its ensemble with no exclusions whatever. It seems to me the work of art should take in the entire horizon."[3]

A revealing personal comment accompanies this statement of allegiance: "As I have a horror of the role of disciple, I would not be able to accept one [screen] exclusively and in its entirety." In other words, this early we can see that Zola would insist on his personal label, *naturalism,* because it would set him apart from his fellow realists. As he told Edmond de Goncourt in 1870: "After the analysis of infinitesimally small nuances of feeling carried out by Flaubert in *Madame Bovary,* after the analysis of artistic, plastic, nervous things such as you have done, after these *jewel-works,* these finely chiseled volumes, there is no room left for the young, nothing for us to do, nothing left in the way of creating characters. It is only by the number of volumes, by the power of creation, that we can impress the public" (*Journal,* August 27, 1870). With these avowals, we can, for the moment at least, consider Zola's naturalism as nothing more than a personal banner that he waved as a member of the army of realism.

In the first instance it was indeed by the number of volumes that Zola set out to impose himself upon his generation. The twenty volumes of the Rougon-Macquart series are a series of hammer blows for public attention and approval. *Thérèse*

Raquin and *Madeleine Férat,* which preceded the series, show an early presence of tendencies that are discussed later, but they are not of great moment in themselves. The so-called Three Cities and Four Gospels novels that follow the Rougon-Macquart are thesis novels and far outside the realistic canon. As we narrow the scope of our examination it should be noted that not all the Rougon-Macquart novels are realistic. The most obvious is *Le Rêve,* an idyllic fairy story of a young girl and her prince charming who, after surmounting obstacles, are united in marriage, only to have her die in her husband's arms as they leave the church. (Zola admitted in his sketch for the next novel that he now wanted to get back "into the real world.") Much the same judgment must be applied to *La Faute de l'Abbé Mouret,* which begins with an examination of the earthy resistance of a small Provençal parish to its saintly priest, and speedily degenerates into an allegory about the Garden of Eden, replete with tag names and other explicit parallels. This work is important, however, as an early statement of the fertility theme that becomes the symbolic center of some of the later novels in the series. On quite different grounds *Le Docteur Pascal,* the concluding novel in the series, must be ruled out as unrealistic. Its function is to wind up the story of the two families and to draw certain scientific-philosophical conclusions. The slight action rests on a literary parallel: the love of Clothilde and her uncle Pascal is compared to the love of Abishag and King David.

We are left, then, with seventeen volumes of the Rougon-Macquart series upon which our assessment of Zola's realistic—and naturalistic—practice must depend. As the preface to the first novel, *La Fortune des Rougon,* tells us, the author conceived of the whole as "The Natural and Social History of a Family under the Second Empire," a unity that was felicitously, if unexpectedly, rounded out "when the fall of the Bonapartes, which I had need of as artist and which I had always considered the fated end of the drama, without daring to think it would come so soon, took place and gave me the terrible and necessary denouement for my work. It is as of today complete;

it whirls within a closed circle; it becomes a picture of a dead reign, of a strange epoch of folly and of shame."

The general notes in preparation for this vast work give us an idea of Zola's attitude toward basic realistic tenets. Eschewing politics and religion, he wants his study to be "a simple piece of analysis of the world as it is. I merely state facts. It is a study of man placed in a milieu without sermonizing. If my novel has a result it will be this: to tell the human truth, to exhibit our mechanism, showing the hidden springs of heredity and the influence of environment." A second interesting reflection has to do with Zola's reaction to Taine's admonition to make a depiction general and strong. Since Zola is conducting experiments (he does not yet use that word, but the idea is there), he feels he must turn to the exceptional "like Stendhal," avoiding too great monstrosities but taking particular cases of brain and flesh. In addition, since he wants to be "purely naturalistic, purely physiological," Zola wishes "no more description, or the least possible. . . . The laboratory process, though long, is the right one." Likewise he wishes to avoid epithets and to conduct his style in a magisterial manner so that his books will be "simple *procès-verbaux.*" In general, these remarks indicate adherence to the sobriety and impersonality of realism, though there are some interesting deviations, especially when Zola views the conduct of a novel as essentially a logical *deduction*. It seems possible, even at this early date, that he is too much addicted to what he conceives of as scientific process and too eager for strong effects. In other words, some of the elements of naturalism are here, even though formulation of the doctrine is still to come.

Because he proclaimed that he was going to write the natural and social history of an age, Zola's contemporaries and disciples were ready to acknowledge that he had done so. Yet the truth is that Zola was never more clumsy than when he tried to make a close attachment between fictive and actual events. Fortunately in the Rougon-Macquart these attachments are more tenuous than one might expect; the series as a whole makes no effort at sustained historical reference. We accept the necessity by which *La Fortune des Rougon* and *La Débâcle,* occupying initial and terminal points in the historical continuum, must relate closely to actual events, but we may discern in the difference between them something of the difficulties their author encountered as he developed his design. The first novel is local and specific. Except for the fact of the coup d'état of December 2, 1851, and the armed demonstrations that broke out against it in Provence, there is little embarrassing burden of historical event to get in the way of the novel. On the other hand, *La Débâcle,* important and imposing as it is, suffers from the handicap of trying to deal with too much historical material and in too great detail. It would have been enough for Zola to write a novel confined to showing the incredible blunder at Sedan, which by its confusion and waste would have been a tacit indictment of a criminally incompetent government. But he was not content with that. The capitulation of the French armies, the siege of Paris, the various stages of the communard uprising are all treated in summary fashion, so that the final quarter of the novel is little more than a poorly assembled and occasionally sentimental compendium of history. The Commune could have provided material for another novel, but it did not belong in this one.

For the most part, however, Zola is wary of attachment to specific events. We rarely know or need to know in what year we are. There is no steady procession of time as we move through the series until three of the last novels, *L'Argent, La Bête Humaine,* and *La Débâcle,* are joined together as part of the climactic frenzy of the reign. But then *Nana,* written years before, is also part of the catastrophe of the Empire. Occasionally we get a fixed point of reference by means of a well-known event or a specific date: the Salon des Refusés, the Orsini attempt on Napoleon III's life, the death of Maximilian in Mexico, and the Exposition Universelle at the high point of the Empire. These attachments do not get in the way of the novels; they merely give an air of verisimilitude without burdening the action (with the partial exception of the Orsini affair, which is an integral part of *Son Excellence Eugène Rougon).* More persistent as referent for those novels that are set in Paris is the rebuilding of the city under the aegis of Baron Hausmann, the demolition of the old quartiers, the cutting through of the new boulevards, the building of the great central markets. This activity is equated with large-scale speculation in land, and that in turn with the unbridled luxury and depravity encouraged by the regime. As for historical personalities, *Son Excellence* and *La Débâcle* excepted, Zola is very sparing indeed.

The main organizing principle of the series, the famous family tree of the Rougon and Macquart families, turned out to be a delusion and a burden. The idea of summing up an era by means of the chronicles of a single family, even when proliferating from a double source, is novelistically, not to mention logically, absurd. In addition, it forces the narratives into a kind of straitjacket. For example, the monotonous appearance of degenerate and sickly children from the tainted stock becomes ridiculous; they have no being in their own right and are merely a mechanical restatement of the givens about heredity. The novels would work just as well if the family relationships did not exist beyond, possibly, the grouping of the three brothers, Eugène, Aristide, and Pascal Rougon, for in terms of family as well as in terms of history the series turns out not to be a continuum but a mosaic, a judicious sampling of a society at a given time and place, a study of environments *per se* in which the particular human specimen under examination needs no intricate antecedent history. The fact that Nana is Gervaise Coupeau's daughter is important, but more by reason of environment then heredity, and the fact that Claude, Etienne, and Jacques Lantier are brothers, and half-brothers to Nana, is of no importance whatever. The reappearance of a character in another novel has little connection with his first appearance. Jean Macquart is central to both *La Terre* and *La Débâcle*, yet his appearance in one novel in no way supports his presence in the other, though the two novels do suggest the mythic figure of the rootless modern man.

Whatever reservations we may have today about Zola's use of social history and a family tree to produce a unified history of an age, they cannot be allowed to destroy his importance and his influence. Novelists found in Zola's novels as a group a broad and exciting canvas that they tried to duplicate, often patterning it to a more perfect design than his. In nearly every European literature there has been something like the Rougon-Macquart. Writers have traced families and the movement of social history, although it is less usual for them to have done both at once. (Notable combinations of the two are to be found in Roger Martin du Gard's *Les Thibault,* in John Galsworthy's novels about the Forsyte family, and in Thomas Mann's *Buddenbrooks.)* For better or worse, to his successors Zola stands for the *roman fleuve* that attempts to sum up an era or a movement, and he has provided one of the impressive, if illusory, patterns for the novel of our time.

Actually Zola's explorations and expropriations of subject matter on a smaller scale are a good deal more impressive. Time after time among the novels of the Rougon-Macquart he has added new territory to the literary domain. *La Fortune des Rougon* and *La Conquête de Plassans* present the bourgeois society of a small town in terms of power structure. *Le Ventre de Paris* shows the special milieu of the great central market of Paris, and *Au Bonheur des Dames* provides a detailed picture of a great department store and its effect on traditional commerce. In *Nana* we have the demimonde, scarcely a new subject but somewhat more down to earth than earlier novels of the kind. *L'Oeuvre* observes the world of the artist, at that time not yet a hackneyed subject. *L'Assommoir* is *the* proletarian novel of the nineteenth century; *Pot-Bouille* attempts a similar summing up of the Parisian middle class. The depressed mining areas and a strike by the miners are the subject of *Germinal,* rapacious rutting peasants that of *La Terre,* and the disorder and waste of war that of *La Débâcle.* If these are not always new subjects, they are freshly studied and are for the most part divested of conventional trappings of sentiment and romance. In the aggregate these novels are proof that every kind of social situation may be exploited by the realist.

If milieu is important, so is the particular kind of scene or action portrayed. Zola's search for the typical is nicely summed up in an interview reported in *L'Evénement* for March 8, 1889:

> You know how I proceed. First of all I have the idea of the world in which my novel is to take place; then I seek out and settle on an intrigue, which is almost always provided by the world in which I wish to situate my drama.
>
> When I have set up my model, "the monster," I concern myself with documents; I seek them out with care, and if often happens that these documents completely modify my idea of the novel.
>
> My work is "settled" only when I have all my documents and I have discovered the reflexive effect of subject on documents and of documents on subject.

Only when the general preparation was complete did the author allow to emerge, by a kind of parthenogenesis, characters who were suitable to the milieu and to the action. There is no doubt that in general Zola adhered to the idea of the average in respect to both action and character, though as we have already seen, he was from the beginning drawn to the limited and exceptional case as the more striking. (Indeed, he followed the quoted description of his method by the admission that in the present case—he was writing *La Bête Humaine*—he wished "to make a dramatic tragic novel, something 'nightmarish' like *Thérèse Raquin. . . .")* In spite of this deep seated inclination, however, Zola does not in the Rougon-Macquart place a single exceptional character in an important situation until he comes to Jacques Lantier in *La Bête Humaine.*

His major characters, even when they are possessed of unusual energy and reach considerable heights, are close to the norm in their basic characteristics. The two characters who achieve the most, Eugène and Aristide Rougon, have no outstanding quality except perseverance; a less vigorous personality, Octave Mouret, is merely a successful opportunist. Or to take an extreme case, if we turn to Nana the person, not Nana the symbol, we see that she is no epitome of evil but is an ordinary, limited, vulgar woman. A particularly good case in point is Etienne Lantier in *Germinal.* In the older novel he would have been cast as a Moses to lead the miners out of bondage. In *Germinal* we see his inability to do so because of the limitations of the situation and his own mind.

Less consistently, the actions of the novels are also kept within the bounds of the ordinary, again with the egregious exception of *La Bête Humaine,* though sometimes there are incidents within an action that bear the stamp of the romanesque. *Son Excellence Eugène Rougon* is conducted with exact propriety as the title character undergoes the ups and downs typical of a politician to whom power is more important than principle. *La Débâcle* is a restrained and powerful war novel as long as it lets war appear in its inherent confusion, and it falls down when the sensational and contrived intrigue of Goliath, the German spy, is introduced. From one point of view the most exceptional central action of all the major novels is the strike in *Germinal,* but in this instance the exceptional is carefully brought back to the ordinary. The strike is unsuccessful; there is little of the heroic about it, though we have to admit that Souvarine's destruction of the mine is another matter.

The great innovation made by Zola so far as subject matter is concerned was his challenge of the taboos relating to physical functions, particularly sexuality. No doubt crusading zeal entered into this, but this challenge was a necessary outcome of his reading of human nature as dominated by physical causality. Zola could not escape showing the physiological man and woman, and particularly the copulative, reproductive man and woman, with clinical objectivity. It is this aspect of his work that provoked the shrillest and most vehement outcry, although one suspects that the charge of obscenity was often a smoke screen for antagonism on other grounds. *Thérèse Raquin,* his first novel, published six years before *La Fortune des Rougon,* caused such a furor that Zola wrote a defense and a rebuke to the critics as a preface to the second edition. In this preface, Zola challenged his critics for their lubricity of mind when they should have seen his attitude as scientific, one of carrying out "on two living bodies the work of analysis that surgeons perform on corpses." Given this approach, he argued, the cruel love of Laurent and Thérèse contained "nothing that was immoral, nothing that would arouse evil passions."

This outcry was redoubled as the years went on and came to the point of explosion over *La Terre*. Though Zola was never hailed before the courts for obscenity, some of his followers were, and his books were put under judicial ban in England and strong social and moral prohibition elsewhere. This condemnation sprang first of all from his insistence on the physical nature of man and on the primacy of physical behavior. For better or worse as far as the future of literature was concerned, Zola demanded and largely won the freedom of the city with respect to admitting and depicting the so-called lower elements of behavior. As one critic puts it, Zola showed "sexual life intimately bound and woven into social life, as one of the substantial causes, perhaps the most fundamental, of all actions and reactions . . . sex life omnipresent and omnipotent, as a perennial and dominant *leit-motif.*"[4]

To the reader today Zola seems modest and nonprurient in his handling of sexual activity. Accounts of sexual encounters are sparse in detail and neutral in tone. The violent first encounter of Laurent and Thérèse is described in six words: "The act was silent and brutal." The multiple adulteries of *Pot-Bouille* are largely free of circumstantial detail. Nana's subjection of her lovers forms the erotic substance of the novel; the sex act is taken for granted. In *Germinal*, where copulating miners bestrew the landscape, this phenomenon is treated with respect and without lewdness. A remarkable instance of restraint occurs in the opening scene of *La Terre*, in which Françoise, who is taking her cow to be serviced by a neighbor's bull, is quite without embarrassment as she guides the bull's member into the cow while Jean Macquart looks on. (The treatment here should be compared with the very similar passage in John Steinbeck's *The Grapes of Wrath*, the point of which seems to be that it is the occasion for a dirty joke.) There are certainly a few occasions when the desire to titillate gets the upper hand, especially in *La Curée, Le Ventre de Paris*, and most gratuitously *L'Argent*, where Saccard and Baroness

Sandorff are discovered in abnormal coitus. If there is falsification, it is in the tendency of the author to desex his protagonist when he is engaged in other intense activities. Eugène Rougon, Claude Lantier, Jean Macquart, and even Saccard seem at times to have less than normal sexual responsiveness, so intent are they on other pursuits. In general, a decided sense of sex as a casual, unidealized, often brutal appetite can be drawn from the novels, which has little in common with either the sickly hothouse atmosphere of *La Curée* or the idyllic innocence of *La Faute de l'Abbé Mouret.*

To balance the assertion that Zola adheres generally to a *juste milieu* for both characters and action, it must be admitted that he is constantly beset by a penchant for the romantic, the sensational, and the mythic, and is not always able to prevent their intruding into the observed and sober fabric of his fiction. There is, for example, no scene in realistic literature that goes further beyond the boundaries of realism than that of the death of Antoine Macquart in the final novel, where the old man, saturated by a lifetime's consumption of alcohol, burns slowly with a blue flame until he is utterly consumed, only a heap of sludge remaining on the floor. Most of Zola's excesses are less outrageous than this. There are some conventional romantic situations in his studies of high life or the demimonde. The conquest of Octave Mouret by Denise in *Au Bonheur des Dames* is handled in a manner to bring joy to the readers of women's magazines. More often Zola falls prey to sensationalism. *La Bête Humaine* is less a study of criminal mentality than it is a horror tale. There are such inharmonious incidents as the beating of little Lalie in *L'Assommoir* and the mutilation of Maigrat in *Germinal,* which undermine the sobriety of those works. There is also a tendency to pile horror upon horror at the end of a work, especially in the later novels, as in *La Terre,* in which Françoise is pushed upon a scythe and left to die by her sister and brother-in-law, who then smother the old father and set fire to his body.

When we consider the clarity with which Zola envisaged his method, it is surprising that until the publication in 1877 of

L'Assommoir, the seventh in the series, his new approach did not produce any overwhelming popular impact. It was this novel that gave incontrovertible evidence of Zola's originality and controlled technical skill. As we read through the entire Rougon-Macquart we conclude that in only a half dozen or so of these works does he show himself master of a new way of writing. Today we cite *L'Assommoir, Pot-Bouille,* and *La Terre* for one kind of excellence, and *Nana* and *Germinal* for another, with *La Débâcle* resting uncertainly between these two groups because the novelist's means were not equal to his ends, which were in any case uncertain.

When we examine the novels preceding *L'Assommoir,* we find that Zola's force is there. His poetry and his taste for strong effects are all too evident, but his ability to evoke actuality is sporadic and is diluted by recourse to convention. These works suffer from some general disabilities: the difficulty of getting the Rougon-Macquart apparatus into operation; an excessive occupation with the social thesis—the rottenness of the Second Empire; a propensity toward melodrama; and, on occasion, an inflated and hectic rhetoric. Within limits, the first novel, *La Fortune des Rougon,* gives an adequate view of provincial mediocrity and stupidity after the coup d'état, but it does not stop there. We also get a picture of young Silvère Mouret and his sweetheart Miette, a girl of thirteen, whose idyllic love is shattered by the fall of the Republic. They join the marchers, and at the end of the scene Miette reverses her cloak so that the red lining will show as she bears aloft the red flag of the marching men, becoming a poster picture of revolutionary ardor.

The most interesting of the early works is *Le Ventre de Paris,* though in it we encounter a significant kind of failure to achieve the level of realism. Here Zola has almost got his bearings. He sets out to examine a unique and isolatable milieu, Les Halles, one of the tangible improvements of the imperial regime, but for all that a typical microcosm. Zola provides a satisfactory cross section of its denizens, and recounts in detail their jealousies and petty intrigues, organizing the action not too arbitrarily around the rivalry of Lisa, *la belle charcutière* (a Macquart), and another stall keeper, *la belle normande*. The family tree is unimportant here; while the social thesis is vaguely present, it does not impair the overall accuracy of the representation. What does flaw the work is resort to melodrama and to poetizing. Lisa's brother-in-law Florent, an escapee from French Guiana and a republican sympathizer, is too prominent. His absurd plots and the rigamarole that surrounds his betrayal remind the reader of Balzac's Vautrin. He is too large and romantic a figure to set alongside the average scale of the market people. The two scales are not compatible; Florent's romantic intrigue clashes with the day-to-day realism of their lives.

The other problem that arises in this novel is one of treatment of detail. Physical data are present in abundance as we observe the operation of the markets, both below and above ground, and as we look at the heaped-up products of every variety and color that move in and out of Les Halles to satisfy the appetites of Paris. There is an appeal to sight and taste and smell, and an overwhelming assault on the senses which came to be one of the hallmarks of a Zola work, though never again rendered with such pictorial intensity (except perhaps in *Au Bonheur des Dames,* where it is the myriad-colored fabrics of the department store that are arrayed in dazzling impressionism). Unhappily the author never decides through what lens to view these data. Part of the time he is sharply photographic—if the term can be extended to sensory impressions other than those of sight. He reproduces the experience of the markets in overpowering rawness. But part of the time he is an impressionist painter making a visual poem of these materials. It is to that end that Zola introduces the painter Claude Lantier, modeled after his boyhood friend Cézanne, as a kind of roving eye. Either way of seeing is artistically legitimate, but the two do not go together. In view of the way he depicts human actions, Zola, to be consistent, should have used the harsh, raw images of unretouched photography for things as well.

After the mediocre beginnings just described, suddenly—so

it seemed to the contemporary reader and so it still seems to us today—Zola emerged as a master realist with the publication of *L'Assommoir.* It has by general consent been characterized as the archetypal naturalistic novel and the high point of Zola's writing in that mode, if not the greatest of his works. (For sheer power many readers prefer *La Terre* or *Germinal,* which go beyond realism–naturalism.) *L'Assommoir* is a coherent and beautifully articulated work without a major flaw. It maintains authorial objectivity; it exhibits the techniques of the cross section and of the large representative block of action; it avoids the tendentious and the symbolic almost entirely. The subject of the work is the hopeless, stultifying life of the Parisian worker. Although there was an early tendency to misread the novel as a temperance tract, Zola himself puts us straight on this in his preface:

> I wish to show the fatal decline of a working-class family in the pestilential milieu of our industrial faubourgs. Beyond drunkenness and unwillingness to work are the breakdown of family ties, the filth of promiscuity, the progressive apathy of proper feelings, and then as a denouement shame and death. It is simple morality in action.

The milieu shown is a confined one, la Rue de la Goutte d'Or in Montmartre and the adjacent area, a quartier bounded, as the novel says, by the slaughterhouse and the hospital. It is made up of small shops and of tenements. It seems without contact with anything but itself, as it stews in its own distillation of poverty and despair. The characters do not escape from Paris; indeed they scarcely get out of the quartier. This is emphasized on Gervaise's wedding day, when to escape the rain the guests troop down into Paris to visit the Louvre, where they are ridiculously out of place and hopelessly lost. Their lives are implacably bound to shop and factory and tenement; their horizon is limited by the nearest tall building. Their modest hope is somehow to stick it out in minimal comfort and die in their beds.

In this novel the cross section is developed in a comprehensive and convincing way. Gervaise Coupeau is the prime example of people living in this environment, and she is worth attending to because she is in fact better, that is, capable of more effective resistance, than most of those around her. If her decline is accepted as inescapable, then that of the others must be also. She works hard and she fails. Her failure can even be seen as stemming from her success, as being the necessary concomitant of it. When her shop prospers, she is in a position to indulge herself a little. Thus she spends more money on food, takes time off for feasting, and so destroys the economic well-being that makes this indulgence possible. Coupeau's decline is parallel to that of his wife and precedes it. There may be a degree of contrivance by which such an abstemious and hardworking man should suddenly change his whole personality pattern and become a loafer. If so, the fault is in the handling, not in the observation, for part of the supporting cross section is made up of people just like him, the reason for whose unwillingness to work the novel does not bother to trace. They have given up before the novel begins: Bijard, a drunkard, who beats his wife and daughter; Coupeau's drinking companions, Bibi-la-Grillade and Mes Bottes, not to mention the anonymous workingmen whose desperate carousing provides background sound effects.

Examined fairly closely are four middle-ground groups, the Boches, Virginie and her policeman husband, the Goujets, and the Lorilleux, all of them basically decent people who are trying to keep their heads above water. Virginie's failure as a shopkeeper is exactly parallel with what happens to Gervaise. The Lorilleux, who are so intent on storing up a competence that their human responses have atrophied, are an indication that even the most single-minded determination is unlikely to be enough; in addition, they are potential victims of failing strength and of the business cycle. The Boches keep afloat by toadying to whoever is on top and incontinently deserting those whose luck has turned. The Goujets, mother and son, are the most provident and self-disciplined of people, but even for them the future is hazardous. The impressively muscled Goujet, whom Gervaise visits at his forge, will be able to earn a living only so long as he has physical strength, and there are indications that even before his strength declines he may be replaced by a machine.

Another dimension of the cross section is in terms of age. The younger generation growing up is represented chiefly by Nana, vicious and knowing beyond her years, an artificial flower of the muckheap who runs off with the first man who beckons and thereafter is a woman of the streets (in this novel at any rate). What other fate is there for the product of such an environment, unless it be premature death as in the case of little Lalie? At the other end of the scale is Old Bru, long past the age of employment, who lives in utter destitution, and Mother Coupeau, an unwelcome burden on her three children during her last years. Youth, age, and the provident and improvident poor are all before us, all bound to the same fatality, though at different points on the wheel.

The effect of these horizontal expansions is to give a picture of a milieu as it bears upon people at large. Gervaise's centrality is diminished, or at any rate blurred by this broad spectrum. Zola has here avoided the dangers of a single life; with such buttressing of other cases it cannot be charged that he has selected an exceptional case in order to support a thesis. In much the same way Zola gets around the problems involved in presenting some twenty years of a character's life. There is little that can be called plot; what there is of narrative pattern is in its broad outlines dictated by life itself. It is here that Zola's invention of the block technique comes to the fore. We see the life of Gervaise Coupeau in great scenic blocks that show characteristic activity of different kinds in dense detail and with considerable vividness, though in this novel with little dramatic use of dialogue. There are thirteen chapters, each in its way a monumental resumé of a certain aspect of the life described. The opening chapter has at its center the fight at the neighborhood laundry between Gervaise and Virginie over Lantier, giving us the tone of the community and establishing a jungle-warfare image. Some of the following chapters are dramatically concentrated, particularly the one describing Gervaise's wedding day or the one describing the great gluttonous feast on her saint's day. Some of the chapters are more general and depend on summary narrative, centering on making a living, the situation of children growing up in such an environment or of the old miserably declining in it. Given the cause-and-effect relationship involved in this work there is no need to relate events in close sequence. Dipping in for strategic examples is enough so long as temporal continuity is maintained (though even a radial symmetry would be possible in this sort of work once beginning and end are established).

One of the most significant technical advances of this novel is the use of vulgar speech. What Zola did is not easy for us to assess today after a hundred years in which the vernacular has rung more or less true in the novels of all nations. For *L'Assommoir* the author actually consulted basic works on popular locutions and compiled a dictionary of vulgar language, which was much parodied by his contemporaries.[5] The expressions used are so exactly right for the milieu that in reading we scarcely notice them. Certainly today they no longer present a challenge. (Oddly enough, this is not true of the next novel, *Nana,* where vulgarity is flung in the reader's face. The producer of Nana's play keeps telling his interlocutor that his theater is *un bordel* [a brothel], and when Satin, Nana's lesbian friend, is asked what she is doing as she waits in front of the theater, her answer is, "Je m'emmerde.") Use of vulgar language is usually indirect. There is very little of it in dialogue; rather it is assimilated in such a way that mental attitudes and processes are summarized in such terms. Possibly this was a precaution against giving too violent a jolt to the reader. In any case it is a shortcut, though to the ear of the twentieth-century reader this often has the effect of a parody such as Joyce produces with intent in the Polyphemus and Nausicaa episodes of *Ulysses.*

Zola was well aware of what he was doing. In the preface to *L'Assommoir* he concludes that what upset readers was not the content but verbal innovation: "People were upset by the words. My crime was to have had the literary curiosity to gather up and press into a carefully wrought mold the language of the people . . . and to rejoice in its crudeness, in the unexpectedness and force of its images. It is a feast for burrowing grammarians. Nobody has perceived that I wished to make a permanent contribution to philology, which I believe is of lively historical and social interest." This resort to the language that people speak is generally characteristic of the later works of the Rougon-Macquart, most notably *La Terre*. Inasmuch as Zola makes no effort to reproduce consciousness directly, a summary stream of consciousness in which people think and express themselves colloquially is an invention of importance.

Third-person omniscient point of view is the characteristic Zola stance. He seems to have had no difficulty in adopting it and shows no self-consciousness in using it. Thoughts and emotions are therefore secondary, and changes or developments in personality are not really posited as significant. All of this contributes to the air of an "experimental" novel. Even if we credit the rat in a maze with thoughts, what we can observe is his behavior in the maze. The Zola character, endowed with certain oversimplified inherited traits and dominated by simple behavior patterns, is turned loose in a circumscribed situation and watched as he or she works out a pattern of behavior. These actions should bring no real surprises and should be self-evident in their meaning. Therefore, there is no need for authorial intervention, though we must concede that some characters, especially Dr. Pascal in the final volume, are ill-concealed authorial mouthpieces as they philosophize or rhapsodize over the meaning of it all.

The almost perfect objectivity of *L'Assommoir* does not belie the presence of Zola's two weaknesses, his tendency toward sensationalism and a growing desire for symbolism. The first is almost completely under control in this novel. The one incident to which nearly everyone takes exception is the case of little Lalie. The irony of this is that the incident was drawn from a newspaper account, but the fact remains that by its heightened quality it jars with the more pedestrian account of human misery which makes up the novel as a whole. Perhaps Coupeau's delirium tremens is also a little too special, but in a novel in which the ravages of drink is a principal index of desperation it is probably acceptable.

This novel is the one instance where Zola manages to create a metaphor of the whole work without going beyond his data. The symbolic center of the novel is the vitriol machine, the destroyer of lives, which we see doing its evil work in the bar named *L'Assommoir*. (Zola found this word in a dictionary of slang to denote a bistro of low stature.) Certainly the product of this machine is lethal, and there is ample evidence in the novel of its destructive power. However, there is also a verbal play that leads to a more complex understanding. *Assommer* means to *stun* into insensibility (with special reference to cattle being readied for slaughter). Thus, it is the stunning, dehumanizing effect of the lives that these people lead that breaks them. The vitriol machine eventually appears to be less cause than effect. Resort to it is made in order to deaden the pain of the blows that the environment has inflicted, though such resort accelerates the degeneration. Without question we have here a use of symbol that goes beyond the basic idea of realism, but it does grow naturally out of the data themselves and on an immediate level is perceived or created by the characters themselves. The machine or the bar is a natural object in a specific environment that has a specific symbolic meaning for the people in that environment. We perceive it both in their terms and in the more expansive terms of the novel, where the title itself becomes a significant part of the frame of reference. We properly conclude that it is the total environment that destroys. The fact that this is pointed up by symbolic means certainly does not contradict what is otherwise demonstrated, or raise the statement beyond what it would be in any case.

Though of considerably less power and range than *L'Assommoir, Pot-Bouille* (with a title also drawn from a dictionary of slang) is important for the consolidation of the techniques we have been discussing. The novel surrenders the dominant symbol of the earlier one for a neat pattern of irony, but within the framework so set up it uses the cross section with great skill, avoiding even the concentration on a single character that we have with Gervaise. The action covers two years and is vaguely presented from the standpoint of Octave Mouret, a young man on the make for both sex and money. Physically the locus is a new apartment building, described as the epitome of middle-class luxury and respectability. While various of the tenants are followed outside, the action primarily occurs within the building and exhibits the difference between its outward decorum and the moral squalor of the people who inhabit it. The novel is built on the simplest of foundations, the casual, or accidental association of a representative group of people on board ship, in a hotel, in an office, in an army unit—the possibilities are legion and they have all been employed *after* Zola. In this novel the elements are more closely tied together by family relation-ships than is usual or necessary, but we still get a sense of a sufficiently random sampling.

Two of the later novels, *La Terre* and *La Débâcle,* are also successful in letting the facts speak for themselves without undue manipulation, though with some heightening. The for-mer is the work that provoked the famous attack of five minor writers on Zola in 1887—the so-called *Manifeste des Cinq.* It is a scarifying work but, on balance, an honest one. It strikes directly at the myth of the happy peasant, of man in a state of nature living an idyllic life on the land. By use of a limited cross section the novel shows the peasant, on the contrary, as brutal and brutalized by the life he leads. It is as crushing as *L'Assommoir* in its effect and even more stark in its demonstra-tion. Here again we are largely free from the Rougon-Macquart incubus. Jean Macquart, the brother of Lisa and Gervaise and a native of Provence, comes as a hired hand to the wheat-growing region of La Beauce, south of Chartres. To the extent that Jean is a man of integrity and good sense, he stands in contrast to the peasantry under study, and his expulsion at the end of the novel emphasizes the subhuman quality of the peasantry. His position as a stranger is a means of giving perspective to, and underlin-ing, a major peasant characteristic, an insularity and ingrained suspiciousness toward all that comes from beyond the bounds of the immediate horizon. This work is less dramatic in presentation than some of the others, partly because it covers a period of three years, but mostly because it must portray the repetitious, unchanging nature of peasant life. It uses scene sparingly in favor of narrative summary.

The keynote of this work, its latent symbolism, is the passionate struggle of the peasant, who is dominated by two appetites that are fused into one, a desire to possess the land and an urge to brutal and direct satisfaction of his sexual needs. To this end the novel abounds in images of the peasant's relation to the land in gross sexual terms, and his general nature is expressed by unusually varied and primitive animal imagery. There is a scene in which Lise and a cow give birth simultaneously, once and for all establishing the identity of peasant and brute creation. A more covert development of the same theme is the unwillingness of the community to support a priest, which culminates in Abbé Godard's departure and his statement that he will leave the parish to live like beasts. There is an unceasing and relentless demonstration of the primitive, bestial, violent struggle that is peasant life. The soul-crushing labor on the land pits the worker against crushing obstacles in the natural environment: hailstorms that destroy crops in a moment, the desperate effort to save the lives of cattle, the searing summer drought. There is a kind of animal rage, as the peasants pit themselves against danger from the elements to complete the harvest, with the result that they are hardly distinguishable from beasts of toil; they reek of sweat and animal odors.

The main action on what one might call a human level is the struggle for succession to the land within a single peasant family. Old Fouan and his wife, who are unable to work any longer, decide to divide their holdings among their three children in return for maintenance and an annual income. This is the beginning of the end for them. There is delinquency of payments, failure to provide maintenance, and hostility deepening to such a point that the mother dies of a blow. After living alone for a time the old man goes to the house of one child after

another, quarreling with each, until at last he wanders outdoors
for a night like Lear on the heath. In the end, when he has been
robbed of his money and securities, he is treated like an animal,
deprived of human contact, and finally smothered to death lest
he tell of a crime that he has witnessed. In contrast to the old
man is his elder sister, called *La Grande,* who knows that only
by financial independence can she keep alive and who therefore
mercilessly exploits those around her. At eighty-nine, after
being almost raped by the grandson whom she has terrorized
and enslaved, she is able to summon up enough strength to kill
him with a blow. Of the three Fouan children, Fanny, married
to Delhomme, a peasant of some substance, maintains a degree
of decency, but she too makes life unbearable for her father.
The elder son, known in the community as Jésus-Christ, is a
drunkard and ne'er-do-well who steals from his father. Buteau,
the other son, is a powerful, stubborn man, dominated by
passion for the land and ready to sacrifice every human instinct
to his desire for possession. After some years he marries Lise,
whom he had earlier got with child. He lives with her and her
sister Françoise, joining their portion of land with his own and
undergoing agonies of loss when Françoise marries and takes
her land away from him. Buteau is beset by desire for Françoise's body, and his wife in an equally exacerbated rage for
possession is willing for him to take her sister so as to get
possession of the land.

This picture is filled out by other contrasting situations in the
community. We become acquainted with the farm of La Borderie and its owner Hourdequin. Here too passion erodes the
soul. The farm is failing because of obstinately bad weather, the
depressed economic situation, and peasant resistance to improved agricultural methods. Hourdequin too, obsessed by
sexual desire, is dominated by his housekeeper, who sleeps with
every groom and laborer on the farm. Of the other background
figures the most interesting are a couple named Charles, who
have retired with a substantial fortune realized from a brothel
they have run in Chartres for thirty years. They are in despair
over the way that establishment is being run by their son-in-law

and are delighted when their granddaughter, whom they think they have brought up in ignorance of their activities, undertakes to marry the Delhomme son and with him to save the family business.

This novel has two major flaws. Twice there are electoral contests in the region that give rise to discussions about the farm problem in a changing economy, somewhat in the fashion of Tolstoy's *Anna Karenina*. These discussions are not fully developed; they add nothing to the novel except a reminder that there is a world of forces outside the narrow community under study. The discussions dilute the sullen introversion on a brute level that is the essence of the novel. The other flaw is Zola's characteristic excess in the piling up of sensational events. Those events at the end of the novel, in particular, are too violent and come in too rapid succession. Françoise, pushed by her sister, falls on the point of a scythe and dies. Old Fouan is smothered to death and his body is burned. At La Borderie, Tron sets a trap for Hourdequin, who dies, and then burns the farm buildings in a rage when the housekeeper spurns him. There are other questionable touches. One may take exception to the sobriquet Jésus-Christ and to the chapter in which he carouses to a continual fanfare of farts, which seems a deliberate challenge to reader sensibility, as do the incest of Palmyre and Hilarion and the latter's attempted rape of *La Grande*. In a work in which the good is so notoriously absent, there should be a little measure in the presentation of evil. There is quite enough sexuality without including incest, however well authenticated it may be in rural areas. There is no need to discredit the accuracy of the depiction by indulging in a Fourteenth of July explosion of violent actions at the end.

However, *La Terre* is admirable for the consistency of its texture. This, as mentioned earlier, cannot be said of *La Débâcle*. Both novels offended special interests in their day, but *La Débâcle* has benefitted from the subsequent respectability of war novels, whereas *La Terre* has suffered both from the initial insults it received and from a twentieth-century cult of the primitive that sentimentalizes life close to the soil. What is excellent and original about *La Débâcle* is its restricted focus and basically unheroic action. This is not the first time that a battle has been seen through the eyes of an individual participant, but both Fabrice in *La Chartreuse de Parme* and Pierre in *War and Peace* were outsiders who had casually intruded into a battle. In Zola's novel the point of reference is that of a continuous participant from the retreat at Mulhouse on the Rhine plain to the capitulation at Sedan. Zola has used a pattern that is often employed in the twentieth-century war novel; he has taken a squad as group protagonist. Actually, Zola confines himself pretty much to two members of the squad, Jean Macquart, the corporal, an experienced soldier because of his prior service in the Italian campaign but a man unschooled in ideas and sensibility; and Maurice Levasseur, who has a higher level of social experience and education. What the two men see and feel is the focus of the novel. This is presented in small bits of experience, some of it trivial, much of it for its time in fiction shockingly bloody and brutal. None of it is heroic in the traditional sense. Such heightening as occurs is largely the result of an implicit contrast between Maurice's automatic civilian responses and the grim actuality of military life.

The weakest part of this overall picture of battle is the tight relationship between bystanders and participants by reason of family connection or friendship. This raises certain of these incidental characters above the anonymous misery of the mass and engages our sympathies for individuals, which changes the distance from which we generally view these events. This is one reason why the part of the novel set in Paris during the Commune is a mistake. It ceases to be a general picture and becomes a poignant and unbelievable duel between Maurice and Jean Macquart, ending in a situation in which the latter must kill his former comrade.

Whatever their occasional weaknesses of execution, the novels we have been analyzing are essentially realistic in their statement. The other Zola, the one who goes beyond the direct impact of data, comes to the fore in *Nana*, which was published only two years after *L'Assommoir*. This is a remarkable turn-about, for though he was tempted to enhance the real by way of symbol and myth, Zola had up to this point kept such a tendency under control—with the evident exception of *La Faute de L'Abbé Mouret*. With *Nana* he turned overtly to this other vein, the one which, for better or worse, was to dominate later conceptions of what naturalism was. The format of this novel is much the same as that of its predecessor: a view of a segment of Parisian life presented in large blocks of material so dense and varied as to give the impression of representing the whole. Fourteen chapters cover the three years of Nana's career in the theater and higher prostitution, all of them scenic in their basic organization, though they contain a good deal of summary narrative. To a degree unusual in Zola's work, Nana is present in and dominates all these scenes; they would be nothing without her, which is not true of the relationship of protagonist and setting in other novels. The scenes have no emphatic logical connection. What emerges from them is the completeness of Nana's destructive force, brought to a culmination in the thirteenth chapter by a kind of roll call of the victims of her voracity.

From the first she is more symbol than woman. She emerges more and more clearly as a blind force of nature exciting man's latent sexuality which, when violently aroused, can destroy him. The first full description of Nana states: "Nana was smiling still, but her smile was now bitter, as of a devourer of men." There is a certain imagistic obviousness in the name of the play in which she appears, *The Blonde Venus,* and on opening night her appearance on stage causes an almost palpable feeling of rut to sweep over the audience. Nana's capricious and insatiable fornications are a prodigy we accept because we have accepted her larger-than-life nature. What she feels and what she offers cannot be called love; it is a darker corrupting power. In Chapter 7, an article written by one of her lovers calls her "a golden fly which has flown up out of the dungheap, a fly which has taken death from the carcasses tolerated along the roads and which, humming, dangerous, sparkling with the brilliance of jewels, poisons men merely by lighting on them in the palaces which it has entered by the window." This symbolic potential for destruction accompanies her throughout the novel. However, her hyperbolic role produces a curious contradiction. In her physical magnificence and corruptive power she remains uncorrupted (except in her submission to Fontan and her pursuit of the lesbian Satin). Why then subject her to an ugly and agonizing death? The answer is that other symbolic needs of the novel intervene at the end. Her death is made to coincide with the agony of the Empire, which is equally poisoned.

The most revealing way to indicate the departure of this work from realism is to point out that here protagonist and destructive force are one and the same, whereas normally Zola shows one or more of his characters destroyed by forces that are separate from them. Even when inherited elements enter into play, there is such a separation. This condition of being worked on keeps such characters in a subordinate position. The only way they can become inflated is as victims, but this is avoided by keeping them on the level of ordinary and representative human beings. Nana, on the contrary, is a colossus, even though when we look at her closely we see that she is the most ordinary of creatures. Thus the issue is clearly joined: Has Zola undertaken to portray that segment of society known as the demimonde, or is the novel an apocalyptic vision of destruction by evil? Whatever it started out to be, the latter is what the novel became. It is brilliant in its massing of detail in some of the tableaus (notably that of the horse race at Longchamp), but such substantive brilliance is subordinate to something else, to a conceptual structure that goes far beyond the evidence. Nana is not just a representative whore; she is an embodiment of evil. She is not just a body that a finite number of Parisians may enjoy; she is a nemesis which takes the measure of the Second Empire and destroys it.

The particular process of symbolism just described is not

followed in *Germinal,* but that novel too goes beyond the literal and ventures into the area of symbolism in other and even more complicated ways. In *Germinal* the life in a Flanders mining community is well and fully documented. But from that realistic base rise structures of symbolism that wrest the data into new patterns of meaning, leading to a curious ambivalence, since the symbolic statement contradicts that of the experiental data.

The basic structure of the work is again a cross section, at the center of which is the Maheu family, a group protagonist, buttressed by their neighbors, the Pierrons and the Levaques. Life and work in the Montsou mining area are presented in the usual large blocks, but this material, dense as it is, is merely a backdrop for the specific action, the developing revolt of the miners that culminates in a strike. Because of the social dynamics involved, there must be a second cross section, though a perfunctory and skeletal one, of the representatives of wealth and ownership. Here we have a threefold grouping of the Hennebeau, Deneulin, and Grégoire families—management of large-scale enterprise, independent small-scale owner, and dividend-eager shareholders. By the presence of these two cross sections we speedily become aware of the class struggle. The precise direction of this struggle is left open, for there is a third spectrum in the novel, this time of people representing different formulas by which to achieve social justice: Ma Brûlé, who stands for mass uprising, reminiscent of the French Revolution; Rasseneur, who represents Fabian Socialism; Pluchart, who stands for the Second International; and Souvarine, who represents Anarchism; not to mention the two minor figures of the Abbé Ranvier and the Abbé Joire, who stand for the attitudes of the Church toward the problem.

The central action is the collision that arises out of the confrontation of these forces, which is unusual in Zola. No longer do we have a chronicle of a dead reign, which is therefore static, but a study of process, which necessarily looks to the future. Moreover, to some extent this process must be seen as one of attitudes and ideas going on in the minds of the characters. Furthermore this conflict comes to a head in a crisis situation which, though not at all Dostoevskian, parallels the explosiveness of the Dostoevskian novel. What we are shown is a situation in which environmental circumstances have become unbearable, generating a resistance that culminates in a strike which is doomed to defeat because of the obvious inequality of the adversaries. At the end of the novel, so far as the literal data are concerned, the *status quo ante* has been restored on a slightly more hopeless level, since the miners are worse off than before, their losses far outweighing those of the mine owners. (The statement that the strike has been a fatal wound to the Empire is not substantiated.) Thus the conclusion is pessimistic; the miners cannot win because of their inferior power; they are doomed to a condition of slavery. If they revolt again, they will be put down again with equally crushing force. Moreover, there is no real basis of understanding between the two factions and no identity of interest. Since all the doctrinal approaches represented in the novel appear inadequate, we conclude that there is no way out of the impasse.

But this literal statement is only part of the novel, which contains also two symbolic patterns that lead to a contradictory conclusion. First of all, there is a schema of loosely Marxian orientation by which we see the confrontation of bourgeoisie and proletariat. This corresponds somewhat roughly to the facts of the novel but goes beyond them in the significance it draws from them. This local struggle on the industrial front is raised to the level of a universal; it becomes the class struggle wherever carried on. It therefore must be viewed from the vantage point of the teleology inherent in Marxist doctrine. Even though the workers appear to fail, in the broad perspective of history they can only win, since that is the fated end of the class struggle. Symbolically in the novel old Bonnemort (the Maheu grandfather), inheritor of generations of proletarian misery, is able even in his paralytic state to strike out blindly and kill Cécile, the hope of the bourgeoisie. Rhetorically at the end of the novel as Etienne Lantier walks away from the scene of defeat, we are told that a black avenging army will burst through the mold of repression to reap the harvests of a coming age, a promise that is in direct contradiction of the defeat we have just witnessed.

A bridge between this ideological orientation and an even more diffuse organizing myth is the *fact* of the miners' fertility, which is well documented. The miners' indiscriminate and uncontrolled procreation both characterizes their debased state and constitutes their hope. The affluent bourgeois are sterile: Cécile Grégoire is the sole child of her parents and she is killed. The Hennebeaus have no children; the wife is carrying on an adulterous affair with her nephew, and the husband envies the free and easy sex of the miners. Deneulin's daughters are, after he loses his mine, doomed to sterile spinsterhood. Thus the rulers will be unable to reproduce themselves, and the miners must prevail by reason of their replenished and expanding numbers.

From the very first page of the novel, where we see the mine through Etienne's eyes as some sort of monster gorging itself on human flesh, the mythic framework of death and regeneration is enunciated with mounting intensity. The mine disasters, including Souvarine's willed destruction, are central to this. The whole process of life that the miners know is one of thralldom to death, yet they triumph over it. Symbolically, Catherine reaches physical maturity and carries Etienne's seed for a moment as she dies. Etienne literally emerges from the underworld when he is rescued from the mine, and his whole Montsou experience is to be seen as a sojourn in the underworld, which he enters in winter darkness and from which he departs in the spring. The triumph of spring over winter is attested by perennial human experience; so by analogy the novel gives assurance of the triumph of social justice over bondage and misery.

What this amounts to is the introduction of a kind of mystical meliorism, which contradicts the tight causal premises of naturalism. This is fairly pervasive in the later works. At the end of *L'Argent* there is a philosophical passage assessing the catastrophe that has occurred. First, human experience is characterized as "unjust and ignoble like nature"; then this is countered by the recognition that money, an agent of destruction, is also a fertile element:

> . . . beyond the stirring up of so much mud, beyond the crushing of so many victims, all that abominable suffering by which humanity pays for every forward step, is there not an obscure and distant goal, something higher, good, just, positive, toward which we go without knowing it, and which swells our hearts with an obstinate need to live and hope?

Such sentiments are present in as early a novel as *Au Bonheur des Dames,* in which Denise, witnessing the crushing of small businesses by the great department store, concludes that "this was good, that it was necessary to have this manure of misery for the sake of a healthy Paris of tomorrow. Yes, this was the role of blood, every revolution had need of martyrs, the march forward was only over the bodies of the dead." In his sketch for this novel Zola had noted: "a complete change of philosophy; first of all, no more pessimism, not a conclusion about the stupidity and sadness of life. . . . In a word, go along with the age, express the age, which is one of action and conquest, of endeavor in every direction." In the philosophical summarizing of the final novel we get a reiteration of this idea. Dr. Pascal passes on to Clothilde his faith in humanity, "his final faith in a better world, when science had given men an incalculable power." There is also faith in the rightness of history, in the beneficence of the process of survival of the fittest, and finally a belief in the brotherhood of all living things: "Ah! animality, everything that drags itself along and complains beneath mankind, what immense sympathy must be accorded it in a history of life!"

Even if we posit a mystical strain to be present in Zola from the start, we must be struck by his novelistic movement away from the scientifically verifiable, the empirically observable man of the present to the putative man of the future in whom a growth beyond the physical has taken place. We must conclude that his naturalism, so-called, was two things. It was the more

or less scientific view that Zola set forth in *Le Roman Expéri-*
mental (1880) and other critical statements, and it was a later
mystique that endowed all life with purpose and salvaged from
the workings of Darwinian and Marxian determinism a belief, a
faith, in future improvement. It is never easy to determine
which of these attitudes is meant when we encounter the words
naturalism and *naturalistic*. In practice they are likely to be used
pejoratively, suggesting either an extreme of determinism or a
going overboard in some area of realistic depiction. But to some
writers—Frank Norris, for example—these terms suggest a
mystical acceptance of a destructive deterministic process as
bringing the somehow good. Overall, it is the adventitious
elements in Zola's later practice, rather than the rigor of his
earlier formulations, that encouraged writers and critics to
think of naturalism as a distinct literary form, even as a kind of
counterthrust against the realism of earlier writers.

To leave this distinction to one side for the moment, there is
no question that Zola believed in and practiced the main tenets
of realism as it had evolved in his earlier years. He believed in
the objective or impersonal approach; he believed in portrayal
of the average, the norm; he believed in showing a slice of life
rather than using a contrived plot; he believed that language
should be natural, unobtrusive, nonliterary. In his various
discussions Zola advocates these approaches for the naturalistic
novel (and play) and makes it plain that whereas he prefers to
call himself a naturalist, he belongs to the mainstream of
realism. The whole elaborate argument of *Le Roman Expéri-*
mental goes beyond realistic doctrine in only one important
respect: it says that the artist has an *a priori* idea: "The artist
has the same starting point as the scientist; he stands before
nature, has an *a priori* idea, and works in line with that idea."
In other words, the naturalist comes to his examination of
human experience with already fixed conceptions as to the
working of causality. He is, in effect, a pessimistic, materialistic
determinist. He is working deductively from an already established premise, and that premise may be one that he accepts
from others without himself having arrived at it by induction.

Actually most realists accept such a premise, at least tentatively, but they do avoid the rigidity that Zola has set down; they seem to depend more on observation than on formula, with the result that their novels are more flexible, more varied, and, perhaps, more generous in their depictions of human beings, though they come out much the same in the end.

We come back, then, to the likelihood that it was Zola's practice, or what some followers wanted to single out from his practice, that provided the basic differentiae of naturalism. Part of this separation merely marks an historical process. Because of the lengths to which he carried his depiction of what is, Zola's writings became intolerable to sensitive natures, who were put in the curious position of accepting milder representations as realistic and erecting a dike to protect them from what they called naturalistic. J.-K. Huysmans, for a time a Zola disciple, puts this distinction in a graphic way: "According to some, and, it must be admitted, according to the most widely received opinion, realism would seem to consist in choosing the most abject and trivial subjects, the most repulsive and lascivious descriptions, in a word, in bringing to light the sores of society. After removing the ointment and bandages which cover the most horrible sores, naturalism would seem to have only one goal, that of probing them to their frightful depths in public."[6] In other words, it is possible to say that the public seized upon the term naturalism as a means of saying to the realists "thus far and no further," as a means of blocking off by condemnation territories where some writers went too far.

Beyond this, however, in Zola's practice, not in his theoretical discussions, there were certain salient elements that could become the constituents of a different doctrine. Five of these, with varying emphasis, seem to be present in most formulations of what naturalism as a separate entity is. The first of these, strong emphasis on the lower physical functions, especially sex, has been discussed. It is difficult to see how this could have been excluded from any realistic depiction of humanity once taboos had been successfully removed. To exclude sex from realism would be to eunuchize it and to make it tell less than the truth.

Nonetheless, for a time at least this was one of the characteristics of naturalism in popular estimation. Secondly, Zola by choice, and perhaps by conviction, diminished the role of mind in human behavior, taking a position like that of the epiphenomenalist or of the twentieth-century behaviorist. In such a work as *L'Assommoir* internal states have little importance, and seem to be at most accompaniments of action on the external plane. The people are moved around physically by physical forces, which constitutes an effective, if tacit, denial of the importance of mental forces.

From this, as a third element, comes Zola's celebrated ability to portray the action of crowds. Since human beings are in the main hardly distinguishable components of a milieu, Zola often shows them as a mass engaged in collective action or reinforcing an individual action by a kind of chorus presence. Nearly every one of Zola's novels has at least one episode in which this is to be seen, from the marching republicans of *La Fortune des Rougon* to the entrapped army in *La Débâcle*. In the background of *L'Assommoir* is the drunken noise of the biweekly payday, "la grande quinzaine." *Au Bonheur des Dames* has two magnificent portrayals of crowds at department-store sales. *Nana* shows the rut of the audience when the Blonde Venus appears and the excitement of the onlookers at the Longchamp races. Most notable of all is the march of the miners in *Germinal,* which is the most intricate exercise of this sort that Zola ever composed. The march is presented in three movements: the chasing of the rabbit Poland by the children, the lacrosse game of the workers, each leading in to the random course of the strikers as they flow erratically across the countryside. Here there is depersonalization by means of language. "Shouts arose." "Rumor ran along." There is use of part for the whole, with reference to arms, feet, and hands, as constituent elements of the mob. The depersonalized elements are posed against an indeterminate landscape, one that is vast and limitless, such as a snowy plain, and lighted in such a way as to flatten out individual characteristics by a dazzling sun or the obscurity of night. Metaphorically the crowd is characterized by animal imagery, but to this is added the metaphor of natural phenomena in excess; sea, flood, tempest, storm, and even the medical image of a deep-seated abscess bursting, culminating in an image of mania and religious exaltation. It is in scenes like these that the source is found for later realist depictions in which personality is almost entirely absent, for example, in Theodor Plievier's account of the defense of Stalingrad, and in Jules Romains' depictions of Paris going to work in the morning or the mass destruction at Verdun.

Animal imagery as applied to human beings is a fourth Zola characteristic, perhaps the one that has most invited imitation. The effect is reductionist, if not denigrative, for the consistent use of lower animals as a means of comparison has the effect of leveling humanity to the status of nonhuman kind. This is not a new device, for Shakespeare, to cite an obvious example, makes telling use of it in such plays as *Richard III, Othello,* and *King Lear,* but in Shakespeare its use is dramatic; it points up by contrast the debased nature of a specific personality, though this may be generalized on occasion. Zola is consistent in his application of such imagery, which is applied to all and sundry. It insists on the primacy of instinctive behavior and on the unimportance of will or judgment or choice. It is most prevalent in *Germinal,* where one after another of the characters is equated with an animal. The priest picks his way along the road like a fat cat; Jeanlin is a monkey and later, in his recidivism, a weasel; Maigrat is a tomcat; the haulers in the mine steam like overburdened mares. From such an imagistic base it is impossible not to see the crowd as a group of wild, stampeding animals and the whole mining community as unthinking creatures buffeted by a storm of external force. On one famous occasion in *L'Assommoir* an animal serves as a commentary on human action. After Gervaise's lavish saint's day feast, at which the whole neighborhood has caroused to the point of inert repletion, the scene ends with the picture of an alley cat greedily picking the bones of the devoured goose. Some fantastic adaptations of this dominant animal imagery have been made by later writers such as Jack London and Frank Norris; to them it was a recognizable hallmark of naturalism as they understood it.

Accompanying this basically physical and depersonalizing depiction of mass men is a fifth characteristic of a different kind. This is a basic pessimism. Things run downhill. No man achieves his desire. Human motives are base, and human achievements, such as they are, are futile. However promising the beginning of the race, it will end in disappointment, destitution, and death. There is a slow grinding down of the human creature by the very process of living; at the end man is without even the illusion of dignity, a wounded and dying thing. This grim and intransigent formula is certainly part of what has come to be called naturalism by those who came after Zola. It is a "no exit" philosophy with a vengeance, and it has been interpreted by some as excluding any other sort of ending. It does not seem that Zola is as adamant about the relentless application of this formula as those who have come after him, but in the hopeless running down of lives which he shows he certainly has given encouragement to such a reading.

Set off against these five characteristics are two others of quite different nature that are also cited as elements of naturalism. Zola is definitely responsible for both of these, though not for the unthinking aggrandizement they have received. One is gigantism, a process by which the drab and commonplace particular takes on the lineaments and importance of a universal, usually by reason of the inflation of some symbol or myth. We have observed the presence of this tendency at least from *Nana* on. It is most obvious in such major characters as Jacques Lantier in *La Bête Humaine*, Buteau in *La Terre*, or Maheude in *Germinal*, but it is not confined to these works. Jeanlin exhibits it to a slight extent, as do Chaval and Catherine in *Germinal*, not to mention Count Muffat or Satin in *Nana*. Just as this tendency contradicts the limited scale to which realistic depiction is committed, a second characteristic already mentioned contradicts the meaninglessness and the pessimism of these representations. Without exception the novels we have been discussing turn out badly, but as we have seen with particular reference to *Germinal* and others of the later works, in spite of what they show there is present within them a faith in the beneficent processes of the universe, an implicit meliorism, which rests on three ideological foundations. Zola believes in the ability of science to resolve human problems, even extending that ability to the experimental novel, which he manages to see as a branch of science. He has a similar faith in the outcome of struggles for survival in the biological sense (a Darwinian notion) and in the social sense (Marxian). Zola does not examine or question this tripartite faith. He asserts it increasingly until it becomes dogma in the works after Rougon-Macquart.

Zola's philosophical position is therefore a curious one. More than any of his realistic contemporaries he subscribes to belief in the scientific doctrines of his time. He is clearly a materialist, a determinist, and inferentially a pessimist in the main outlines of his doctrine as expressed in *Le Roman Expérimental.* He has no reservations about the efficacy and accuracy of scientific method; he has no patience with assertions that there is an unknown, some region of experience inaccessible to reason which science is powerless to explain. Zola's demonstration of man's limited state is strictly geared to the findings of physical science, showing him to move in a narrow and painful course, the sport of the external world and of his own genes, his end determined from the beginning without possibility of evasion or appeal. This position, though philosophically tenable, is not humanly comfortable, and sooner or later all but the most disciplined of thinkers will seek a way out. Zola's way, though vaguely formulated, is in the direction of creative evolution. Within the implacable matrix of causality there exists an unknown, an X-factor, expansive and capable of bringing change. Thus, to repeat the lesson of *Germinal,* those very forces that doom the miners to eternal servitude at the same time contain a seed which under certain conditions will change from latency to an active state, thereby adding a new and fertile element to a causality that appeared to be rigid.

The truth of the matter is that Zola is too various, or from the point of view of his detractors, too undisciplined, for it to be possible to reconcile the contradictions that exist between his critical statements and his literary practice. The best statement of Zola's fundamental position is one he made to the critic Jules Lemaître in a letter of March 14, 1885, at the high point of his career:

> I accept your definition very willingly, "a pessimistic epic of human animality," on condition, however, that you explain the word "animality" to me. You locate man in the brain; I place him in all his organs. You isolate man from nature; I do not see him without the earth from which he comes and to which he returns. The soul which you shut up in a being I feel to be dispersed everywhere, in that being and outside him, in the animal whose brother he is, in the plant, in the stone. . . . My characters think as much as they should think, as much as people think in current life. . . .[7]

These remarks come as close to describing the core of Zola's reading of humanity as we are able to get. He does without question locate the vital center below mind and soul; he does see men as subject to the same forces as crush other species, and he is willing from that standpoint to admit the appropriateness of the word "pessimistic" to describe his "epic." But the latter word carries contradictory implications of grandeur and significance that go beyond the purely impersonal laboratory observation.

The Zola depiction is, in fact, far warmer, far more compassionate than that of Flaubert or the Goncourts and, illogically, far more hopeful than theirs. In a way he was caught by the rigor of his demonstration of how man fares against environment (and heredity) with which he began analytically. Zola seemed as he moved through successive volumes of the Rougon-Macquart to rebel against the necessity by which he showed his characters bound, to begin to take sides with them against adverse forces, and to seek for them an escape from the prison of circumstance that it had once been his prime purpose to depict. For a man of his ebullient temperament it was impossible to reject the somehow good, to deny purpose and promise to the human adventure. Without wishing to carry the parallel very far, we see Zola anticipating the Reverend Gail Hightower in exclaiming "Poor mankind!" and with typical enthusiasm determining to do something about that condition as he launched into the works of special pleading with which he closed his career.

5

Leo Tolstoy

The world described by Tolstoy seems, at first glance, to be the most ample of those depicted by the major realists. This impression of breadth of canvas is in part the result of the impact made by *War and Peace*; in part it is the result of Tolstoy's technique, which is both wide-ranging and leisurely in its assembling of data. Upon reflection, however, one realizes that Tolstoy, like the other realists, is necessarily limited as to the segment of life that he portrays, and that there are definite boundaries beyond which he rarely ventures.

In general, too much is made of the autobiographical sources of Tolstoy's art—we must remind ourselves that they are to be assumed for any artist—but we must recognize that his particular position in the Russian society of the nineteenth century gave him a vantage point with a wide perspective and provided him with certain experiences that served to broaden the scope of his novels. Since Tolstoy was a spontaneous realist, utilizing the materials that came to hand as the basis for his writing, we should not expect him to be a researcher or documenter. In general this is true, though we find that a late work like *Resurrection* depends heavily upon research, and we come to realize that *War and Peace* also depends on the gathering and verification of historical data. The rest of Tolstoy's fiction springs from observation, from the accidents of experience. Since that experience was broad, it is perhaps occasion for surprise that his world is no more extensive than it is.

Tolstoy's depiction has as its base the upper class of the country, the seminoble, semipatriarchal landowning class who were the chief source of the military hierarchy and of the top level of the Russian administrative service. Their education implied proficiency in French, German, and English, which ensured access to, if not interest in, the ideas of Western Europe. The wealth and position of these individuals made possible extensive travel in the west though it did not necessarily encourage westernization. Within this group there is a kind of polarization between the mundane, sophisticated, and international outlook of their time and class and the simple, unchanging, even anachronistic values of the country properties from which their incomes were entirely derived. Their numbers were limited; they were bound by ties of marriage, and they therefore represented a fairly close-knit, intimate social group.

This is the world of Tolstoy's three novels, of his Bolkonskys, Rostovs, Kuragins, Levins, Oblonskys, Shcherbatskys, and Nekhliudovs, for, whatever the differences in their moral qualities and social orientation, they are obviously members of the same class. It is also the world of Princess Marya in *Family Happiness*, of Olenin in *The Cossacks*, and naturally of the early and autobiographical hero of *Childhood, Adolescence*, and *Youth*. Belonging to this world as functionaries supported by it and assimilated to it are such officials as Alexei Karenin and Ivan Ilych, as well as many peripheral figures. In short, we become intimate with the homogeneous, wealthy, land-based ruling class of Russia, though for the most part we do not see them in the exercise of their power—government as such is not a principal concern of Tolstoy—or in the exercise or abuse of their great wealth, for in spite of the tribulations of the Rostovs and the Oblonskys money plays no great part in Tolstoy's depictions. Instead his novels and stories show the moral being of this group and what life is like for people of this class in terms of a norm that is not a class norm but is universal and transcends class, though naturally he is best able to present it for that social stratum which he knew.

The social stratum of Tolstoy's works does not include simple functionaries or modest landowners; it is never involved in commerce and industry and has few of the characteristics of the middle class. This absence of a middle class in Tolstoy's novels is one of the things that sets him most sharply apart from other nineteenth-century realists, nearly all of whom took that social level as their automatic subject matter, to such an extent that there is a temptation to define realism as the depiction— usually critical—of the bourgeoisie. Whereas those writers were attracted to a world that was coming into being and sought to show a social truth that went beyond conventional and antiquated descriptions, Tolstoy ignored in large part what was emerging in favor of a thorough description of what had been.

The most necessary corrective to standard descriptions of Tolstoy's world has to do with the part played by the peasantry. Here the facts totally discredit a sentimental myth. The Tolstoyans, disciples of the later messianic figure rather than of the novelist, were interested in Tolstoy's religious and social sympathies and thus represented him as placing great emphasis on the serfs, the most lowly members of Russian society. Whatever their importance in Tolstoy's social thinking, the peasants have little place in his fiction. What we find are some rather surly serfs on the Bolkonsky estate, a few happy figures in the hunting sequence, and the philosopher Platon Karataev on the road from Moscow in *War and Peace*. The world of *Anna Karenina* includes peasants in the mowing scene and Levin's coachman, and there is Gerasim in *The Death of Ivan Ilych* and a whole peasant village in *Polikushka*. There is a considerable array of the unfortunate and downtrodden, some of them peasants, in *Resurrection,* and above all the drunken, brutal, avaricious family in the play *The Power of Darkness*. In short, there is a minimal presentation of the lower orders on which Tolstoy's privileged segment of society rests, and except for *Polikushka* no attempt is made by Tolstoy to show extensively what peasant life is like. Given the degree of social tension present in Russia before and after the emancipation of the serfs in 1861, it is a matter of surprise to observe the absence of such tension in Tolstoy's novels. This world has its recalcitrant clay, and there are efforts to mold it into various shapes, but of social dynamics there is next to nothing.

Tolstoy's few departures from the social norm are chiefly the result of his military service in the Caucasus and his presence at the siege of Sevastopol during the Crimean War. Within his depiction of the norm there is great care to show ordinary people and ordinary situations. The most outré actions are those of Dolokhov in *War and Peace*, a man who by the violence and nonconformity of his behavior shatters the stillness of the Tolstoy stream. The most unusual action of all is the murder committed by the husband in *The Kreutzer Sonata*, but this is muted by the retrospective nature of the narrative. Anna Karenina too goes beyond the bounds of typical behavior, and she too disturbs the quiet of the Tolstoy world, forcing the reader to reevaluate Tolstoy's conception of normality. One has to conclude that although violence is less crude and less intrusive in the social level shown by Tolstoy, mental and moral suffering are certainly not absent.

The gamut of personalities that Tolstoy shows is fairly narrow, just as is the gamut of society itself. One reason for this is the fact that Tolstoy confines himself largely to external behavior. He does not deny internal states; indeed he presupposes them, but the primary data of his observation have to do with the way people act, and the range of human action that he shows is not extensive. With the more compulsive actions arising from sexual and criminal drives largely blocked off, with the physical desperation of poverty scanted, and with the physical and moral suffering of war in some ways played down, what is left is a valid but limited, though at the same time universal, segment of experience. Of all the major realists Tolstoy is the least sensational, the most determined to cling to what he conceives to be the norm of experience. On the whole, he does not see suffering as part of that norm. Death, with which Flaubert and Zola on occasion shock us, is part of the natural process to Tolstoy and is to be accepted as such. The exceptional deaths of Polikushka and Anna Karenina do not invalidate that attitude.

The unusual thing about Tolstoy's world, in *War and Peace* at least, is that he does not hesitate to reinstate history as an area for the realistic novelist, thereby providing an example of tremendous importance to later writers. If we cling to the idea of Tolstoy as a spontaneous realist, we see that his use of the Napoleonic Wars is an extension of his experience, drawing on what he had heard from survivors of the invasion of Russia and from the intense activity of a mind obsessed with that great event. In his note on *War and Peace* Tolstoy defends himself for doing this. On the one hand, he asserts the right of the artist to use historical materials differently from the historian, since the latter is concerned with the results of an event, whereas the artist is concerend with the event itself. On the other hand, Tolstoy says he is not guilty of imaginative reconstruction: "Everywhere in my novel that historical personages speak and act, I have invented nothing, but have made use of the materials which I have found and which in the course of my labors have amounted to a whole library. . . ."[1]

The use of history verifies the fact that Tolstoy is on the whole antiromantic. Childhood is nonidyllic; the discomfort of adolescence is more evident than any halcyon qualities. Love is a mixed experience: there is an element of unhealthy self-deception in Masha's attraction to a much older man in *Family Happiness*, as there is a flagrantly unsuitable quality in Sonya's love for Nikolai or in Olenin's self-delusion about the possibility of love for Maryanka. The exotic scene—the Caucasus—is brought into focus, if not actually debunked, in *The Cossacks* and *Hadji Murad*. Upper-class society is generally shown as foolish and corrupt, rather than glamorous. And war, first in *Sevastopol* and then in *War and Peace*, is largely, though not completely, deromanticized—because of the patriotic responses invoked the battles described do retain a certain heroic grandeur. The peasant, man in a state of nature, is brought down to earth, though at times a bit equivocally. Finally, the divine afflatus of religious fervor is deflated. Princess Marya's interest in God's Folk is seen to be an escape mechanism; Prince Andrei's yearning for celestial peace is sterile and a denial of life; Lidia Ivanovna's piety is sheer egoism supported by charlatanism. This demolition of romantic attitudes in Tolstoy's works is largely incidental. He is not so much antiromantic as he is completely independent of fashion. Tolstoy shows things as he sees them. In the beginning he is an artist obsessed by the need to depict truly; in his later years he is driven by the desire to expound moral Truth and repudiates his earlier works. The two ways of writing cannot be reconciled, but they do spring from the same source of independence and originality.

It is hard to say whether Tolstoy's world appears today to be more of an anachronism than those of his realistic peers; it is a temptation to say that it is. A century later, at the culmination of a long process of industrialization and urbanization, we may feel a nostalgic attraction to Tolstoy's world but we know that it does not exist and that the terms of human experience on which it is built are not meaningful. Today an acceptable depiction of preindustrial life would have a struggle for existence that was more bitter and a sense of deprivation that was much more acute. In part, a feeling of anachronism is inevitable for later readers of all realistic works. In proportion to their faithfulness to the external data of time and place these works are doomed to be period pieces. Yet, since the prime subject of such writing is what it is to be a human being, it ought to be possible for the period piece also to be timeless. If any of the older realists has escaped anachronism, Tolstoy has.

Tolstoy's first work, though autobiographical in content, is cast in the form of fiction. On his arrival in the Caucasus in 1851 Tolstoy undertook to write what he called "my novel." The first part, *Childhood,* was published in *The Contemporary* for September 1852. (This moved Turgenev to write a month later that the author would go far.) *Boyhood* ànd *Youth* appeared in the same journal in October 1854 and January 1857, respectively. Tolstoy's original plan called for a fourth part recounting his period of riotous living. Undoubtedly he shied away from this because he did not wish to exhibit his debauchery or could not conceive of truthful terms in which to exhibit it without violating his concept of decorum. (It must be observed that, with the exception of *The Devil*, Tolstoy avoids circumstantial treatment of sexual impurity.) *Sevastopol*, a series of three sketches written at the same time as the autobiographical accounts, has the immediacy of an eye-witness report. These first works show a preference for use of the first-person point of view; it is only in the later parts of *Sevastopol* that the author discovers the advantage of a third-person approach. There is a movement away from telling to showing in these formative years, with the highest point of showing being reached in *War and Peace*. Beginning with *Anna Karenina*, though the third-person omniscient continues to be dominant, there is a regression from showing to telling; flashes of earlier brilliance of scene, however, illuminate the latest works for short periods. This development is not illogical; rather it reflects the changed goals of the author. As his didactic interest mounts, he wants to argue his case, and this can be seen in the texture of his writing, except when enthusiasm for the sense experience gets the upper hand.

The Sevastopol sketches show how rapidly Tolstoy learned his craft. The first sketch is a piece of reportage and is rather literary in treatment. It is in the second person; that is, the reader, "you," will see this and that under the guidance of the narrator, whose "I" is largely suppressed. You, the reader, are taken to a hospital and confronted with the sight and *smell* of fifty amputees and seriously wounded men, a scene made lively by a couple of pages of dialogue. You are finally taken to the dangerous fourth bastion where you are subjected to shellfire. The whole is framed by descriptive literary passages about the scene itself. It has the general lineaments of a set piece written by any war correspondent in any modern war, one written without the author's necessarily having experienced battle. The work also has a conventional note of patriotic reassurance. The new Czar Alexander III took such pleasure in it that he ordered it translated into French; in that form it appeared in a Brussels newspaper the following July.

For the second sketch Tolstoy undertook to describe a specific event, an engagement on the night of May 10–11, which he had passed in the fourth bastion. This is a much more direct, raw, and veridical representation of war; it worried the editors of *The Contemporary* and infuriated the censors, who riddled it with deletions. This piece is presented much more directly by the use of scene than in the first sketch, though it is marred on occasion by overanalysis, and it makes extensive use of dialogue between French and Russian soldiers during a truce. The piece concludes with some reflections of theoretical literary cast:

> Where is the depiction of evil which must be avoided? Where is the depiction of good which must be initiated in this novella? Who is the villain and who is the hero? All of them are good, and all of them are bad. . . .
> The hero of my tale, the hero whom I love with my whole soul, whom I have undertaken to reproduce in all his beauty, who has always been, is, and will be always admirable is truth.

This was too much for the editor, who felt it wise to add the words: "But we didn't begin this war," and so on.

The third and longest of the sketches is the most developed as fiction. The time is the end of August 1855; is Sevastopol *in extremis*; army organization broken down. There is a great gathering of officers at a posting station awaiting conveyance into the city. There we meet a Lieutenant Kozeltsov, who is returning from convalescent leave, and his younger brother Volodya, who is on his way to the front for the first time. The attitudes and responses of Volodya are developed at length, especially his fears and dreams of glory. We see the city and the bastion through his eyes and participate in the battle with him. The scene shifts to the older brother at his station, where he is mortally wounded, and then back to the battery commanded by Volodya, who is killed in an assault by the French. The deaths of both brothers are casual and underplayed. The events speak for themselves until at the end there is a withdrawal to the elevation of the omniscient observer to permit a description of the emotions aroused by the defeat and the loss of the city. This third piece is in technique close to the battle sequences of *War and Peace*, though it is much less dramatized by dialogue. By giving glimpses of common soldiers as well as officers in characteristic attitudes Tolstoy has begun to demonstrate his skill and economy, achieving mass and variety by quick, incomplete sketches in which the part serves for the whole. Above all he has begun to disengage himself from the mass of autobiographical data toward a fictional reshaping of the experience in a form that has no direct connection with him.

Between this work and the grandiose achievement of *War and Peace* there is to some extent a regression. The stories written during those years are no longer based directly on Tolstoy's personal experience, but they withdraw from direct scenic treatment and sometimes seem a bit argumentative. This is most true of *Family Happiness*, a short novel that reaches a fairly shattering conclusion without adequate documentation. Tolstoy reverted in this work to a first-person narrative, which is necessarily retrospective if a long action is involved, so that the end—the state which the narrator has reached before he begins to tell the story—is bound to condition and mute the beginning. Masha, a lovely young girl without experience, falls in love with and marries a man twice her age. She finds after a time that the disparity between them because of age and degree of emotional maturity is a source of increasing friction, which undermines affection and makes communication difficult. She finally concludes that her youthful incandescence was wrong and that well-being consists in a placid, prematurely middle-aged submersion in the duties of family life. In many respects Masha is a prestudy of Natasha of *War and Peace*, but this first effort sacrifices immediacy to generality. We see Masha's actions only as she reports them and, because she is a sentimental young girl given to bursts of "wild ecstasy," her report actually falsifies. It is neither a detailed analysis of romantic illusion nor an externally objective depiction. The result is that it gives the impression of proceeding deductively, of summoning up only the minimally necessary data in support of a preestablished conclusion. Even the crisis at Baden in which Masha sees the error of her ways and is frightened back into a life of sane values is not given adequate scenic treatment.

The Cossacks, which avoids the difficulties of a first-person narrative, is a better work in much the same vein.[2] Olenin, as a man, suffers from the same kind of youthful illusion as Masha does as a woman. Having lived a licentious and unsatisfactory life in the city, he flees from his failure, only to repeat it in a new environment, which is ostensibly that of infinite romantic possibility. The novel is thus romantic and antiromantic at the same time, and it does present the Caucasus as a locus of primitive, natural responses devoid of the artificiality of the sophisticated city. Luke and Maryanka are noble savages, the former in particular being endowed with heroic stature. The mountains are beautiful and uplifting; the life of the village is colorful and spontaneous. Yet we see these elements without any sentimental haze. Uncle Eroshka, the great huntsman, is a liar and a scrounger. The fighting between Cossacks and natives is a sordid, meaningless affair, and Luke dies a meaningless death. Above all, Olenin does not fit in. Whatever the value of this life for those who belong to it, it has no relevance for him, and he has, in fact, in a subtle way repeated the failure from which he fled in Moscow. The weakness of this work is that it seems too bare a sketch, one which is ultimately programmatic with minimal support of detail. Certain scenes are excellent, especially that of Olenin's leave-taking, but there are not enough of them. We do not get the immediacy of scene to be found in *Hadji Murad* some fifty years later, where the cold, objective assessment does not seem to be harnessed to a prior judgment.

Polikushka, the third major work of this intermediate period, is more truly realistic in both conception and treatment. Its subject is peasant life, and within its short compass Tolstoy manages a considerable variety of characters and situations. He shows the proprietor, the overseer, and several peasant types. The action is of the simplest, even though it is twofold: The misadventures of Polikushka, who loses money he has been sent to collect, and the decision made by the peasants as to whom they will send to the army to fill their draft quota. These two strands are interwoven only to the extent that they are simultaneous and culminate in the scene in the village between Polikushka and the draftees. Having seen the interior of Polikushka's hut and having witnessed the reaction to his death, having been present at the debate over whom to conscript, and having seen the attitude of the men who are being sent off to the army, we are able to conclude that this is what life is like in a peasant village. For the first time with Tolstoy every stroke counts: The ineffectuality of the *barin* is set forth in the barest terms, as is the vanity of the overseer. The one weakness in the work is the suicide of Polikushka, which seems in excess of the facts and appears to be directed at the reader's emotions. We learn that an earlier version of this novella erred even more in this direction, for there the peasant Dultsov was turned into a stereotype of avarice, whereas in the final version Dultsov is the agent of returning the lost money and has no thought of keeping it for himself.

The subjects of all these works seem to be too big for the narrative means employed. It is not altogether reasoning after the fact to assert that Tolstoy needed a big canvas. The process of maturation of Masha, for example, which covers a period of years, or life on the Caucasian border as it involves Russian soldiers, Cossacks, and *abreks*, or the quiet desperation of a peasant community are actions that need the support of more varied and more specific data than these short works can provide. Tolstoy was not Chekhov. Tolstoy did not have the gift of the single illustrative incident that in Chekhov's hands somehow expands to convey the whole. As we see in our consideration of Tolstoy's two great novels, his interest was in the countless minutiae of daily life that make up the experience of living. For this he needed, and found, the big canvas. Without the major achievement of his two great novels Tolstoy could not have imposed himself on the world of literature as one of the great figures, for it is only in the novels that he shows his true greatness, a greatness that he attempts to deny in later years.

The simplest way to come to grips with *War and Peace* is immediately to challenge Sir Percy Lubbock's charge that it is imperfect in design[3] (though we must admit serious lapses in execution), and then to show what the novelistic organization is and how it contains and directs the vast flow of the novel. These elements must be inferred from the work itself, independent of statements about the author's intention and disregarding the accidents of formal division into parts. Since the novel was published serially and revised periodically over a number of years, there is no clearly definitive version.

The most important element in *War and Peace* is its showing the maturation of a representative group of young people under the impact of the specific and unusual events of war. This is not primarily a historical novel, but the historical events are one of its dimensions and permit a structural arrangement of extreme importance. To put it another way, a novel about maturation could, and usually does, take place against an invented background of private and (in the case of realistic novels) commonplace events. This is pretty much the case in *Madame Bovary* or *Anna Karenina*. In *War and Peace* the fact that the author has used history as a backdrop is fraught with consequences, but that historical framework should not be allowed to obscure what the main lines of the action really are. Also we should not be misled by the title, borrowed, as it happens, from Proudhon's book on social justice. It is merely a convenient rubric, an umbrella that covers everything, not an indicator that points to some sort of meaningful contrast or alternation—a conclusion, however, that can only be verified by examination of the novel. In fact, the background of the multiple protagonists is basically one of peacetime interests and pursuits. Like their whole generation, and many other generations before and after them, they are caught up in the whirlwind of war that forces, but does not exclusively determine, their development. Like everybody else the protagonists of the novel resume their normal lives when the war is over, with changes in outlook, but change of some sort was inescapable with the passage of time.

As we become acquainted with the considerable number of young people who appear at the beginning of the novel, we have no way of knowing which ones are to be important and which are to be only background figures. Gradually by emphasis and repeated appearances these personalities sort themselves out; some are static, others undergo continuing development, and it is the latter whom we must follow. As we proceed through the novel, it becomes apparent that there are five lives under closer scrutiny than the rest: three men, Pierre Bezukhov, Andrei Bolkonsky, and Nikolai Rostov; and two women, Marya Bolkonsky and Natasha Rostov. For one reason or another we have relegated to the sidelines the three younger Kuragins, Denisov, Dolokhov, Vera, and Berg, and particulary Boris Dubretskoi and Sonya, both of whom initially appeared to be of prime importance. Though these young people are not all the same age, which would be too contrived, they are all under thirty and within reach of each other in the process of maturation. They therefore constitute a cross section of Russian youth from a medium to high level of society. With the exception of Bolkonsky and Dubretskoi they do not move in the very highest circles, but neither do they by origin or acculturation fall below the level of polite society—a limited segment, but the one that Tolstoy knew best.

As previously indicated, certain of the characters recede into the background as the novel develops. Some become stereotyped almost at once; others, like Boris, promise to be central and are allowed a certain development before they lapse into the posture that is to characterize them for the rest of the novel. Among the major characters the two women necessarily play a smaller role than do the three men, if for no other reason than that their activities are almost entirely domestic even in a world subject to war as well as ordinary vicissitudes. The novel moves back and forth from one of these major figures to another. Four of them appear in the epilogue suitably married to each other—in the style of the older novel which is perhaps unnecessarily tightknit for realistic depiction. No one of them is *the* protagonist; to none of them does the narrator overtly give his preference. Rather, in Zola's terms, Tolstoy seems to have set up an experiment by which he undertakes to see which of the characters are successful and which ones fail, a body of data from which some conclusion may be drawn about how to live a good life. The meaning of the novel is the patterns these characters develop against a background of minor characters and historical personalities.

At the risk of making the novel appear to be more narrowly schematic than it is, we can see in each personage a characteristic excess or deficiency. Nikolai Rostov is *l'homme moyen sensuel*, average in his responses, conventional in his enthusiasms and prejudices. For that reason he is not very interesting to many readers, but for the same reason he is absolutely vital and central to the novel's statement. His potential is less than that of Pierre or Andrei, but his capacity for deviation from the right way is also less. Pierre Bezukhov is the enthusiast, the man of emotion. He leaps first and reflects afterward; he lives at a high pitch of feeling, which is both his strength and his weakness. Prince Andrei Bolkonsky is a man dominated by intellect, or at least a man whose intellect dominates emotion. It is difficult for Andrei to respond spontaneously; he is immediately critical of others and of himself. He is an absolutist in his ideals and, to the surprise of many readers, this absoluteness is sharply repudiated in the course of the novel. The natures of the two women are more simply drawn: Natasha is too spontaneous, too outgoing; she has to be chastened into a more matter-of-fact understanding. Marya is too withdrawn, too inclined to sensitivity and inhibition; she must be brought out.

The reader should not contemplate these separate lifelines in isolation or become a partisan of one against the others. These main characters all have their faults; they all have their potentialities. This is not a novel that creates a sympathetic character and puts him through his paces in meeting obstacles in order to leave him triumphant and the reader glowing with satisfaction over the character's triumphs. These lives take on meaning as they are related to each other, not necessarily by tight interconnections of plot but by encountering similar experiences. We compare their responses and derive an understanding from their variation. In contradiction to what was previously suggested, to place Nikolai in the center of the story would be a mistake; yet we must see him as important in his ordinariness, as constituting a kind of norm, a measuring stick against which to evaluate the rarer natures and behavior of Pierre and Andrei. We must not be put off by Pierre's bearishness or find him too sympathetic because we share his enthusiasms. Above all we must not place an excessive value on Andrei because he is highborn, because he is an intellectual and a man committed to the ideal, or because of the religious overtones of his questing. In fact, he shows up as a nay-sayer, as a man who gives up his hold on life for the sake of the frozen perfection of the blue sky. Since the novel at no point suggests that life is not good, Andrei's way is a mistake; he has missed the meaning of life by relinquishing it.

It is the exhibition of the natures of these characters in a variety of situations that accounts for the great length of the novel. They are also involved in historical, or pseudohistorical, situations at the same time, and this permits one set of narrative events to be effective on two levels at once. A twentieth-century realist would probably not permit lives of his or her characters to be as closely intertwined as Tolstoy does, but in consideration of the length of the novel a shortcut had to be taken somewhere. Certainly this interrelation of the characters in Tolstoy's novel is a convenience for the epilogue, where the moral center to which the surviving characters have come by different routes can be shown in a single scene.

What happens to these characters against a background of more static figures *is* the novel, but of course it is not all of the novel, which must be understood in terms of all the structuring devices it contains. Of these the first to consider, because it is the most neutral in effect, is a pattern of the cyclical nature of life. Though the work falls short of the normal twenty to twenty-five years for a generation—it begins in 1805 and even with the epilogue extends only to 1820—we are continually reminded of the repetitiveness of the life process in general and of particular kinds of experience with which the novel deals. Old Prince Bolkonsky in his last days recalls the time when he was a young general on the banks of the Danube—in Suvorov's war under Catherine, not in the campaign against Napoleon with which the novel begins. Sitting on the sidelines at Natasha's first ball, her mother remembers her own first ball. And so it goes: the essential experiences must be gone through in every generation. As a further means of stating this important truism we have the sight of young Petya going off to war in 1812 in the same access of enthusiasm as that felt by his brother Nikolai in the Austerlitz campaign seven years before. In the epilogue, young Nikolinka, Andrei's son, in his zeal for questioning is beginning to trace his father's footsteps. This insistence on a cyclical pattern is a way of insisting that human experience is basically unchanging and that the quest or the ordeal remains much the same, whatever the time and place. By this means the heightened historical backdrop is deemphasized. The same questions, the same partial answers, the same fumblings are to be observed in eras of historical splendor and fury as in the most pedestrian of times.

Another organizing principle in the novel, which has been often noted and often criticized, is the contrast between city and country, which becomes a contrast between the artificial and the natural, and ultimately develops into contrasting intellectual and moral orientations. This has many permutations. It begins in a simple way with a contrast between formal St. Petersburg and natural Moscow, between Anna Scherer's soirées and the relaxed life of the Rostov household; this is echoed later on by the contrast between the incapacity of the Czar's court to save Russia and the spontaneous and effective resistance of the population of Moscow. This is rapidly expanded to a contrast between the general formality and sterility of city life and the life-giving naturalness of the country, and is crowned by a denial of formal patterns of thought in favor of an intuitive understanding, which, in turn, becomes a denigration of Western ways of thinking in contrast with the natural Russian way.

For a large part of the novel Pierre is caught up in the artificial. We see him in Anna Scherer's salon, at Count Bezukhov's house, married to Hélène Kuragin, and involved in the sterile and pedantic mysticism of the Masonic Order. His development consists of sloughing off the unnaturalness of various restrictive ways of behavior and thought so that his natural self may finally emerge. His moment of truth comes in contact with Platon Karataev on the weary road west from Moscow. In Platon artificial modes have no place; instead he is endowed with intuitive insight that permits him to see what is important without wasting energy in vain struggle. Naturally enough the vision Pierre gains from Platon fades with the passage of time, but we are told, with perhaps too obvious a narrator guarantee, that decisions which formerly had been difficult for Pierre became easy, that he had no difficulty in distinguishing between the essential and the accidental in his life. However, as an important qualification, even at the very end we find Pierre on the fringes of a conspiracy resembling the Decembrist plot, caught up in a formal program that by definition is doomed to failure.

Nikolai and Natasha may be considered together, since they spring from the same background. They succumb in varying ways to the temptations of a formal and empty way of life; Nikolai gambling, for example, because of a youthful desire to do what other people do; Natasha almost eloping with Anatol in resentment over the unnatural rigidity of her engagement to Prince Andrei. But they are both naturally attuned to the simple and true, as we see with Nikolai in the hunt scene and Natasha at Uncle's, where she spontaneously adopts the rhythms and postures of the peasant dance that she has never seen before. In an emergency each rises to the occasion and does what he or she has to do without pausing to analyze or complain. Nikolai rides onto the Bolkonsky estate and rescues

Marya, just as he later unhesitatingly undertakes to support his mother and to rebuild a life out of the wreckage of his father's estate. Natasha's role is less substantial, more inferential. She nurses Andrei and later she governs Pierre wisely.

Prince Andrei is the one who does not escape the manacles of formalism. By social connection and by analytical cast of mind he is severely shackled from the beginning. Spontaneity has been frozen in him. He is "correct" toward his wife; he is incapable of give and take in human relationships generally. Andrei can accept Speransky, a political figure, only as a perfect being; once he sees Speransky's feet of clay Andrei repudiates him. Andrei's program for running his estate is just that, a program, which, though efficient, has little concern for the human beings for whom it is devised. He yearns for the empty perfection of the blue sky as he lies wounded at Austerlitz, and he surrenders to it after his wound at Borodino. His sister shares some of his difficulty. A victim of the logical martinet who is their father—he makes her study mathematics —she seeks escape in effusive emotion—yearning over God's Folk, writing letters to Julie Karagin—but she is brought back to a sane and natural way of life by the realities of war and marriage.

The principal exhibit on the side of form is the Kuragin family, a uniformly unprepossessing group. Prince Vasily is an accomplished courtier, with all the superficiality the word implies. His son Ipolit is a mental defective, whose courtship of Marya is a maneuver in his father's game of family advantage. The other son, Anatol, is a debauché, and the daughter Hélène is a sensual egoist. (It is not without significance that she dies from an attempt at abortion or miscarriage—a denial of the life force.) Pierre marries Hélène out of conformity with what the world expects of him and is forced to repudiate her if he is to live in harmony with himself. Marya refuses to be affianced to Ipolit and Natasha compromises herself with Anatol, who through Pierre's agency is ostracized from society. By association the whole artificial world of the upper classes is touched with the Kuragin taint. Since French is the language of that world, the use of this language becomes a convenient sign of artificiality. It is this world that draws Boris Dubretskoi permanently into its ranks; once he has made a calculated marriage of convenience with wealthy Julie Karagin, he ceases to be of interest to the novel. On a more pedestrian level we see Vera Rostov and her husband Berg drawn to this same sphere, their ambition being to have a salon like everybody else's salon.

This contrast characterizes the novel's overall approaches to life. Systems, because they are formal and artificial, are wrong; the spontaneous, intuitive response is right. Andrei consistently shows the sterility of intellectuals, though when he gives in to his feeling for Natasha the dead oak tree bursts into leaf. Pierre's eagerness for formulas is reduced to absurdity when he tries to find a numerological schema by which he can identify himself as the one destined to kill the Beast of the Apocalypse, Napoleon Bonaparte. Marya and Sonya are caught by sentimental formulas that have little to do with living reality. The former escapes; the other becomes a hanger-on of the Rostov family, a sterile flower.

On the level of historical characters and events this contrast is simple and forthright. The *right* way is that of Kutuzov and by extension of the Russian people, as a kind of mystical body; the *wrong* way is that of the theorizers, the formalizers, men who automatically delude themselves and others by believing in the efficacy of artificial systems. Napoleon is the notable example of this on the French side, but there is a difficult problem in presenting the Czar. He belongs to the wrong element by class and background and formality of role, but he is the father of the Russian people, who are right. The solution is to take him out of circulation almost entirely, though not without some damage to his image. A number of memorable scenes dramatize this contrast of approaches to life, the most pointed being the council of war in which general after general warmly espouses his own doctrinaire plan, none of which have much to do with the actuality of the military situation. Kutuzov, who knows this, is shown sleeping through the discussion, waiting patiently to resume the limited control of events possible to him, which amounts to letting the events develop as they must without losing any more men than he can help.

Unfortunately in this part of the novel Tolstoy suffered a failure of nerve, apparently being afraid that the actions would not speak for themselves as they do on the fictional level. The result is the introduction of annoying expository-argumentative passages beginning in Part IX, which is so damaging to the objective tone of the novel. The failure here is not one of design but one of execution. Not only is the argument out of harmony with the fiction, but it is intense and repetitious and rides roughshod over some incidents so as to negate the very heart of the effort. This culminates in the second epilogue, a philosophical tract of personal and wayward train. Unfortunately by position this nonnovelistic element has the last word.[4]

Leaving the content of the epilogue for the discussion of Tolstoy's philosophical position, we must look at some of the techniques that support the novel and produce its unusual freshness. Above all the author is skilled in the kaleidoscopic presentation of scene. The simplest way of analyzing this is to say that there are no big scenes in the novel, but that what seem to be big scenes are rather countless vivid scenic bits that serve to give the work its appearance of boundless, fluctuating variety. It is this free form of scenic treatment that has been the marvel of Tolstoy's readers. Zola later developed a presentation of detail that was notable for its density and for the fact that it went far beyond what any observer, even the most trained one, would be likely to see. The result of his techniques is a rigidity and static quality that contribute to the effect of a set piece. The Tolstoy scene, at its best in *War and Peace*, does not work in this way. It is a mosaic in which the whole is more than the sum of its parts. We shift rapidly from one part of the whole to another; we are rarely given an orderly, analytic approach. Thus the units presented, in a mixture of narration and dialogue, are psychologically manageable, small enough to be taken in and assimilated as the reader proceeds.

One means to this end is the use of some limited human

viewpoint as a point of reference. At Borodino we view the battle through Pierre's eyes; that is, his physical position and responses, as well as the responses of the soldiers and officers, are the battle. This depiction contrasts ironically with the attempt to picture the disposition of troops with which the scene begins. It is scarcely less evident that the account of the confused situation in Moscow after its capture is carried out in the same way. Central to our notion of the confusion is Pierre's involvement as it is summed up in his problem of restoring a lost child when his whole being is set on finding Napoleon and assassinating him. This is buttressed by other limited actions, of which the death of the presumed traitor Vereshchagin is a kind of historical set piece, but among which Berg's single-minded determination in the midst of growing chaos to acquire a piece of furniture is very effective. A similar example is the scene of Kutuzov's council of war in a peasant hut that is viewed through the eyes of the little girl Malasha, who has no idea what is going on but is on the side of "Granddad," that is, Kutuzov.

Tolstoy's method of characterization is similar to this. A single physical or moral characteristic may immediately stand for the whole person if he is a background figure, or it may serve as a quick point of reference for a developing character. The short upper lip of Prince Andrei's wife is an example of the first method, and Princess Marya's luminous eyes an example of the second. Whether it be for scene or characterization, Tolstoy early discovered that the part can effectively stand for the whole and that bombardment by all relevant data is not only unnecessary but potentially inimical to the ends of realism. This is a discovery of the utmost importance, which permitted an escape from the Balzac-Zola type of inventory; above all it permitted movement and therefore life. This is not to say that Tolstoy carries this technique to its ultimate limits. His sense of the novel is too tightly knit for that; he keeps the whirling kaleidoscope within rigorous bounds. Moreover, he bridges gaps in the scenic presentation by means of description or summary narrative, thereby giving the reader a sense of direction and stability. In short, he provides a controlled formlessness, which is, of course, not formless at all.

The second great Tolstoy novel, *Anna Karenina*, is structurally similar to *War and Peace*, though on a smaller scale, and it is even more tightly controlled. The materials are three domestic situations, those of the Levin and Oblonsky families and the triangle involving Anna, her husband, and Vronsky. By reducing the cases studied to a limited number, Tolstoy has run the risk of making the demonstration arbitrary and rigid, particularly as there is a temptation to ignore the Oblonsky family as the midpoint in the spectrum and to see the novel as a sharp contrast between extremes, which indeed does happen at the end when we listen to the opposed philosophies of Anna and Levin. This final touch, however, is one of supererogation, since whatever conclusion is drawn about the right course for human behavior is arrived at inductively by examination of the cases under study. Whereas in *War and Peace* the subject was how to adjust to the world by way of fruitful maturation, in *Anna Karenina* the subject is narrower, though perhaps only a rephrasing of the more general question. We now look at family happiness, asking what makes a good marriage and by extension a good society. There is a basic assumption here that marriage is by its function good and necessary to society; there is no effort to explore nonmarriage as a way of life.

The structure in this novel is a cross section and more a logical schema than in *War and Peace*. The three families do not, at least superficially, start out together. Instead they have only one thing in common, the element of striving, but they are radically different in where they are at the beginning of the novel, let alone at the end. And there is virtually no effort to fill in the background with minor instances of the same kinds of problem. This amounts to saying that *Anna Karenina* is both more restricted in scope and more intense than *War and Peace*. Almost as long as the latter, *Anna Karenina* is nonetheless conceived in terms of an economy that is not found in the earlier work. But the criterion of selection of materials is much the same in both cases: situations of normal experience to be lived through and reacted to in somewhat different ways. The Levin household is one that, in spite of severe initial difficulties, gets increasingly on the right path and manifests natural, spontaneous responses to the perennial round of experience. The two households of which Anna is a member collapse because of the absence of right attitudes, and because of a formalism that masks emptiness. In the middle, the Oblonskys limp along; their situation is undermined by wrong action, yet there is enough understanding of the primacy of family for them to subordinate or control egoism and so keep the enterprise going. Just as in the case of Nikolai in *War and Peace*, the importance of the middle cannot be overemphasized. It is where most human experience falls; the more extreme cases take on validity as they refer and attach to the middle, for taken by themselves they would appear incapable of providing a basis for generalization.

There is no stirring background to the events in *Anna Karenina*, though there is preoccupation with the social question of the age, how to develop adequate social institutions in the aftermath of the Emancipation. Thus the narrative events are much simpler than in the earlier novel. They are the ordinary experiences of courtship, marriage, childbirth and childrearing, domestic organization, and social and community life—in short, the materials with which a women's magazine of that day and this deals so badly, because it does it so untruthfully. (As previously noted, because of the social level depicted money is less important than it generally is in works of this kind, but then is rarely important in Tolstoy's works, which sets him apart from other realistic writers.)

Without extending the parallel too far, we can see much of Pierre in Levin; in Karenin there is a dessicated Prince Andrei; and Stepan resembles Nikolai's father, the feckless Count Rostov. Although there are evident similarities between Kitty and Natasha, or between Varenka and Sonya, the women in this novel go beyond what is offered in *War and Peace* since they are shown active in the domestic area. Whereas in *War and*

Peace maturation is conceived of as forgetfulness of self in the broad sense of belonging to humanity, and there is little stress on familial obligations until the epilogue, here the characters grow or shrink as they achieve self-forgetfulness in that sphere. Levin initially appears before us as too sensitive, too self-conscious; he has the capacity for love but worries it to death. Early we see him skating with Kitty in graceful harmony and self-forgetfulness when his reflexes take over. Later, and more impressively, we see him mowing with the peasants, after his initial awkwardness achieving a natural physical rhythm and moral identification, which is the way life ought to be. Kitty, because of her inexperience and social pressure, is dazzled by Vronsky and by her dreams of playing an unnatural role in the brilliant world of high society. Like Natasha, Kitty pays for her failure of insight and for her active error with a general breakdown, for which time and the natural resiliency of the human organism—not doctors—provide the only cure. Rigidity is condemned; growth, and growth in the right direction, is the great underlying law of life. Kitty achieves this growth. She nurses her husband's dying brother and rejoices over her pregnancy; she is attuned to the basic life forces. Stepan's weaknesses are those of good nature. He never does learn to control his appetites, but neither does he stray into the encapsulated isolation of complete egoism. Dolly is subject to the temptations of the world of society; to Levin's disgust she teaches her children French. She is jealous of the luxury and freedom of Anna's establishment in comparison with her own, but she regains perspective after a short time, returning gladly to her natural state, in which, absorbed in being a mother, she never has time to develop her own egoism.

The triangle of which Anna is the center is much more complicated and presents by far the most subtle relationships that Tolstoy ever described. In the last analysis it is impossible to fix the blame for the failures that arise from this unnatural situation. It is enough that each of the three principals suffers absolutely for his or her fault and that Anna's two children are innocent victims of these unhappy circumstances. Anna's egoism is to some extent unexpected. Its appearance after years of her being a submissive and undemanding wife is not explained. Suddenly she wants everything, love as well as respectability, and she is never able to limit or to define the new role that she chooses, so that by her unreasonableness she wrecks both what is and what might have been. Vronsky seems at first to be the most shallow of the three. We are early shown in his *lessive* scene that he is a man who takes his being from social form, and we tend to sympathize with him for being caught by forces of passion that carry him beyond the support of forms. Yet the horse race, at which he kicks a fallen mare in an outburst of anger, is a reminder that Vronsky has his share of egoism, that he values the maintenance of his glittering role in the world, and that he is capable of self-abnegation only to the extent that it is in conformity with the role he has assumed.[5] At the end of the novel Vronsky falls back on the one role left him, that of the man weary of life who goes off to get himself killed in an irrelevant war.

Toward the end the novel becomes a kind of dialogue between the doctrine of self-abnegation and the doctrine of egoism, setting up a philosophical contrast for which there is no middle. Anna, riding in a carriage to the train and her final perverse self-assertion by suicide, agrees that life is a struggle for existence and that it is hate alone that binds men together. Levin, reflecting on his experience since marriage, marvels at the sense of well-being and the rightness of feeling that have come over him, but he also recognizes that perfect self-forgetfulness is impossible and that he will go on backsliding and trying again for perfection. This tendency toward abstract dialogue in the last part of the novel is the culmination of one of the chief structuring elements in the work. As in *War and Peace* there is a contrast between country and city, between the natural and the artificial. St. Petersburg is the locus of vanity. It is the home of Alexei Karenin, the servant of sterile form, who can never slough off the bonds of that formalism and whose genuine emotion takes him no further than the sterile practices of spiritualism and a fraudulent religiosity. It is also the place with which Vronsky is identified. The adultery is committed there, the horse race occurs there, and Anna's disastrous appearance at the opera, which marks the final blow to her real being, occurs in the capital. (The opera itself is a sign of the arrantly artificial, as Tolstoy states with amusing exaggeration in *What Is Art?*) Moscow is perhaps a middle ground in this work, since Oblonsky is associated with it, and it is characterized by futile but less dangerous practices than St. Petersburg. But it is the country that really nurtures men. All the best domestic scenes are there, and most of the novel is set in the country. The famous haying scene, Kitty with her child, and many other vignettes exemplify the good life in the country. Some of the minor characters quickly manifest their incompleteness when they are set down in this country milieu—to the extent even of Veslovsky's being expelled from this paradise by Levin.

Whereas *Anna Karenina* examines a much narrower situation than does *War and Peace*, it too has its extension to a kind of historical level. In addition to looking at happy and unhappy families, the novel is concerned with the great family, Russia herself, and the relation of the different social entities that make it up. This is a very Tolstoyan answer to Chernishevsky's question, "Chto delat?"—"What is to be done?" It is carried out on a surprisingly broad scale. Karenin as a bureaucrat is considering schemes for the handling of native populations. Sergei, Levin's brother, is a social theorist whose book fails and who fails personally in that, wishing to propose to Varenka, he is unable to talk about anything but mushrooms. Vronsky attempts to set up a model estate, but his imposition from above, without heart, is a failure. The Oblonskys let their estate run down in a relationship of exploitation, not the true marriage with the soil and peasantry that Levin seeks to bring about. There is a good deal of talk about the kind of local government to be instituted for the enfranchised serfs. This level of the novel does not drive toward any explicitly formulated program, but it is clear enough that the same attitudes are needed in general social organization as in the family.

One reason for what readers generally take to be a more

somber tone in *Anna Karenina* is its much less extensive use of scene. This is not the brilliant revolving stage, bringing one group after another to the front, that we find in *War and Peace*. There are scenes of some magnitude and of unforgettable intensity, but they are fewer in number, are on a somewhat more elaborate scale when they do occur, and are more clearly harnessed to the task of specific demonstration. Here we do not have life in its abundance, but life limited to that which is immediately relevant to the book's subject. As a partial compensation for lack of scenic vividness, Tolstoy does make an advance in the presentation of internal states. In *War and Peace* what the characters feel comes out chiefly through what they do and say. Only rarely does Tolstoy experiment in other directions, notably when Nikolai Rostov on the battlefield has something of an interior monologue as his mind moves by auditory association through the series, *tache, sabretache, Natasha.*

In *Anna Karenina* it is not enough to show externally what happens to the characters. An important part of what they undergo is suffering, and suffering is necessarily internal. Vronsky, the man contained within a code, can without too much diminution of his being be shown externally. We watch him as he adopts one conventional posture after another, and we are content to infer what he feels in the narrow gamut of feeling that we think is open to him. For the other characters there is need to get beneath their exteriors, and Tolstoy uses a number of devices for this purpose. With Levin it is a combination of summary stream of consciousness and soliloquy, conventional and clumsy though the latter is. With Alexei Karenin there is an effort at a kind of expressionism, especially in the sequence dealing with a discussion of divorce at the Moscow lawyer's office and at a dinner party that evening. With Anna there is a genuine effort to get at the core of her suffering. The use of the symbolic figure of the *muzhik* and the recurrent dream she has are part of this, though the device is more literary than psychological, especially when Vronsky dreams a similar dream. There is actually a rudimentary interior monologue as

Anna rides to the railway station. What goes on in her mind is chaotic, is minimally structured, and is interrupted and diverted by the impingement of external data that she registers. This episode, as noted, is part of a somewhat formal philosophical argument, but there is also an attempt at a radically new technique.

Since the moral and intellectual crisis by which Tolstoy became a didactic writer rather than an artist coincided with the later stages of his composing *Anna Karenina*, it is not to be expected that the works of his last years—over thirty years, to be precise—should show much of interest in the technical development of realism. These works are, however, often instructive as a means of evaluating the earlier writings, and the artist did occasionally reassert himself in them. Of these works, *The Death of Ivan Ilych* (1886), *The Power of Darkness* (1886), *The Kreutzer Sonata* (1891), *Master and Man* (1895), *Resurrection* (1899), and *Hadji Murad* (1912) have an important place in the Tolstoy canon. Of these, only *Resurrection* has the dimensions of a novel. It is realistic, if we dare use that term for any part of it, only to the extent that Tolstoy documented himself on the life of prisoners and the operation of the judicial and penal systems. Based on an actual incident recounted to Tolstoy by a friend, the novel starts out dramatically when Prince Nekhliudov is called to jury duty and is present at the trial of Katusha, whom he had seduced two years before and thus started on a life of prostitution. Although it is evident that the girl is not guilty of the crime charged against her, she is convicted and sentenced to four years in Siberia. The Prince, now remorseful, determines that he will get the conviction reversed and marry her. Fortunately for the veracity of the novel, she turns him down, and resurrection comes to both of them; to her because she changes her corrupt ways and to him because he ceases to be an aristocratic parasite and devotes himself to social justice.

The central characters in the novel are wooden, and the narrative events amount to little more than the framework for a conducted tour of the infamous workings of the Russian social system. The novel is undermined to the point of collapse by its insistence on a thesis, though this is not very explicitly formulated, for in addition to the immediate concern about the miscarriage of justice in the courts and prisons there is measured out a heavy dose of Henry George economics. The strength of the work lies in the incidental portrayal of the many "little people" whom the Prince encounters in prison and on his way to Siberia. Tolstoy's eye was still good when he kept it on the object, and the incidental characters, whose being is almost entirely independent of the thesis, are lively and memorable. In a way this novel is Tolstoy's *Crime and Punishment* without the intensity or psychological acuity of Dostoevsky. The moral suffering does not really come through, though the physical degradation is clear. Overall it makes one think of the typical American novel of social protest of the 1930s, powerful at times but also ridiculous in its heaping up of instances of social injustice.

The Kreutzer Sonata is even more unsatisfactory, also because of a thesis. In writing it Tolstoy warned himself against "the desire to make a work of art," that is, a work of vanity. The narrative framework is provided by an account of a train journey taken by the first-person narrator, in the course of which there is a general conversation about contemporary morals, divorce, and the like—ten pages mostly in dialogue with an excellent differentiation of speakers. Out of this comes a seventy-five page monologue by a man who killed his wife; the account is punctuated only by the most perfunctory interruptions on the part of the original narrator. In spite of the artificial format this is a remarkably vivid and exact description of a marriage that has gone to pieces and it gives good insight into the state of mind of the husband (though none at all into that of the wife, whom we see only through his eyes). When taken by itself the narrative is of a not unpromising psychological kind, but unfortunately it is harnessed to a theory and used in support of the thesis. It becomes ridiculous, especially since, as in *War and Peace*, it is accompanied by a fifteen-page epilogue that restates the thesis as direct argument. The love-hate dualism, moreover, though Dostoevskian in insight, is conveyed in terms that are more logical than psychological. As in *The Devil*,

Tolstoy is a prude about sexual relationships and so denies himself the kind of substantive data that would be most useful for the narrative.

The Death of Ivan Ilych and *Hadji Murad* are by common consent two of the novelist's greatest works, emerging luminous from the didactic darkness of the last years. The subject of the first is the deadly mediocrity and ultimate meaninglessness of the average man's life, in which conformity with respect to possessions and career robs life of individuality and meaning. The technique here is original. The opening section is a vivid dramatic scene showing the response of Ivan Ilych's family and colleagues to his death, reducing it to an event no more important than an impediment to a planned evening of whist and demonstrating by the objective correlative of a pouffe with jack-in-the-box springs the mechanical existence of people living in the world described. The story then proceeds by rapid narrative summary to state that the dead man's life had been most terrible because it was most ordinary. Only at the end does the work come back to the use of scene in order to show the impact of death on Ivan Ilych and to contrast the falsity of his life with that of his peasant servant, Gerasim, another Platon Karataev, and a more convincing one. This work is a triumph of narrative art, and whatever doctrine it contains springs from the facts and is supported by those facts. If the work exhorts, it does so only in the minimal sense of asserting that commonplace lives could be other than what they are and that even commonplace people, like Ivan Ilych, have the capacity to recognize their error, though this does not imply the miracle of conversion or the possibility that the dying man, if reprieved, would have changed his ways.

Except for a brief symbolic framework, *Hadji Murad* is presented strictly as objective narrative. At the beginning there is a first-person narrator who recalls that he once chanced upon a thistle growing along the road which attracted his attention by its beauty and vitality, one which, when he returned a few hours later, lay broken and dead by the random destruction of a cart wheel. This reminds him of the story of a native chieftain in the

Caucasus whose fate is of a similar inconsequentiality. That story is told in the third person with the quick movement of scene and the objectivity of viewpoint that characterized the best parts of *War and Peace*. Though the story would seem fated to sentimental treatment, it does not receive it, for Hadji Murad is never shown out of the perspective of his limitations and situation. Similarly, though the Russian official world is egoistic and inhumane, the satire that it receives is kept within bounds. Hadji Murad through circumstances not subject to his control was caught up in a process that he was incapable of withstanding and became a casualty—like the random thistle along the road.

It is not possible to overstate the importance of Tolstoy the novelist for later writers. Perhaps he has done more in the long run for the novel than Flaubert and Zola because of the more genial quality of his world.[6] Certainly Tolstoy's example provided a corrective for the exaggerated distancing that is characteristic of the French realists generally. He avoids the rigor of their determinism. Although committed to a basically external approach, Tolstoy never denies the presence and vitality of internal states, allowing his characters to work out the patterns of their lives to an accompaniment of the feelings that are part of that experience. This makes it possible for the reader to participate with them in that experience instead of holding them at arm's length as exhibits wriggling on a pin.

Yet when we examine Tolstoy's philosophical position as it appears implicit, and sometimes all too explicit, in his works of fiction, we are struck by the fact that his outlook is not so different from that of his French contemporaries as we may like to think. Tolstoy too is a determinist; his characters cannot evade the impulsion of casuality any more than can those of Flaubert and Zola. Tolstoy too sees human beings subject to forces that are indifferent to them and in their implacability capable of destruction. Yet his characters are not automata, and their awareness of their predicament and their struggles to extricate themselves from it are important parts of their experience. This is best summed up in the terms by which Tolstoy examines the problem of free will versus determinism in the second epilogue of *War and Peace*. If, he says, the events of human existence be examined from a sufficient distance—from another planet, for example—by an omniscient observer, then the only possible conclusion is that man is the creature of necessity, that he has no free will, and that his every act is the result of the convergence of myriad antecedent causes. To assert otherwise would be to speak nonsense and to reduce the universe to a condition of chaos. But only deity—or in our day conceivably a computer—has the necessary distance and omniscience to take this view. Therefore such a statement, although true in the abstract, is actually false in terms of the experience of the individual, who, involved in the process of living, must act under the illusion that he has free will and that his choices and his decisions are open and important. For practical purposes this illusion of free will means that he has free will, since his actions, and the thought and emotion that precede and accompany his actions, will be based on that assumption.

Whatever Tolstoy's status as philosopher, this statement is of the utmost importance in terms of the realistic novel. Through it he finds a way out of the impasse created by his doctrinaire contemporaries. He escapes the reduction of human beings to puppets, which is the likely outcome of the Zola demonstration. Tolstoy makes it possible for his readers, also suffering from the illusion of free will, to find interest and significance, even solace, in the doings of his fictional creatures. His mirror is actually more accurate because it reflects in truer perspective and does not flatten out his picture, as would be the case from a remoter elevation.

Though a determinist in the abstract sense, Tolstoy is not a pessimist. He neither denies nor lingers unduly over the evils and catastrophes of existence. His emphasis is certainly not on an inevitable running downhill of personal existence and of social institutions. Death is final but not an obscene indignity. He charts in detail the disastrous career of Anna Karenina. He shows Hadji Murad to be a blind casualty of circumstances. There is that within Prince Andrei which leads him obstinately to surrender life. But they are on the whole exceptional cases. Tolstoy's emphasis is on a human capacity within the boundaries of a general determinism somehow to intuit the response which is life sustaining and by means of trial and error to adopt a way of life that is viable and even satisfying. This is certainly not to be done by reason, by subtle analysis, but by a process deeper than reason, one almost of primitive sentience. This is the wisdom of Kutuzov, who attempts to align himself with the forces he feels are operative in the universe and to put as few obstacles in their way as possible. This is something that Pierre and Nikolai and Levin have to learn through experience, something that Natasha and Kitty to a large degree have innately, though they can be swerved from the proper intuitive course. What the major Tolstoy works show is that not only does life mean intensely but it means good, and that the course of events, the whole direction of the great abstract deterministic design, is beneficent, or at least not predominantly antagonistic to man.

It would be easy to translate this vision into traditional religious terms, for the obduracy with which some Tolstoy characters persist in the wrong direction can certainly be equated with the sin of pride, and in general the necessity to ride with the current, to learn not to thresh around in futile striving resembles basic forms of Christian quietism. Yet in the earlier and major works Tolstoy's faith is a secular one. He is not speaking in terms of religious salvation but of well-being in this life. His is a halfway station between the strict scientific determinism of his French contemporaries and the primitive Christianity of Dostoevsky. It is a personal vision abstracted from reality as he has observed and experienced it, and thus it is open to criticism by those who claim that his interpretation goes beyond what the facts will support.

This leads to the question raised much earlier in this chapter as to whether Tolstoy's representation is an anachronism, whether it squares in essentials with the world as we observe it today. Certainly the world in which his characters move is different from ours. It is one of stable and permanent social forms, one of fairly limited chances to go wrong, one where physical or moral isolation is so rare as to be almost negligible. Personal crises are cushioned by the presence of these norms, not exacerbated by the absence of any norms whatsoever. There appears to be remarkable agreement as to what the right way is. Difference lies rather in the capacity to discover it and adhere to it. It is a hierarchical world in which each element seems to know its place, for we get little intimation of striving to get out of place.

We are therefore forced back to a basic question as to how much Tolstoy has manipulated his representation by the presence of his sharp polarities: city versus country, the artificial versus the natural, will versus acceptance, intellect versus intuition. In the multifarious life of *War and Peace*, and to a lesser extent in the other works, these polarities seem to emerge naturally as the result of induction, not to be the deductive basis for a didactic statement. If we look at many lives, Tolstoy seems to say, we discover that some are shrunken and made rigid by wrong attitudes, and others achieve well-being by an almost unconscious adoption of right attitudes. The ability or inability to make right choices is part of the human constitution and therefore part of the causal pattern. Apparently, however, it is not fixed, for there seems to be room for maneuver, room for learning even from wrong choices. There is an implicit moralism in this observation. It does not leave open the possibility of reaching well-being by other means. As readers, we tend to accept it as valid where the body of detail about experience is vast and to shy away from it in shorter works, where the bare bones of deductive argument are not fleshed over by luxuriant detail.

If, as has often been suggested, to be a realist is to be alienated from the world that one observes or portrays, then Tolstoy is not a realist—and neither is Chekhov or Galdós. But the validity of such a definition is open to question. Alienation may actually be a violation of objectivity, an *a priori* position of an intellectually fashionable kind. Someday we may decide that Tolstoy had the last and right word after all when he said to Gorky, with reference to Dostoevsky's turbulent view of the world: "It is all so much simpler."[7]

6

Fyodor Dostoevsky

To include Dostoevsky among the realists of the nineteenth century is to stretch the term to the breaking point. Yet to omit him is to ignore one of the major streams of realistic innovation, and the one which has been most influential in the twentieth century. It gets us nowhere, moreover, to attempt to resolve this dilemma by recourse to Dostoevsky's own formula of a "higher realism," since this merely leads us into an area of metaphysics where the assumptions are antithetical to the philosphical grounding of realism. It is better to accept at the start that Dostoevsky's writing is mixed, that he never sets out to be a reporter in the ordinary sense, that he truly wears his realism with a difference.[1]

Still it is important at the outset to look at Dostoevsky in the terms that we have used for other realists. Even though his major interest is elsewhere, he too necessarily handles a world of external and verifiable data; he shares at least some common ground with a Tolstoy, a Zola, or a Galdós. We can say that there is a Dostoevsky world just as there is one for each of these other writers, even though it is often overlooked by critics in their absorption in other aspects of his work. In theory it is very little cluttered with physical or social data of a representative

167

sort, as is attested in a passage in the notebooks for *The Possessed*: "I shall not describe the city, the environment, the manners, the people, the situations, the relations and the curious changes in these relations in the provincial life of our town as the result of ancient immemorial customs. . . . I do not have time to concern myself with portraying our little corner. I consider myself the chronicler of a curious particular event that took place among us. . . ." He goes on to admit that occasionally he will provide a few indispensable pictures of daily life, but he reasserts at the end of the passage that "I shall not concern myself especially with descriptions of our current way of life." This statement, though it is only a casual note, does serve to indicate the direction of Dostoevsky's interest and shows one respect in which he is set apart from usual realistic practice. The "curious particular event," the point of tension and explosion on which the action of a Dostoevsky novel centers, is the focus of attention; the background of detail is at best incidental. Dostoevsky is, to be sure, inconsistent in his comments on this point, for he wrote his friend Strakhov in 1869 that one does not achieve realism merely by falling back on the everyday run of things, but at the same time he takes a stand for documentation when he said: "I have reached the irrevocable conclusion that a novelist ought to become acquainted in minute detail with the multiple historical and current realities that he is going to depict."

Dostoevsky's repudiation of the factual density of Zola is to be expected, but he is also severe toward Tolstoy and Turgenev, whom he finds static and old-fashioned. In *The Diary of a Writer* for 1873 he complains that "Our artists . . . insist on observing certain phenomena of reality . . . and on representing in art certain types only at the moment when, having had their day, they are on the point of disappearing and must yield place to others more in conformity with the times. The result is that we are always being offered what is old as something new." Again in *The Diary* for 1877 he laments that "A large part of Russian life has remained outside observation and has not found its historian. In any event I am certainly right in stating that the life of the nobility, brought under the light in too high relief by our writers, is too limited and too separated an aspect of Russian life." In principle, it would seem that Dostoevsky participates in the general, realistic repudiation of conventional subject matter. Yet his drive toward innovation is not consistent. There is nothing as old-fashioned as the kind of plot to which he was addicted; on the other hand, there is nothing as new-fashioned as his revelation of complexity of behavior under a condition of stress. It is the latter orientation that successive generations have valued and emulated even as they have wrung their hands over Dostoevsky's absurdities and willful confusions of plot.

Dostoevsky has often been regarded as one concerned primarily with "the insulted and the injured," with people on the fringes of society, with oddities cut off from the support of social forms. Such a conclusion comes largely from examination of his early works and arises also from too exclusive a concentration on the isolates in *Notes from Underground* and *Crime and Punishment.* It is certainly not borne out by the other works. On the contrary, we find that there is generally a middle-class environment, a world of decent people and decorous social forms, a world in which the struggle for existence is not on the simple level of predation, a world of government officials and country landowners—in short, a bourgeois world in many of its substantive elements, however much it may differ in emotional intensity.

Dostoevsky's first novel, *Poor People* (1846), does not examine a segment of life; it sets up an artificial situation and squeezes from it as much sentiment as possible. This is equally true of two other early works. *Netochka Nezvanova* (1849) (left unfinished because of the author's sudden enforced removal to Siberia) is a first-person account of a young girl's life in three rather discontinuous stages. The whole is suffused with romantic feeling and mystery and is raised to a high point of emotional anguish. There is some psychological analysis, such as the subjugation of a child by her stepfather as part of the war between husband and wife. On the other hand, the adults are generally wooden; there is no psychological complexity there. The other early full-length work, *The Insulted and the Injured* (1861), can only be considered a good old-fashioned nineteenth-century tearjerker, with an evident Dickensian provenance, even to the name of little Nelly. In this work contrivance, malefic plots, and some amateur detective work confirming the guilt of the villain take precedence over observation. The most promising exceptions to this charge are other early works that explore a vein of social comedy. *Uncle's Dream, The Village of Stepanichikovo* (in English usually entitled *A Friend of the Family*), and *The Gambler* are entertaining examples of that genre. These works have an excellent eye for detail and are important in showing another side to the "morbid" Dostoevsky. They do not, however, mark an important advance in realism, social or psychological. If we seek for the source of Dostoevsky's mature orientation, both philosophical and literary, we must find it in his experience of prison and Siberian exile from 1849 to 1859. Certainly thereafter his works are much less literary in the imitative sense, and his conception of the mystery of human personality has infinitely deepened.

Notes from the House of the Dead (1860–61) is documentary to a degree that Dostoevsky never sought to reach again. In its way it is one of the great works of the nineteenth century, since it is a direct transcription of an experience all too frequent in Russia that had not previously been the subject of literature—a precursor of Aleksander Solzhenitsyn's *Gulag Archipelago*. Chekhov later also wrote from firsthand experience about the life of the deportees on the island of Sakhalin, but he was only a temporary observer. Tolstoy too in *Resurrection* gained power by identifying with prisoners about to go into exile, but again from the outside looking in. Though by no means artless, Dostoevsky's account is vivid, it is balanced and controlled, and it is without literary posturing. The first-person narrator, a thinly disguised authorial voice,[2] Alexander Petrovich Goryanchikov, has left a manuscript that Dostoevsky purports to have found after Goryanchikov's death, "a narrative of his ten years in prison," in which are to be found "strange fragments, abominable memories set down without order, convulsively as though to ease himself." The narrator makes a plea that attention be paid to this "world of fallen men, an absolutely new world, one which has remained impenetrable until now."

The narrative is remarkable for its objectivity of tone. While Alexander Petrovich reflects with some frequency on the dehumanizing effects of detention and flogging, he does not argue but is content to let the account of daily life, the pervasive melancholy, and the brutal punishments speak for itself. If there is any structuring in this work, it is directed toward showing the full gamut of responses to prison life in a manner that is neither rigidly analytical nor topical. Most of the material is narrated in an equable, matter-of-fact tone, but on occasion the treatment is scenic. There are pages of sustained dialogue in language that is down to earth and unliterary. There is no effort to probe the minds of the convicts directly, though Alexander Petrovich by telling of his own inner states provides a basis for access to the feeling of others, about which he also speculates and generalizes. The leisurely and repetitive manner of the narrative diminishes its impact in one way but adds to its truth. Whether or not this book contributed to Dostoevsky's skill in writing novels, it shows that he did learn how to present common suffering humanity in a setting that is sufficiently concrete to carry conviction and that he did here escape completely from the half-world of the grotesque.

When we turn to the five major novels written in the last two decades of the author's life, we have a more solid basis for assessing the nature of his world. These vary in the amount of external data that they present, but they can all be considered to come to grips with some aspect of reality, social or psychological, whatever their success as finished works. Of these *The Possessed* and *The Brothers Karamazov* are by far the most substantial in their presentation of social background. *A Raw Youth* and *The Idiot* occupy a middle-ground position in this respect, and *Crime and Punishment* exists almost in a social vacuum.

On its simplest level, *The Possessed* comes close to being a comedy of manners, since it is rich in observation, though uncontrolled in its tendency to melodrama. It is its failure to keep to this simple level that makes it the unsatisfactory, albeit challenging, novel that it is. One segment of the novel is devoted to an examination of the higher levels of provincial society as we see it at the Stavrogin country estate of Skvoreshniki and the neighboring town. The vacuity of life at Varbuara Petrovna's and her sterile relationship with Stepan Trofimovich, the vanity of provincial society, the incapacity of the governor, and the emptiness of literary and scientific pretension are all matters for comedy, culminating in the hilarious fiasco of the benefit for indigent governesses. These events and situations should have no grave consequences and at most should be permitted only limited excess of eccentricity and overdrawing, though even in such a limited context Dostoevsky goes overboard with the flight and death of Stepan Trofimovich.

The other half of this novel, that involving "the conspiracy," is not based on observation or genuine documentation (in spite of Dostoevsky's claims to the contrary) and is hysterical in its revulsion and fear. It is organized as a logical demonstration: first, a cross section of various kinds of unstable youth, then showing on the scale of intense melodrama the blight that their doctrines and attitudes bring. Here there is a piling up of horrors: the murder of the Lebedkins and their servant in a fire that is incendiary in origin; the plotting and death of the criminal Fedka; the fortuitous death of Lise at the hands of the mob; the murder of Shatov (and the gratuitous deaths of his wife and infant); the suicide of Kirilov as an exemplification of his beliefs; and finally Stavrogin's confession and suicide. There is a sharp difference of method and tone in the two parts of the novel. The work does not hold together, in part because what was supposed to be a binding element, the Stavrogin-Tikhon dialogue, is undeveloped or, as happened with the confession, suppressed. It is no wonder that critics have abandoned this novel as a work of art and prefer to use it as a mine of the author's ideas.

Certainly it is that. In a way it is an answer to both Chernishevsky's "What Is to Be Done?" and Turgenev's *Fathers and Sons*, since it is suffused with the turbulence of post-Emancipation questioning. It is also a study of a society plagued with a frivolous ruling class and a brutal, dehumanized intelligentsia. At the very beginning we are given a sketch of the moral and intellectual ambiance: "It was a peculiar time; something new was beginning, quite unlike the stagnation of the past, something very strange too, though it was felt everywhere, even at Skvoreshniki. Rumours of all sorts reached us. The facts were generally more or less well known, but it was evident that in addition to the facts there were certain ideas accompanying them, and what's more, a great number of them."

When we reach the climactic events of Part III there is a further indication of this ferment:

In turbulent times of upheaval or transition low characters always come to the front everywhere. I am not speaking of the so-called "advanced" people who are always in a hurry to be in advance of everyone else (their absorbing anxiety) and who always have some more or less definite, though often very stupid, aim. No, I am speaking only of the riff-raff. In every period of transition this riff-raff, which exists in every society, rises to the surface, and is not only without any aim but has not even a symptom of an idea, and merely does its utmost to give expression to uneasiness and impatience. . . . What constituted the turbulence of our time and what transition it was we were passing through I don't know. . . . Yet the most worthless fellows suddenly gained predominant influence, began loudly criticising everything sacred, though till then they had not dared to open their mouths, while the leading people, who had till then so satisfactorily kept the upper hand, began listening to them and holding their peace, some even simpered approval in a most shameless way.

The important thing here is not the adequacy of the conservative narrator's assessment of the situation, but the fact that the elements so described have their being in a concretely established social setting. The characters are not vaguely conspiring in dark St. Petersburg taverns or gossiping in vaguely delineated drawing rooms. Not only do they have a definite physical locus, but they are members of a community in which the relationships have meaning in terms of the functioning of the social whole. Varvara Petrovna is, or has been, the grande dame of the district. Lembke is the governor, whose stupidity facilitates a breakdown of social organization. The conspirators are not demons summoned out of the air but are known personalities with local affiliations. And the repercussions of these events are not shown in abstract ideological terms but in terms of the relations of these people.

The action of *The Brothers Karamazov* is also contained within a community, or rather a Chinese box of communities, and in spite of the heavy concentration of symbolic elements, this novel too must be understood initially in down-to-earth terms. As Ralph Matlaw has pointed out, the fundamental level is always the literal one, since the strategy of Dostoevsky is "to express the sublime in terms of the commonplace."[3] There is a town—"our town," says the anonymous narrator—called Skotoprigonevsk, a name which might be Americanized as "Roundup." We do not get a comprehensive cross section of this community, but we see enough of its average citizens to gauge the nature of public opinion and conventional ideas and to encounter a wide variety of human judgments and errors. An adjunct to the town, the monastery, is another community, beset by the same varieties and incapacities of human response. Also in a central position are a number of families, who constitute the basic physical and symbolic units of the novel. Each of these families fails to function properly in its own way, but they also have in common a general imperfection that is disastrous to their members. Kolya Krasotkin has been fatherless since infancy. The Snegirov children have an emotionally disturbed father and a simple-minded mother. Madame Khokhlakov is a widow, to Lise's distinct harm. Katerina Ivanovna has

been betrayed by her trust in her father. In the foreground the
Karamazov family is governed by a buffoon, who is also a
sensualist and an egoist, and none of the four sons has ever
known the care of a mother. The explosion of events that is the
novel takes place within this tight-knit, tangible community.
The reader cannot map the topography of the town, but is given
a reassuring sense of familiarity by the substantial descriptions
provided.

This is not true of the other three novels. A known place, St.
Petersburg, is merely the lightly sketched locus of complicated
and often erratic human relationships. In *The Idiot* we see
Prince Myshkin as an appendage of the Epanchin family in the
city and at the summer resort. The soirées, concerts, and
birthday celebrations are normal middle-class activities that we
accept without question though they are not minutely described. There is even less substance in the background of *A
Raw Youth.* Arkady is whisked from one set of ambiguous
relationships to another; scenes set in the auction room and the
gambling den are striking because of their rarity. Finally, in
Crime and Punishment (and *Notes from Underground*) this lack
of concrete detail is extreme. The city is vaguely defined,
impersonal, and essentially hostile. By reference to a few fixed
points, the rooming house, the police station, the tavern, the
haymarket, and the Neva, we are rescued from complete
abstraction, but essentially it is merely a stylized stage set.

In the last analysis, the Dostoevsky world is one of people,
not of things. To avoid the Scylla and Charybdis of romantic
overdrawing and of classical universalization he had to present
recognizable, run-of-the-mill persons, not exceptions or abstractions. Dostoevsky was well aware of this problem but was
unwilling to accept the idea of the norm espoused by other
realists. At the beginning of Part IV of *The Idiot* the narrator
offers a long disquisition on this subject:

> There are people whom it is difficult to describe completely in
> their typical and characteristic aspect. These are the people who

are usually called 'ordinary,' 'the majority,' and who do actually make up the vast majority of mankind. Authors for the most part attempt in their tales and novels to select and represent vividly and artistically types rarely met with in actual life in their entirety, though they are nevertheless almost more real than real life itself. . . .

Yet the question remains! What is an author to do with ordinary people, absolutely "ordinary," and how can he put them before his readers so as to make them at all interesting? It is impossible to leave them out of fiction altogether, for common-place people are at every moment the chief and essential links in the chain of human affairs; if we leave them out, we lose all semblance of truth. To fill a novel completely with types or, more simply, to make it interesting with strange and incredible charac-ters would be to make it unreal and even uninteresting. To our thinking a writer ought to seek out interesting and instructive features even among commonplace people.

In a literal sense Dostoevsky's characters do not adhere to the norm, yet to admit this is to give too much support to the widely held idea that he is interested only in isolates, men who live out their destinies in a singular, anguished struggle. This idea derives from acquaintance with the man from under-ground, with Raskolnikov, and with Ivan Karamazov, though it seems that these two novels show that isolation is abnormal and bend their efforts to reintegrating these strayers from the proper path, or to sketching out the terms on which such reintegration might take place. Raskolnikov and Ivan are, as it turns out, average in their essential humanity: It is not possible either to be a superman or respectfully to hand back one's ticket to God. Admitting that the circumstances exhibited are height-ened, we can accept the idea that Dostoevsky does in his way draw close to a norm which he defines in terms of anguish and struggle. Oddly enough, the dangerously exceptional figures in his writings are certain abstract embodiments, romantic aber-rants, who are novelistically useful but whose natures are static, since they merely serve as foils to the representative central characters. The following are some examples at random: Sonya and Svidrigailov (though the latter has another function, that of *double*), Nastasya and Rogozhin, Pyotr Verkhovensky, Lambert, and Father Zosima. There is little by way of nuances in these figures; they exist as embodiments of good or evil without qualification and are effective and useful as characters in a morality play. There are also figures who are cursorily contrived caricatures who exist only for the purposes of satiric demolition. Luzhin and Lebeziatnikov or the various conspirators in *The Possessed* are the worst examples of such depersonalization. There are also the contrasting lawyers at Dmitri Karamazov's trial, where the interest is less in legal process than in the opposition of egoism and intellectual shallowness.

In Dostoevsky's novels there is a strong emphasis on young people, reminiscent of Tolstoy's great gamut of young people trying to find their way in life. In *Crime and Punishment* there are Raskolnikov, Razumikhin, and Dunya; Ganya, Ipolit, Lebedev's nephew, Burdovsky, Vera Besedev, and the three central characters in *The Idiot*; the whole gallery of young men plus Lise and Darya in *The Possessed*; Arkady, his various brothers and sisters, his friends and acquaintances including the young prince in *A Raw Youth*; and the three Karamazov brothers—all form the center of their respective novels, creating an ambiance of seeking and striving, of dynamic potential and self-scrutiny. There is a sense of infinite possibility in these novels because of the uncertainty of issue. The important characters are not finished because it is impossible for a man to be finished short of the kind of avatar to which the Zosimas and the Makars ascend after years of probation.

This dynamism results from an essentially new conception of human nature. Novelists and dramatists before Dostoevsky usually provided characters who were the product of analysis, or at any rate of fragmentation and resynthesis. Either there is a dominant tendency of personality, as represented by the Elizabethan notion of humors, a tendency toward abstraction growing out of classical generalization, or an overdevelopment of unilateral imbalance and excess to the point of monstrosity as in the romantics. In any of these cases, even the last, the fictional personality is accessible to rational understanding and reducible to logical explanation. This is true also of the character drawing of most realists. Zola by asserting the primacy of hunger and sex falls back on a monolithic conception that differs from these previously given descriptions only in its exclusively physical causality. All his life Dostoevsky inveighed against such overly analytical approaches on the ground that they merely touched the surface of a personality.

What Dostoevsky insists on is the varied, confused, unexpected, and contradictory elements of a personality. He denies the previous monolithic conceptions in favor of a pluralistic view, and he works from external signs into obscure and covert inward states. What a man says is not as important as what he does, but what he does is subject to misapprehension unless our insight can reach beneath the surface to what he is, a welter of contradictory impulses and desires. At once we confront a paradox. Realism depends on that which is publicly accessible, open to inspection and verification. Yet the materials of which we are speaking are by nature hidden, at best verifiable only by private introspection, and therefore carrying no assurance of their validity. Here there is a chance for invention of the worst kind, the very fault of the romantics against which the realists were forced to rebel. Dostoevsky certainly incurred attack on those grounds from his early readers, yet gradually his public was won over, once prejudice and preconception had been dissolved by the force of his creation or readers had, perhaps, found verification within themselves. There is danger here that life may too readily come to imitate art, that readers may feel an obligation to discover within themselves maelstroms at least as turbulent as those which agitate Dostoevsky's fictional beings. Be that as it may, if over a period of a hundred years readers have with increasing agreement come to attest the truth of these portrayals, they may be called realistic. Moreover, there has been independent verification, at least in broad terms, by depth psychologists, notably Freud, who gave Dostoevsky the accolade in a famous, if somewhat wishfully argued monograph.[4]

Dostoevsky's view of human nature is advanced *logically* in the first part of *Notes from Underground*. There the speaker attacks the materialist thesis, in particular the validity of the Utilitarian doctrine. It is not true that human beings act from a sense of their own self-interest. Indeed, they frequently act against it, and it is necessary that they do so, since they are human. A compulsion to hurt oneself, a tendency to self-abnegation and self-laceration, is as important and normal as self-assertion and regard for one's own interests. Compulsions to drink, to gamble, to indulge in debauchery, to humiliate oneself, and even to destroy oneself are central to Dostoevsky's portraiture and become a kind of signature of his art. He makes capital of psychological confusion and seems to deny that analytical tools can adequately engage with the human psyche, though perhaps the reader ultimately concludes that the apparent confusion is reducible to a new analytical conception of personality, one which is, however, more profound and infinitely richer in what it contains.

One facet of this reading of human nature is the prevalence of behavior that is aberrant and criminal, of acts that are universally qualified as bestial and degenerate. These acts, associated by Freud with deep springs of sexuality, are by Dostoevsky given a more general form and origin. In his characters there are frequent instances of the death wish, culminating in the suicides of Kirilov, Stavrogin, and Smerdyakov, and in the attempted suicides of others. There are two major instances of perverse sexuality, the detailed history of Svidrigailov, which ends in the dream of the child harlot, and the rape of a little girl by Stavrogin, who by deliberate inaction has complicity in her subsequent suicide. Shocking as these acts are to the novelist's contemporaries, it is necessary to point out that they represent the furthest range of the abnormal in his depiction and that there are whole areas of perversity to which he scarcely alludes.[5] He is remarkably restrained and reticent for one who saw so clearly, and he shows no tendency to exploit such materials for sensational ends. It is a great distance from Dostoevsky's novels to, say, John Updike's *Rabbit, Run!* or Hubert Selby's *Last Exit from Brooklyn*, to name two well-known modern works.

Hard as it is to believe at first, the emphasis of Dostoevsky is not upon great sinners or monsters; it is not upon case histories that would grace a textbook of the abnormal, nor is it upon the pathological and the morbid. Rather, his emphasis is upon suffering, upon the tortured and volcanic inner tension between right and wrong, between logical and illogical, between conformity to an imposed outward pattern and an obdurate inner necessity that demands a kind of self-destructive independence of being. With the exception of Stavrogin, who is not really developed as a paradigm of corruption, and Svidrigailov, who as a double exists in a different novelistic dimension, there are no central characters of outstanding corruption in these novels. Instead there is a recognizably human range of fairly ordinary people who are lighted up from a new angle, that of their inner turmoil. We run a gamut from the explosive physical state of epilepsy in Prince Myshkin through the mental infirmity of Maria Timofeevna Lebedkin and Katerina Ivanovna Marmeladov to the self-lacerations of those who are generally mentally and physically sound. Even Father Zosima has gone through this inner turmoil; indeed, he must, for to be so torn is as inevitable in the human condition as is corruption of the body after death. As a result of this conception of the operation of the psyche, there arises a picture of man as dynamic but incomplete, always in a state of becoming, which is of paramount interest for purposes of dramatic presentation, while the attainment of blessed stasis, the doctrinally posited end for this process, is in the novels always deferred, if for no other reason than that it is not open to description.

The key to these characters is their suffering. That is the great human drama as Dostoevsky sees it. It is a condition that is irremediable as far as tinkering with causality is concerned. With Zola and his group suffering is physical, and the result of environmental cause in large part and therefore capable of removal or amelioration by a change in environmental conditions. Zola is under the spell of the materialist doctrines of the nineteenth century. Dostoevsky anticipates the twentieth-century discovery that the improvement of material conditions of life does not necessarily bring moral or personal well-being and may indeed entail a kind of moral recidivism of violent and illogical intensity. His reading is also close to the traditional Christian view, for original sin and inner turmoil are one in essence. It is for this reason that he can move rapidly and smoothly from a level of realistic psychological description to one of Christian allegory. If the terms are not precisely interchangeable, the process may be said to be the same, though the psychological reading stops short of arrival at grace, whereas the Christian reading does not. Though this level is discussed later, it is well to point out here that in the interest of psychological truth Dostoevsky frequently leaves his suffering creatures in a state of suspension, where they find internal warfare intolerable but cannot make the leap to the composition of opposites necessary for Christian beatitude. The classic example of this is Ivan Karamazov, who at the end suffers from "brain fever," a generalized form of breakdown that comes from unresolved tensions.

Once we as readers become familiar with Dostoevsky's point of view and methods, we accept what he shows as being in no way extraordinary because in fact he rarely takes us beyond the bounds of normal experience and, except for some irritating absurdities of plot, does not subject us to sensational and outlandish occurrences. It is the techniques that he employs that must now come under examination. Like his realist peers he had to devise means to represent the world as he saw it. It does not take us long to discover that of the major realists Dostoevsky is the least attached to the doctrine of impersonal narration. It could be argued that he feels a need for the psychological

closeness of the first-person approach, were it not for the fact
that *Crime and Punishment* and *The Brothers Karamazov*, the
most controlled of his novels, are really in the third-person
omniscient form.

The earlier novel *Poor Folk* uses the epistolary device,
which in this instance has no basis of verisimilitude whatever.
The majority of other early works employ a straight first-person
narrator, though a third-person stance might have been better.
For the social comedies there is a certain ironic usefulness in
having a first-person narrator who is also a participant in the
action, especially in *The Gambler* and *The Village of Stepanchikovo*. This form is the only possible one for *Notes from
Underground*, which is an elaborate and strident soliloquy in
which tone is almost as important as content.

The five major novels offer no fixed pattern or progression
in this respect. *Crime and Punishment* is the one that best
handles the impersonal approach. Events are presented sharply
and without commentary except for what resides in them and
their symbolic framework. We are not told the relationship of
Raskolnikov and Svidrigailov but are left to figure it out for
ourselves. We have difficulty in distinguishing between dream
and waking and receive no guidance from the narrator. Only in
the epilogue does this attitude of withdrawal falter, a further
proof of the incompatibility of the epilogue with the rest of the
novel. The final form of this work grew out of an earlier
first-person version. There is preserved a "Journal of Raskolnikov" in which the hero is the speaker, and in the notebooks
for *Crime and Punishment* we learn that Dostoevsky was
uncertain about how to handle point of view. He vacillated
between confession and narrative in the third person: "If a
confession, certain passages will not be chaste and it will be
difficult to explain why it has been written." But he finally made
up his mind: "One must suppose that the author is an OMNIS-
CIENT AND IMPECCABLE being who exhibits to everybody
one of the members of the new generation."

In *The Idiot* the basic position is third-person omniscient, but this narrative voice often slips into the first person and provides or withholds information and comment at will, though admitting that he ought merely to put things down and abstain from explanation. At the beginning of Part III the narrator engages in an essay-diatribe for three pages, but otherwise the novel mostly has the air of removed, objective statement. *The Brothers Karamazov* provides another variation. There is a distinct, though unnamed narrator, a commonplace sort of man who is concerned for the reputation of "our town" and views the events of the murder and trial with the myopia and vulgar curiosity of the townspeople. This voice fades out for long periods, and even when it is present does not interpose itself seriously between the reader and the events recounted. Since there are many situations to which the narrator could not have had access even by report, overall this work is about as objective as *Crime and Punishment*.

In contrast, *The Possessed* and *A Raw Youth*, though fairly late works, are first-person novels, albeit handled in different ways. In the former a minor participant, Anton Lavrentevich G . . . v, is the narrator. He is a strawman, a mere device, unimportant except that as a friend of Stepan Trofimovich he is present at a good deal of the action and is sedulous in gathering information about the rest of what happens. His are an excellent pair of eyes for reporting the social comedy that makes up part of the work, but the lack of cohesion of the novel produces a split in his personality since he cannot maintain the same kind of first-hand account of the conspiracy and is driven to speculation of a shallow and unconvincing kind. The narrator of *A Raw Youth* is the protagonist, Arkady Makarovich Dolgoruky, who writes his account a year after the events have taken place. He states at the beginning that he will limit himself to setting down events and will make every effort to avoid irrelevancy and, more particularly, literary artifice. It early becomes clear that the act of writing is a form of self-therapy: "Perhaps I have been wrong in undertaking to write this: within me there are infinitely more things than appear in words," a fact that, he fears, may lead his account to be ridiculous or misleading. In the course of the novel he comments that the man now writing is radically changed from the man who did the acts described, and, at the end, by the device of a letter from a former teacher to whom Arkady has submitted the manuscript, we get a comment that would be inappropriate from him to the effect that the act of writing has made Arkady "redo" his education. The narrator's position is clearly an important dimension of this work. The very criticism by the narrator of his former self brings into relief what the novel is trying to show, the development from adolescence to maturity. In the notebooks for this novel Dostoevsky comments that while telling the story Arkady is still an adolescent but treats with disdain the adolescent he was a year before. The author there makes another useful observation as well: "If I write in the first person, there is, no doubt, more unity and less of what Strakhov reproaches me for, that is, an overflow of characters and events." In spite of this hope *A Raw Youth* cannot be cleared of such a charge.

Early in that novel Arkady comments that it is "impossible to describe feelings without facts." This incidental remark describes the general problem that Dostoevsky has to solve when it comes to developing action in support of psychological probing. All the realists have to choose new kinds of action, but at least they can choose from what they observe around them. Dostoevsky has to go further. He must find (or invent) plots that are suitable for his purpose of bringing into the open covert elements of human nature or that will permit such subterranean elements to show themselves clearly and accurately. Such actions are not as readily available as one would hope. At one extreme lies melodrama, that is, sensational, special situations that permit the representation of people under pressure but which automatically take the reader away from any kind of general truth. The opposite extreme is archetypical action, where the particular is inflated to such dimensions that we lose sight of the observable human experience as abstraction blots out the concrete situation. Dostoevsky could not help vacillating between these two extremes, particularly since he had an almost uncontrolled addiction to both melodrama and some sort of *higher* meaning.

In all fairness, however, we must remember that in *House of the Dead* we do have a work that never departs from the immediacy of observation, and that in *Notes from Underground* the author takes another and very effective narrative tack, though it is doubtful that this would be useful in a work of greater compass. It begins with the narrator stating his logical position with regard to the mainsprings of behavior. He then supports this position by presenting three isolated instances of his own behavior in narrative-dramatic form. This constitutes argument of pseudo-psychological cast rather than fiction in the usual sense of the term, but it is a solution to Dostoevsky's special problem in that it presents actuality undeformed by the pressure of either melodrama or symbolism.

The best instance among the major novels of incompatibility between plot and subject is *A Raw Youth*. Granting that the givens of the novel are unnecessarily heightened—bastards should have gone out with the romantics—still the basic scheme is a sound and interesting one. Arkady is a decent and intelligent young man whose previous life has given him little in the way of direction or security. His arrival in the new environment of St. Petersburg provides him simultaneously with a family and with the necessity of proving himself as an adult. He seeks at the same time to find his father and to assert his independence of family ties, that is, as he sees it, to be somebody. Dostoevsky puts this very clearly in *The Diary of a Writer* for January 1876: "I took an innocent soul, but one already polluted with the dreadful possibility of depravity, early hate, because of his nothingness and 'accidentalness.' . . ." He says further that he wants to write about a youth who has already left childhood behind and who desires timidly and insolently to take his first steps in life as quickly as possible.

The main outlines of the action to do this are very simple: the events of September 19, the events beginning on November

15, and then, after an interval of illness, the events of late November. We have here the typical Dostoevsky crisis approach: None of the five novels covers in action more than a few weeks of time, though there may be intervals between situations and there is always a good deal of expository filling in of past history. Where this novel gets into difficulties is in having recourse to a mysterious and romantic plot involving both an inheritance and a deadly affront in which Versilov (Arkady's father) is involved, but from which he emerges with honor. Fortunately there are the dramatic scenes in which we see Arkady in a constant turmoil of irritation and resentment as he attempts to feel his way into a balanced relationship with his family and with Tatiana Pavlovna, a kind of honorary aunt. By the end of the novel he does achieve such a relationship, and he has shed much of his adolescent sensitivity and confusion. But it can hardly be said that the romantic trappings of the plot have contributed much to this process.

We have already seen how a similar bifurcation wrecks *The Possessed*. Here, however, the reason lies less in the melodrama itself than in the presence of a thesis that provokes the novelist to melodrama. To demonstrate the dangerous effects of socialistic-nihilistic ideas, Dostoevsky pulls out all the stops and fills the latter part of the story with horrors, culminating in Stavrogin's child rape. *The Idiot* suffers from the same disability, with a difference, for its action, however outré, is thematically controlled. The exhibition is of Prince Myshkin, by definition "a good man," standing against the uses and abuses of this world, in which he is too good to live and from which he is cavalierly ejected at the end. In the strict sense there is no plot, only a series of confrontations rising to a climax with Nastasya's murder and the deathwatch shared by Rogozhin and the Prince. There are some heightened scenes, but these do not seriously interfere with the basic demonstration, which is that the Prince, however inexperienced he may be in worldly ways, is always right in the way he meets a situation and in spite of his naïveté has a power to draw others to him.

The two most perfectly constructed novels, *Crime and Punishment* and *The Brothers Karamazov*, are both narratives about the causes and consequences of a crime. Dostoevsky profited greatly from the use of this kind of plot. The heightened action at the point of crisis that murder represents is in harmony with his reading of human nature. By the analytical process of tracking down the murderer and bringing him to justice which it enjoins, a straight path is provided from which it is difficult to stray. Within such a framework, there are narrative complications and proliferations. In *Crime and Punishment* the straight track runs from the murder of the pawnbroker to the point where Raskolnikov gives himself up at the police station. But there is also the parallel of Razumikhin, a figure of uncomplicated normality in contrast to Raskolnikov's normal abnormality. Similarly Svidrigailov provides another kind of parallel, which involves Dunya, who is herself a parallel. These connected lives are the basic object of scrutiny, the actions of young people in a world they never made, or as Porfiry Petrovich puts it, at a time "when the heart of man is troubled." There are also the events in which the Marmeladov family figures, which seem somewhat tangential to the main action. The thing to bear in mind is that since this is a murder story in which the pursuit is internal, the basic pattern is one of a series of collisions of the central character, who caroms off one person after another until he is exhausted and gives himself up.

The organization of *The Brothers Karamazov* is similar but even more complicated. The central facts are the murder of Fyodor, ostensibly by Dmitri but actually by Smerdyakov, and the apprehension and conviction of Dmitri. The two brothers, Ivan and Alyosha, are also involved since all men have complicity in the murder of their fathers. This central action may be said to fall within the realistic framework of experience. Dmitri's emotional turmoil, his confused actions, and his behavior under interrogation and later under sentence of deportation are admirably observed. The course of events suffers less from contrivance than from obscuration.

To generalize about the plots of these five novels, we see that they have in common an intensity of action, a precipitation of personal development through some sort of crisis. None of them covers a very long time. Each of them depends, in part at least, on the arrival of a central character in a new situation. It is Dmitri's return home, for example, that precipitates the murder in *The Brothers Karamazov*.

As suggested, Dostoevsky leans heavily on the scenic or dramatic approach. There is evidence of this even in the early and more conventional works, in spite of the obstacles that a first-person point of view puts in the way. The most vivid part of *Poor Folk* is the scene of humiliation experienced by Makar in his interview with His Excellency. Both *Uncle's Dream* and *The Village of Stepanchikovo* are developed scenically; indeed the latter was first conceived of as a play. There is less use of external scene in *Crime and Punishment* than in the other novels, but there is constant externalization of Raskolnikov's state of mind by quick, fluid, and short scenes such as his saving a girl from suicide, and his dreams themselves have scenic intensity. In *The Idiot* this technique dominates the novel. Each of the four parts is built around one or more scenes: the meeting of Myshkin, Rogozhin, and Lebedev on the train, the visit to the Epanchins,' and the temptation of Ganya constitute the first part; the false charge brought by Burdovsky is the dramatic center of the second part; the impromptu birthday party and Ipolit's explosive actions are the third part; and in the fourth part the chief action is the soirée at the Epanchins,' followed by Myshkin's tracking down of Rogozhin and discovery of the murder of Nastasya. There are numerous subsidiary scenes, some symbolic material, and some retrospective exposition, but the novel as a whole is scenic, for there is a notable lack of effort at filling in gaps of time or information between scenes. This novel in particular gives the impression of being presented on a revolving stage.

In its basic construction *The Possessed* is at least as scenic. After a slow start we find the situation at Skvoreshniki being developed almost entirely as a drama, with a series of scenes in dialogue introducing the various characters culminating in Chapter V, "The Subtle Serpent," which contains the big scene at Varvara Petrovna's in which Stavrogin and Pyotr make their entrance. Part II takes these two characters through separate meetings with various other persons, mostly in dialogue form, and then brings them together in the meeting of the conspirators at Verginsky's. Except for the final narrative chapter Part III is conducted in dialogue to a degree that is remarkable when one considers the disparate materials involved.

It is not impossible to write a dramatic novel in the first person, but in *A Raw Youth* there is less of dramatic immediacy than in the other novels, which is one reason it is less well regarded. However, in spite of a high incidence of expository material and philosophical disquisition, *The Brothers Karamazov* gives the impression of dramatic treatment. It opens with the brilliant and painful scene at the monastery in which most of the characters are present, proceeds by a series of confrontations of these characters, mostly in pairs, uses a roving camera to dramatize Dmitri's actions on the fatal evening, and comes close to stage presentation at the interrogations and trial. All the scenes having to do with "the children" are in dramatic form. Even such recalcitrant materials as the "poem" of the Grand Inquisitor, the dialogue with the Devil, and the homily of Father Zosima are scenic to as great an extent as possible.

All of this is achievement enough, but we are only approaching the heart of Dostoevsky's mystery. In the notebooks for *The Possessed* there is a cryptic phrase: "The reinvention of man and reality," which perhaps carries the secret of the author's technique. Viewing people in the new way that he did, he had to "invent" ways of representing them, of bringing out the truth of human nature, which is the reality (or the most important part of it) that he sought to present. What a character says and does is mysterious and confusing because he does not know why he does it, and may indeed not even want to do it. There is nothing in the conventions of the novel that could handle this mystery adequately, just as the conventions of the drama such as the soliloquy falsify rather than reveal the depths of feeling and motive. To repeat Arkady's statement in *A Raw Youth*: "It is impossible to describe feelings without facts." But what facts can be used? One way out is to use the established technique of analysis, to subordinate action to subtle and complex probing of what goes on in a character's mind. This is essentially what Proust does, threading his way through a labyrinth of more than daedalian intricacy. But in such case the emphasis is less upon the data themselves than upon the process of discovery, of making significant and satisfying patterns that take place in the mind of the narrator and are re-created in the mind of the reader. There is truth there, but it is a subtle and personal truth which, as in the case of Proust, moves close to solipsism. This is not Dostoevsky's way. He believes in a general truth inhering in a visible actuality. Though he does use first-person narration frequently and does fall back on conventional analysis and explanation, this is not the path of his genius. Using the full resources of the dramatic mode, he seeks a way to externalize, to give body and validity to the new and hitherto unilluminated materials with which he has undertaken to deal.

Although Dostoevsky's favorite reality is what goes on inside his characters, we must not overlook the fact that action and perception of external detail are means to this exploration. His characters suffer from hyperreactivity. They cannot move along a street without collision; the simplest domestic gathering is one of incipient tempest. Even the saintly Alyosha has his finger bitten to the bone in a simple encounter with a group of schoolboys. At the Epanchins' Prince Myshkin cannot help shattering a priceless vase. The Marmeladov funeral dinner ends in a brawl. To live is to undergo crises, not to experience a placid recurrence of comforting daily tasks. Nothing more sharply sets Dostoevsky apart from his fellow realists than his indifference to routine and to the repetitive actions of which life is made up. To some extent this explosive atmosphere is the Russian's inheritance from Dickens, but whereas the latter uses a bouncy quality to enhance oddity, Dostoevsky sees energy as something basic to all human nature when it is properly observed and understood. The least composed of his heroes are the ones who emit the most energy: Dmitri rages through town and countryside in an effort to solve his problems of love and money. Raskolnikov is under the spur of obsessive action; even when he is asleep one feels he is in restless movement. In default of any very clear or detailed account of Rogozhin's actions, we identify him with an exceedingly restless and erratic course, his irruptions into and out of the novel being symtomatic of his being.

The fragment entitled "Raskolnikov's Journal" begins with the direction that "The narrative ought constantly to be interrupted by useless and disparate details." There is generally a staccato and interrupted utterance on the part of Dostoevsky's characters, an explosive reiteration of words and phrases, not infrequently fractured syntax. This manner of speech is not phonographic, nor does it faithfully reproduce the cadence and tone of speech and thought. Certainly it is a made thing, not an imitated thing, its purpose being to convey the idea of intense cerebral and emotional activity. From tenor of speech and thought it is only a step to a similar intensity of perception. Raskolnikov, having given little thought to the practical details of committing the murder, finds the axe gleaming up at him from the litter of the porter's lodge. During his fever he concentrates on shreds of cloth, on cracks in the wall. His focus never seems to take in a whole room or a whole situation. The eyes of Rogozhin burn out at Prince Myshkin from the crowd and again from the darkness of a stairwell. The man from underground is aware only of his enemy the officer on the crowded street. In his humiliation at having to undress before the interrogating officers, Dmitri eyes his big toe with loathing. This intensity of perception in turn leads to compulsive action, as perception precipitates act. It also leads to the unrelated act, one out of any clear context, as when Father Zosima bows down to Dmitri at their first encounter.

One way of objectifying thought is to present its formal content, by capsule summary in the case of Raskolnikov's article, *in extenso* with Ivan Karamazov's poem. Soliloquy is another conventional form of bringing the internal out, and the whole of *Notes from Underground* is a soliloquy, which at the same time it attempts to depict the chaos of a mind, undermines the demonstration by the presence of a basically orderly argument. Oddly enough, Dostoevsky does not discover the interior monologue, though he comes close to it on occasion in his *summaries* of mental states. As might be expected, the best examples are in *Crime and Punishment*, as in the following passage after Raskolnikov has an encounter with Razumikhin and Porfiry Petrovich:

> He thought of nothing. Some thoughts or fragments of thoughts, some images without order or coherence floated before his mind—faces of people he had seen in his childhood or met somewhere once, whom he would never have recalled, the belfry of the church at V., the billiard-table in a restaurant and some officers playing billiards, the smell of cigars in some underground tobacco shop, a tavern room, a back staircase quite dark, all sloppy with dirty water and strewn with eggshells, and the Sunday bells floating in from somewhere. . . . The images followed one another, whirling like a hurricane. . . .

This presentation is strictly external. A little later, when the young man is half awake, we get into his mind, though still with the narrator's mediation:

> At moments he felt he was raving. He sank into a state of feverish excitement. "The old woman is of no consequence," he thought, hotly and incoherently. "The old woman was a mistake perhaps, but she is not what matters! The old woman was only an illness. . . . I was in a hurry to overstep. . . . I didn't kill a human being, but a principle! I killed the principle, but I didn't overstep, I stopped on this side. . . . I was only capable of killing. And it

seems I wasn't even capable of that. . . . Ech, I am an aesthetic louse and nothing more," he added suddenly, laughing like a madman.

If we took away the quotation marks and the narrative framework, and forgot about sentence structure and punctuation, we would have something reasonably close to a Joycean interior monologue. However, as the passage continues, Raskolnikov begins to reason too closely with an "in the first place," "secondly," and "thirdly" marshaling his thoughts and taking the reader into the realm of organized discourse.

More typical of Dostoevsky's method is the following passage from *The Idiot*:

> But he had no sooner observed in himself this morbid and till then quite unconscious impulse, when there flashed upon his mind another recollection which interested him extremely. He remembered that, at the moment when he became aware that he was absorbed in looking for something, he was standing on the pavement before a shop window, examining with great interest the goods exposed in it. He felt he must find out whether he really had stood before the shop window just now, five minutes, perhaps, before; whether he hadn't dreamed it; whether he wasn't mistaken. Did that shop really exist with the goods in its window? . . . He walked almost in anguish, looking to the right and his heart beat with uneasy impatience. But here was the shop, he had found it at last! . . . And there was the article worth sixty kopecks. "It would be certainly sixty kopecks, it's not worth more," he repeated now and laughed. But his laughter was hysterical; he felt very wretched.

In this passage we move from external description to a description of feeling to a kind of summary stream of consciousness expressed in the past tense. The second time we go through this sequence the content of consciousness is expressed in the present tense and in quotation marks. All that was needed here was to cut loose from the narrative framework and let Myshkin's thoughts run free without syntactical organization.

Two devices used by Dostoevsky show a considerable

ingenuity and are significant in his efforts to externalize the internal. One is realistic, the other is definitely not; these are the dream and the double. The dreams are striking for their freshness and verisimilitude. In Dostoevsky's hands they cease to be literary and heavily prophetic or symbolic. Instead, in a manner later validated by depth psychologists, they reveal an inner condition. Three instances in *Crime and Punishment* stand out. Before committing the crime Raskolnikov dreams of himself as a small boy witnessing and protesting against the brutal beating of a horse. Critical exegesis varies in the emphasis it places on the components of this dream, but is consistent in its recognition that the dream shows Raskolnikov's subconscious revulsion against his premeditated crime. Completely unequivocal is the so-called reduction dream after the murder in which he strikes unavailingly at the old pawnbroker, who laughs in his face. The frustration that the dreamer experiences is a working out of the covert recognition that his act has proved nothing—putting the deed in a perspective that consciousness has still to reach. The third dream is that of Svidrigailov just before his death when the innocent face of a five-year-old child takes on the allure and sensuality of a harlot, bringing to the lecher a recognition that whatever he touches he defiles. All three of these dreams are presented with overwhelming vividness, to such a degree that the reader is uncertain whether the dreamer is asleep or awake. They make use of disguise and analogue in the manner of real dreams and are a direct projection of an inner state, part of the reality of the suffering psyche in its formulations below the level of active consciousness. Their validity and power are made evident by contrast with the literary dream of the epilogue, which is a set piece with logical and transparent organization and meaning. There are a good many dreams throughout Dostoevsky's novels, most of them falling somewhere between the sharply defined categories that are present in *Crime and Punishment*. They attest to inner disturbance, but are rarely as apt as there, or as patently false as in the epilogue.

The double is a genuine invention on Dostoevsky's part, though the doppelgänger of romantic fiction was already well established. Although the double cannot be called a realistic device, it does forward realistic ends. The term *double* has been used in a number of senses in Dostoevsky criticism and needs to be approached cautiously. In a broad sense it refers to the tendency of a personality to split into conflicting parts—the well-known Jekyll-Hyde pattern. That is what happens in the early novella *The Double*, in a manner that is grotesquely entertaining rather than psychologically convincing. From one point of view we may say that all Dostoevsky's major characters are doubles in respect to the existence of opposed tendencies within them. This kind of opposition of elements is implicit in the prisoners described in *Notes from the House of the Dead*, where the violence of the deeds that have brought them to Siberia and that occasionally earns them additional ferocious punishment is in continual contrast with the kind of decorum that they usually maintain. It is explicit in the pronunciamento of the man from underground, whose mental processes and actions are schematized in this way. It gets its most elaborated development in the presentation of characters such as Raskolnikov, Nastasya, Stavrogin, Arkady, and Dmitri Karamazov, to mention only the most obvious cases. Arkady, from whom we have information at first hand, worries about the duality of his nature at the beginning of his narrative. Later on he points out that "I can as easily as anything entertain two conflicting feelings at the same instant, without my will entering into it," and on another occasion he speaks of his astonishment at the ability of a man like Rousseau to harbor in his heart the highest and the lowest sentiments and responses. At the end of the novel when Arkady has recovered from a kind of nervous breakdown but is upset by his father's cracking up, he says: "I think I am doubling." Later he asks: "What is a double?" and answers: "Nothing but the first stage in a serious mental derangement which can lead to a rather bad end." He concludes that when his father broke the precious ikon, the act was that of a veritable double.

Because this is so predictable a condition in Dostoevsky's characters, its predictability in a way negates the author's contention that human behavior is unpredictable. In other words, there develops a stereotype of inner duality that could become as trite as the idea of humors. It is capable of great variation, however. Often it is attested by a pairing of characters, so that we can see in the companion a tendency that is present in the other but not so predominant or developed. In this sense Sonya is Raskolnikov's double, and Alyosha fulfills that role for each of his legitimate brothers. This is really nothing more than the technique of foils or mirrors, and as such betokens skill but not invention. But in two cases there is a very special way in which a double is used.

The first instance is Svidrigaïlov, an independent being whose existence is attested before Raskolnikov ever meets him and who has his own minor role in the developing plot. But from the time he enters the student's room at the midpoint of the novel we become increasingly aware that he and Raskolnikov have a very special relationship, that they are tied together morally and psychologically. The nature of this affinity is never spelled out, but gradually we come to see that Svidrigaïlov, who is twice Raskolnikov's age, is a forward projection in time and inveterate evil of what the younger man would become if he were to continue on his present course. By this device it is as though the experience of the protagonist were doubled and we participated both in his progress toward conversion, or at least repudiation of his original beliefs, with which the novel ends, and in the total destruction to which he was doomed if he persisted on the path fortunately not taken. Svidrigaïlov's suicide is thus a dramatic enactment of what Raskolnikov's fate would have to be. It is to be noted that the crimes of the two men are quite distinct in detail. The older is sunk in sensuality; the younger seems untroubled by sexuality but seeks by an assertion of will to establish his superiority to other men. This superficial dissimilarity proves nothing. If all is lawful in Raskolnikov's terms, then the specific forms of self-gratification embodied by Svidrigaïlov are subsumed by the revolt of the other. Raskolnikov's crime is the greater for it contains the lesser.

Smerdyakov in *The Brothers Karamazov* is the other indubitable example of this technique, only in his case the relationship is that of hand to mind. Ivan Karamazov makes his revolt against God out of revulsion toward a deity that permits pain and evil. Through this anguish he proceeds intellectually to the conclusion that all things are lawful and that he has no responsibility for his fellow men. Smerdyakov is completely devoid of moral sense, and he is a complete egoist. Hence when Ivan's intellectual position is adopted by him there is nothing to restrain him from action, from putting into effect a kind of categorical imperative in reverse. The relationship of the doubles is less carefully built up in this novel, but there is an air of complicity in Ivan's deliberate absence at the time of the crime. This relationship is complicated, or diluted, by the fact that Ivan also has a dialogue with the Devil, who is clearly an emanation of his own mind. Yet the novel clinches the relationship of Ivan and Smerdyakov symbolically when the former on his way to confront the latter disdains to rescue a drunken peasant, only to reverse his attitude on his return after he has contemplated the effect of his doctrine when Smerdyakov makes his confession. In both novels we have an aspect of personality made flesh for purposes of moral demonstration. Each is a speculative projection, a hypothesis and a warning of what a man might become. No other relationship of pairs of characters works as clearly as these, though it is tempting to link Stavrogin and Pyotr Verkhovensky in this way.

Thus far we have considered Dostoevsky's novels as they represent people in typical and fundamentally human situations. The double certainly goes beyond such representation since it depicts not an actuality but a possibility implicit in actuality. Its justification is to be found not on the level of realistic depiction but in terms of doctrinal statement. It is now time to admit that Dostoevsky always leads us in that direction in his major works, that the inner struggles of his protagonists are not open-ended, that they are, even in their consummate psychological realism, part of a grander design, which is a Christian one, and that a drama of salvation is the capstone of his art. It would be imprudent to make a very categorical distinction between Zola's *Germinal* and Dostoevsky's works in this respect, since each proceeds to raise the realistic data of observation to a higher level of meaning than inheres in them by themselves. But the effort of the Russian novelist is consistently toward this goal. Doctrine comes before facts, and the facts are used ultimately in support of doctrine. Zola's meticulous documentation for the Rougon-Macquart lends itself only on this one occasion to a structure of higher truth. For Dostoevsky higher truth is always the goal. Of his major works *A Raw Youth* is the one that keeps closest to the ground of actuality—which is another reason why it is less well regarded by most readers. In *Crime and Punishment* the representational and the symbolic are so skillfully intermingled that it is easy to think of the novel as exclusively on the realistic level—until one gets to the epilogue. It is the epilogue, different in tone and in substantive detail, that attempts to force the reader to accept Raskolnikov's conversion, that is, the resolution of the inner chaos which has been the object of study of the novel proper. Both *The Idiot* and *The Possessed* start with less interest in the reality to be observed and fail to establish the higher reality to which they aspire, particularly because of the social thesis of the latter.

In *The Brothers Karamazov* the reader is early aware that he is confronting both a realistic and a symbolic statement. The presence of the nonnarrative blocks of "The Grand Inquisitor" and "The Russian Monk" makes such a conclusion certain. In spite of the universally acclaimed religious sublimity of this work, however, it is in a way more open-ended than *Crime and Punishment*. If we accept the premise of universal human rebelliousness, of every man's having within him the wish to kill his own father, we can certainly accept the fact that anguish and depravity are part of every man's lot. None of the brothers reaches a static end; they are all still in a state of becoming when the novel is brought to a conclusion. Dmitri embraces brotherly love and accepts his guilt and the necessity of punishment, but he is not at all sure that he can survive his ordeal. Alyosha, so we are told with some frequency, has still to make his way through the miasma of the human condition, though, to be sure, judging by his influence over the boys, his future is promising. Ivan's future is very uncertain; he is left caught in a moral tug of war that perhaps can have no resolution. His story is that of Raskolnikov without the epilogue. We might say that a kind of realistic tact keeps this novel from falling into the abstractness and doctrinal bluntness of moral allegory, but we never doubt that the novel uses and arranges its existential materials in the interest of higher truth.

Contemporary Russian society, whose creed is one of doctrinal materialism, has found it difficult to assimilate Dostoevsky, who in all his works spoke out against the doctrines on which this new society is based. Early in *The Diary of a Writer* he makes this very clear in an evalutation of Belinsky, to whom he owed his initial literary fame: "Treasuring above everything reason, science and realism, at the same time he comprehended more keenly than anyone that reason, science and realism alone can merely produce an ant's nest, and not social 'harmony' within which man can organize his life. He knew that moral principles are the basis of all things." No doubt for *social* harmony we should read *spiritual* harmony, but in fact the two are equivalent in Dostoevsky's mind. In any event, the locus of man's well-being is in a mystical state, born of inevitable suffering and to be achieved by identification with suffering mankind, and not in a lucky compatibility with the forces of heredity and environment. Again in *The Diary of a Writer* Dostoevsky repudiates those latter forces: "Indeed, this is what the doctrine of environment contends in opposition to Christianity which, fully recognizing the pressure of the milieu, and which, having proclaimed mercy for him who has sinned, nevertheless makes it a moral duty for man to struggle against environment, and draws a line of demarcation between where environment ends and duty begins. Making man responsible, Christianity *eo ipso* also recognizes his freedom." To substantiate this we need only recall Stavrogin's statement that the cause of his acts lay in his will and not in his environment. This freedom has meaning only as it is exercised in the direction of salvation, in the encompassment of the goals set by Christian doctrine. The total Dostoevsky view is neither pessimistic, nor materialistic, nor deterministic, though Ralph Matlaw can point out with some justice that the optimistic view of familial integrity found in *War and Peace* is somehow transformed in *The Brothers* to a view that is considerably closer to that of French naturalism.

The material world, the world explored by reason and served by science, is not a reality for which Dostoevsky has much respect. "The ideal," he asserts in *The Diary of a Writer*, ". . . is also a reality as legitimate as current reality. . . . What is genre, in substance? Genre is an art of portraying contemporaneous, current reality which the artist has . . . seen with his own eyes, as distinguished, for instance, from historical reality which cannot be beheld with one's own eyes. . . ." Similarly he claims that "A genuine artist, under no circumstances, should remain on one level with the person portrayed by him, confining himself to mere realistic truth; the impression will carry no truth." He can only conclude that "I have a completely different view of reality and 'realism' than our realists and critics. My idealism is more real than theirs. With their realism you could not explain a hundredth part of real facts that actually took place. While we with our idealism *have even predicted facts*. It has happened." With such statements we come back to the basic debate of nineteenth-century critics over the ideal and the real as subjects for art. It is evident that Dostoevsky, without hesitation, opts for the former, yet it is equally evident that he has supported this with a wide-ranging and detailed sense of actuality. He has gone beyond realism while using realistic materials. Perhaps E. M. de Vogüé's statement that "No one has pushed realism further than he" means the same thing.

7

Anton Chekhov

During the twenty-four years that he was an active author Chekhov wrote hundreds of stories as well as a handful of plays. Thus it is unusually hard to define the world that he created in his writings. The contours and boundaries of Chekhov's literary world shift with the particular interest, or bias, of critic or anthologizer as from the mosaic of these varied works he creates a pattern to his own liking. Some critics have selected a few of his stories, and on the basis of their subject matter they have made Chekhov into a budding social activist. Princess Toumanova's biography, *Anton Chekhov, The Voice of Twilight Russia,* published in 1940, presents the author as a fin de siècle figure who in elegiac tones depicted the end of the old regime. A favorite twentieth-century formula is to view Chekhov as the chronicler of the human failure to communicate, each of his characters being sealed in his or her own cell of egoism and frustration. There is a perennial difference of opinion as to whether Chekhov is a pessimist or an optimist about the human condition, the same story often serving as support for both points of view. This controversy extends to an interpretation of the plays, particularly *The Cherry Orchard,* to which Stanislavsky gave a melancholy and even tragic interpretation over the protests of the author and to the extreme discomfort of later critics, who see the play as comedy pure, if not simple.

This wide diversity of responses to Chekhov's works on psychological, social, moral, and philosophical grounds is less a sign of critical myopia or perversity than it is evidence of Chekhov's unique position among the realists. It is possible to argue that in holding the mirror up to nature he makes representations so accurate, so *real,* that his artifacts evoke the same diversity of response as does life itself. This merely emphasizes what after all is implicit in all truly realistic writing, that two elements are always in play, the literary object, which in varying degrees succeeds in being a facsimile of actuality, and the multiple perceiver, that is, the minds of readers which, theoretically, are not directed in their evaluation of, or response to, the object. Chekhov may be the greatest of all the realists; he may have come closest to undistorted representation of reality and managed to maintain a completely objective position, so that his works to an amazing extent are unmediated data of experience.

An immediate problem in the evaluation of Chekhov is the nature of the short-story medium, which is his characteristic vehicle. The other writers whom we are considering generally used broad canvases and made the novel—a new kind of novel—the means of their representation of reality. This orientation toward monumental works of prose fiction has carried with it certain inconveniences, but over all the breadth and complexity of the novel form have facilitated variety and completeness. The short story—*nouvelle, novelle, récit, cuento, ocherk,* call it what we will—is something else again. On the whole, in Chekhov's day it was less burdened by restrictive conventions than the novel and was largely free of domination by brilliant antecedent works. The chief practitioners of this form in the earlier part of the nineteenth century were Stendhal, with his *Contes Italiennes,* Mérimée, and Poe. In their various ways they gave the short story distinction and enlarged its scope, but with the partial exception of Stendhal's work their stories cannot be seen as a form of realistic writing. It was the second generation of realists writing toward the end of the century, Maupassant, Chekhov, Verga, and Gorky, who turned to the short story and for some twenty years made it the realistic vehicle *par excellence.*

Chekhov began with what might be called conventional short stories, pot-boilers in every sense of the word, and most critics and anthologizers have ignored them. Chekhov's early stories hover between the gusto of the medieval *fabliaux* and the sophistication of the punch-ending tale. They tell us what amused the author and his readers about Russian life, but they do not tell us much about that life. Yet out of this lighthearted authorship the significant Chekhov stories somehow emerged. There is a notable turn by Chekhov toward seriousness and depth after 1886, which was signaled by the long story "The Steppe," by his receipt of the Pushkin award, and by his increasing concern over craftsmanship. This turning point is not absolute; some of his earlier stories show considerable depth, and a few later ones are trivial. Ronald Hingley, the most recent translator of Chekhov into English, has undertaken to translate all the stories from 1888 on. Many critics consider the forty-odd stories he wrote from 1885 on to constitute the part of Chekhov's *opus* that has permanent value.

While we are defining the nature of Chekhov's *opus*, we must consider his relation to the novel, for his correspondence indicates uneasy ambitions in that direction. Several of his works go beyond short-story length, of which the most important are "The Steppe" (1888), "The Duel" (1891), "Ward No. 6" (1892), "An Anonymous Story" (1893), "A Woman's Kingdom" (1894), "Three Years" (1895), and "My Life" (1896). These works do not encourage one to think that Chekhov would have moved on to the novel. From what we have from his own hand we must conclude that, whereas Tolstoy's short works strike us as novelistic in conception though reduced in content, Chekhov's longer works are little more than expanded short stories.

Even though it is made up of the bits and pieces that a short story shows, the world that Chekhov presents to us is as comprehensive and as varied as that of any of the other nineteenth-century realists. (He completely overshadows Maupassant in this respect, for the latter's range of character and situation is notably limited, and to wade through his collected body of stories is speedily to suffer boredom.) Chekhov's body of stories lacks any consistent locus in terms of either place or social level, though certain boundaries can be drawn. Geographically we are confined almost entirely to European Russia. The rest of Europe figures only incidentally in Chekhov's world, and with the exception of "Gusev," "In Exile," and "Ward No. 6," all of which draw upon Chekhov's trip across Siberia to Sakhalin in 1890, no work of importance is set in the non-European part of Russia. A good many of his stories, especially the early ones, are set in St. Petersburg and Moscow, but those cities merely provide a known background and are not particularized in any notable way. This is also true of Chekhov's considerable use of Yalta as background. We need to know little more about it than that it is in the south, on the sea, and a vacation resort. The point is that place in Chekhov's stories is rarely important, since one place is much like another. Certainly part of what we get from Chekhov's depiction is the essential sameness of life in the Russia of his time. The focal point of historical reference is the Emancipation of 1861, but this is really only incidental to a generally timeless depiction.

An important characteristic of the Chekhov world is a lack of social dynamism, an ignoring or playing down of the process of change. Occasionally a character will discuss the idea of progress, usually as an illusion from which people have to free their minds, but the narratives themselves do not advance the idea that under the impetus of science, or technology, or advanced ideas, or political reform and revolution Russia is getting better—or worse. The most striking instance of social change that Chekhov presents is the well-known breakup of the estate in *The Cherry Orchard,* but this event is chiefly a focus for the responses of a varied set of characters. We have already seen that Tolstoy and Dostoevsky, each in his own way, are also somewhat out of time, but the rural or small-town Russia which

Chekhov represents is less idealized than that of Tolstoy. Similarly, the psychological dynamics of Dostoevsky are generally exhibited in the city and in situations of crisis, both of which Chekhov avoids. Thus, Chekhov seems even closer to the norm than either of his predecessors. If Main Street existed in Russia, Chekhov would have found it and described it.

From the foregoing it is to be inferred that the social range of Chekhov's world is also capable of definition. We must not overlook those characters whom he draws from the upper stratum of society, such as various government officials or the bishop in one of his last stories, but such persons are never shown as among the rich and powerful of the earth. Their situations are always presented in terms of personal problems and solutions. It is the middle range of humanity that is predominant, though there are some striking instances in which the stories dip into the very bottom of the barrel, such cases occurring with greater frequency in the stories Chekhov wrote in the latter part of his life, though not in the plays. Because they are frequently anthologized, "Peasants" and "In the Ravine" are well known, but in this group are also to be found "Peasant Wives," "The Murder," "The Pecheneg," and the early play "On the Highway," which was never produced because it fell afoul of the censor. Of exotics there are few. Easily the most arresting of his characters is the young Tartar in "In Exile." This is almost the only instance of a personality carefully set apart from the Russian norm, but even in this case we must remember that he is only one of a group of exiles, part of a small and fairly normal spectrum of the banished and dispossessed. Another story, "The Black Monk," has attracted a good deal of attention precisely because it is not in the author's usual vein. Chekhov commented on this story in a letter to his friend Alexei Suvorin on January 25, 1894: "I wrote 'The Black Monk' without any melancholy ideas, through cool reflection. I simply had a desire to describe megalomania."[1] This is the only instance in his work of a heightened and genuinely abnormal psychological state.

The world we are shown by Chekhov has relatively little to

do with ways in which people make a living or exercise their professions. Although there are multitudes of people without money, again this is rather a basic background datum—one of the inherent conditions of life—than a social condition to be analyzed for its own sake. This exclusion of substantive data from the workaday world is paralleled by an exclusion of institutional behavior. For institutions involve people in formal relationships, and Chekhov tends to ignore them, because his interest is in the individual response rather than the social. It is this predilection that accounts for the nontemporal, nonspatial quality of his stories, and to a lesser extent of his plays. What he has solved here, almost by accident, is the problem of the particular versus the universal. Chekhov has shorn off the accidental in the lives of his characters and has left only the essential; yet essence, if he can be said to go after it, is presented only in terms of existence. Banal as it sounds, Chekhov's interest is in people, and he has shown them in more variety than any of his realistic peers except Galdós. He has done this without recourse to either gigantism or eccentricity. His characters are no doubt for the most part "little people" in the sense that they are run-of-the-mill samples, but by the time we have become acquainted with them we cease to think of them generically at all.

There is some evidence in Chekhov's letters of his attitudes and intentions with regard to respresenting human beings. To his brother Alexander, an aspiring writer, he wrote April 11, 1889: "Remember, by the way, that declarations of love, the infidelity of husbands and wives; widows,' orphans,' and all other tears, have long since been written up. The subject ought to be new, but there need be no 'fable.' " A decade later, October 11, 1899, writing to G. I. Rossolimo, Chekhov speculated about his range of interests: "I have no doubt that the study of medicine has had an important influence on my literary work; it has considerably enlarged the sphere of my observations, has enriched me with knowledge the true value of which for me as a writer can only be understood by one who is himself a doctor." His passion for accuracy of observation comes out in a letter to A. N. Pleshcheev (February 15, 1890) in which he complained of "the boldness with which Tolstoy treats that which he does not know and which he refuses to understand, out of sheer stubbornness. Thus, his statements about syphilis, about asylums for children, about women's aversion to copulation, etc., are not only open to dispute, but they actually betray an ignorant man who, in the course of his long life, has not taken the trouble to read two or three pamphlets written by specialists." Such statements almost take representative selection and accurate observation for granted. Chekhov is much less a man of doctrine than are many of his predecessors. He has no need to fight windmills. The climate of realism is so well established that he automatically adapts to its ways.

One of the problems that faced Chekhov as a realist was the restrictions of censorship, both official and unofficial. On the whole, he did not fare badly with officialdom, though we cannot know how much he refrained from depicting because of the ever-present shadow of the censor over his shoulder. "On the Highway" was not permitted to be produced because it showed a nobleman reduced to drunken penury. The censor was disturbed by "Peasants" for its stark revelation of the conditions of rural life and the implication that there had been retrogression since the Emancipation, but the cuts demanded by the censor did not seriously impair the work. Chekhov's most interesting pronouncement on the right of the author to show everything came not in response to official censorship but in answer to complaints about "Mire" raised by M. V. Kiselev in a letter of January 14, 1887: Chekhov asserted that although he did not admire sordid literature, he had observed that the great writers of the past "did not fear to grub in the 'dunghill'" when necessary. The fact that Tolstoy and Turgenev avoided the dunghill "does not prove anything; there were writers before them who not only regarded sordidness as 'scoundrelly among scroundrels,' but held the same view of descriptions of *muzhiks* and clerks and all beneath the titular rank." As for the charge that literature may corrupt, he wrote: "Publicists, lawyers, physicians, initiated into all the secret human sins, are not reputed to be immoral; realistic writers are often more moral than archimandrites. And finally, no literature can in its cynicism surpass actual life; a wineglassful will not make drunk the man who has already emptied a whole cask."

He challenged also the conventional position that the task of literature is to raise men's sights by dealing only with the ideal: "Human nature is imperfect, and it would, therefore, be strange to find only righteous people on this earth. But to think that the task of literature is to gather the pure grain from the muck heap, is to reject literature itself. Artistic literature is called so just because it depicts life as it really is. Its aim is truth—unconditional and honest." He concluded this letter with the assertion that since writers are "the children of their age," they must come to grips with the actual conditions of society and he denied that there is any police "which we can consider competent in literary matter."

A couple of years later, still defending "Mire," Chekhov declared: "I shall keep to the truth that is nearest my heart and which has been tested by men stronger and wiser than I. This truth is the absolute freedom of man, freedom from oppression, from prejudices, ignorance, passions, etc." This and similar statements have often been cited as proof that Chekhov was a crusader, a battler for the good, a doughty enemy of the social evils he saw around him. In his heart he may have been, but we must not forget his repeated insistence on absolute authorial objectivity. On a light note he wrote Suvorin on October 17, 1889: "When one serves you coffee, do not think to find beer in it. When I offer you a professor's ideas trust me, and do not search in them for Chekhov's ideas." Two other letters to Suvorin are emphatic about this position. In the first, May 30, 1888, Chekhov declares: "It seems to me that the writer of fiction should not try to solve such questions as those of God, pessimism, etc. His business is but to describe those who have been speaking or thinking about God and pessimism, how and under what circumstances. The artist should be, not the judge of his characters and their conversations, but only an unbiased witness . . . My business is merely to be talented, i.e., to be

able to distinguish between important and unimportant statements, to be able to illuminate the characters and speak their
language . . . And if an artist in whom the crowd has faith
decides to declare that he understands nothing of what he
sees—this in itself constitutes a considerable clarity in the realm
of thought, and a great step forward." In the second letter,
October 27, 1888, he tells Suvorin that it is only obligatory for
the artist to state a problem correctly. "It is the business of the
judge to raise the right questions, but the answers must be given
by the jury according to their lights." Readers are, of course,
the jury.

A letter written a decade later, April 1, 1900, indicates a
continuance of this conviction:

> You abuse me for objectivity, calling it indifference to good and
> evil, lack of ideals and ideas, and so on. You would have me, when
> I describe horse-thieves, say: "Stealing horses is an evil." But that
> has been known for ages without my saying so. Let the jury judge
> them; it's my job simply to show what sort of people they
> are . . . Of course it would be pleasant to combine art with a
> sermon, but for me personally it is extremely difficult and almost
> impossible, owing to the conditions of technique. You see, to
> depict horse-thieves in seven hundred lines I must all the time
> speak and think in their tone and feel in their spirits; otherwise, if I
> introduce subjectivity, the image becomes blurred and the story
> will not be as compact as all short stories ought to be. When I
> write, I reckon entirely upon the reader to add for himself the
> subjective elements that are lacking in the story.

The most often quoted remarks on this subject are usually
presented out of context and are therefore distorted. Chekhov
wrote to A. N. Pleshcheev in October 1889:

> I am afraid of those who look for a tendency between the lines,
> and who are determined to regard me either as a liberal or as a
> conservative. I am not a liberal, not a conservative, not a believer
> in gradual progress, not a monk, not an indifferentist. I should like
> to be a free artist and nothing more, and I regret that God has not

given me the power to be one. I hate lying and violence in all their forms, and am equally repelled by the secretaries of consistories and by Notovich and Gradovsky. Pharisaism, stupidity, and despotism reign not in merchants' houses and prisons alone. I see them in science, in literature, in the younger generation. . . . That is why I have no preference either for gendarmes, or for butchers, or for scientists, or for writers, or for the younger generation. I regard trade-marks and labels as a superstition. My holy of holies is the human body, health, intelligence, talent, inspiration, love, and the most absolute freedom—freedom from violence and lying, whatever forms they may take. That is the program I would follow if I were a great artist.

These remarks show the consistent understanding that Chekhov had of the need for objectivity in his writing. Only Flaubert is as explicit as Chekhov about the need for a separation between evidence and jury, and Flaubert's practice is less pure than is that of Chekhov. This maintenance of objectivity is particularly evident in the Russian's mature work. The great stories of the last decade or so are almost unexceptionable in the way in which they let the facts speak for themselves, and this is true of the plays as well. Whereas in an early story like "A Calamity" the authorial voice may speak of "sham emotions" of the characters, in the later works it is left to the reader to evaluate emotions, attitudes, or actions. Even more important, if the reader after finishing "Ward No. 6" or "Peasants" feels that steps should be taken to remedy those intolerable situations, this urge to action is not Chekhov's fault in any direct sense. He steers clear of weighted and tendentious writing to the very end.

When we examine the techniques that Chekhov develops for the telling of his stories, we must as usual look at his handling of point of view. It is interesting that Chekhov's insistence on objectivity does not prevent him throughout his career from using the first-person approach in either his short stories or long ones. The use of the first person may merely be a device by which to attest to the authenticity of the sample of experience without coloring or qualifying it to any extent. It is possible also that there may be a subtle counterpoint of perception and evaluation between the first-person voice and the characters about whom he tells. In neither case, as Chekhov tells us, are we to ascribe these emotions to him, the writer. It is worth noting that Avrahm Yarmolinsky in selecting stories for *The Portable Chekhov* included only one first-person narrative, an early story entitled "The Privy Councilor." Such a preponderant choice attests to the fact that Chekhov's highest art is identified with the objectivity of the third-person omniscient approach.

Although in this analysis we largely ignore Chekhov's earlier stories, it is well to bear in mind that the various developments in the way of subject and technique that occur in maturity are not incompatible with the more primitive works with which Chekhov began and which, numerically, constitute the bulk of his writing. In those works there are often telling bits of observation, but the people and the situations in which they find themselves are not important, and nothing is revealed about them beyond their obvious superficiality and rigidity. These works were intended to amuse and did so in the traditional fashion of the funny story. They depend on contrivance, usually a trick ending—the O. Henry twist—as in "A Work of Art," "75,000," or "A Chameleon." A related category is that of portraits based on incongruity but in which the human figure becomes more important than the joke. It is not easy to draw a line separating such early works as "Sergeant Prishibeev," "The Lodger," or "A Malefactor," on the one hand, and pieces like "Misery," "Anyuta," and "Vanka," on the other. Certainly the development here is away from the mechanism of the joke and the incongruities on which it turns to a more serious and pervasive incongruity in human attitudes and experience. This increased seriousness has an even more important consequence. The mechanical elements of the early stories have to give way to a technique that is adequate to give life, not rigidity, to what is being represented. In other words, when Chekhov ceased to be a hack writer, he had to find means by which to use the short story for truth, not trickery.

Without trying to separate them too sharply, we can say that Chekhov's major stories fall into two groups, the first written from 1886 to about 1892, and the second, written during the last eight or nine years of his life. In general, those stories in the first group are direct and relatively simple in statement; they attempt to portray accurately and they do not try to encompass too much. The later stories are more complicated and more subtle. But all of these stories bear the stamp of what Yarmolinsky calls Chekhov's quality of "incorruptible witness." Five of the earlier group arouse a degree of uncertainty in the reader's mind as to whether they do not make too overt an appeal to the reader's emotions since they depict situations of loneliness and victimization: "The Huntsman," "Misery," "Anyuta," "Vanka," and "Sleepy" ("Sleepyhead") certainly risk falling into sentimentalism, yet it is hard to convict Chekhov of having tipped the scales except by his choice of subject. In each of these stories the situation is stripped of all but the essential data; none of them involves the passage of time, however much it may be suggested. The huntsman appears after an absence and leaves again; his wife's situation is neither better nor worse than it was before, but we have been made aware of her loneliness by this encounter. Even though the old cabby in "Misery" has just learned of the death of his son, his isolation in the midst of busy Moscow is just what it has always been, except now there is nothing left to sustain his dreams of the future. Anyuta has been used by a medical student. When he sends her away, she suffers humiliation, but again it is hard to see that her situation has really worsened, though he is convicted of appalling egoism. "Sleepy" is more explosive: We see the growing desperation of a young servant girl who never has a moment to herself, a desperation that ends in her strangling the baby as a logical way to get some sleep. The story does smack of the sensational, yet it is played down to the level of a simple *fait divers*. "Vanka" makes the most obvious appeal to sentiment: The combination of the Christmas season and a suffering child is a risky one. Even more dangerous is the element of contrivance, the delayed fuse by which we are made to realize at the end that the boy's letter will never reach his grandfather and that any hope of rescue is entirely illusory. Upon reflection, however, we must see that such a hope was illusory from the beginning since the grandfather's situation was carefully described. Even more significant for our understanding is the inordinate attention given to the dog Wriggles, whose capacity to survive ill treatment is clearly a projection of Vanka's own case.

Another group of five stories shows Chekhov's ability succinctly to sum up a personality or situation without taking advantage of a potential for sentimentality. "An Unpleasant Incident" shows a collision of personalities between a doctor and an orderly in a hospital that is incapable of more than superficial resolution since neither personality can change. The patronizing woman in "The Princess" who has no idea of the figure she cuts as she plays Lady Bountiful to the monastery is a model of quick portraiture. "Mire" is a much more perceptive depiction of a meaningless sexual involvement than "A Calamity," which appeared in the same year. "Typhus" is memorable in that it concentrates on the inability of the convalescent officer to grieve for the genuinely loved sister who has succumbed to the disease. The best of the lot is "The Kiss," which reveals contrasting states of mind evoked by a simple, even trivial, situation. In every one of these stories, even in "The Princess," we are not called upon to judge or give an emotional response. Each of them is impressive by its accuracy of portrayal, by the assured economy with which it presents a recognizable external or internal situation.

Another handful of stories in this earlier grouping, "A Nervous Breakdown" ("An Attack of Nerves"), "The Party" ("The Name-Day Party"), "Gusev," "Peasant Wives," and "In Exile" achieve their end by means considerably more complex, although in each case the situation speaks for itself and is of essentially the same capsule nature as the work just discussed. These latter stories offer a medley of personalities and an interplay between external situation and internal response a good deal more subtle than in the earlier works. In "A Nervous Breakdown," Vasilev who has "a talent for *humanity*," encounters the fact of prostitution for the first time. The clichés with which he has handled this problem intellectually are not relevant to the sordid facts that he now observes. He is disgusted with his friends for patronizing such establishments, and with himself for having gone along and for having been unable to communicate with the women. The experience brings on a painful nervous attack of such proportions that his friends take him to a psychiatrist. The attack runs its course and he returns to the university in no way different or wiser than he was before. There is a suggestion that his nervous vulnerability may be hereditary and that such attacks will occur again, but neither the mental suffering nor the social evil is given special importance.

"The Party" works in much the same way. Olga Mikhailovna, well advanced in pregnancy, finds her responsibilities as hostess at her husband's name-day celebration more than she can bear. The story is carefully restricted to her feelings and responses. At the beginning we have a sketch of her general emotional state. Then there is a series of dramatized situations seen from her point of view. She overhears her husband flirting harmlessly with a young girl; she is caught up in an exchange of social banalities; she goes with her guests to have supper on an island. After the party breaks up she suffers an attack of nerves, quarrels with her husband, and has a miscarriage. At the end, exhausted and under sedation, she has a complete lack of feeling, not the sense of overpowering loss that the situation would demand if viewed tragically. The narrative is effectively carried out; the counterpoint is convincing. In the midst of her *crise de nerfs* she looks at herself and thinks, "I must look a sight." The intensity of her feelings during the endless evening is balanced by her realization that she is seeing everything out of proportion. Only once is the narrative voice intrusive when it speculates as to the husband's thoughts, a passage that is clearly not an emanation of Olga Mikhailovna's mental state.

"Gusev," though exotic in situation, shows a similar collocation of external and internal elements. It too is limited to the perception and response of one person, Gusev, a soldier on shipboard returning from eastern Siberia. His hopeless physical condition is objectified to a degree in that of Pavel Ivanych, a gentleman and a malcontent, to whose complaints Gusev pays little attention. One of his companions dies; Pavel Ivanych dies; and eventually Gusev dies. Yet he scarcely takes in the seriousness of the situation, his mind being occupied with memories and fantasies of home. The movement here is from objective narrative, to dramatized scene, to a kind of summary of consciousness. The authorial presence is occasionally evident, as in the statement "The Sea has neither sense nor pity," and especially in an ironic final passage in which the indifference of nature is contrasted with illusory human attribution of meaning and purpose to nature.

These three stories have a clinical precision that one might expect from Chekhov the doctor but which is, at this stage of his development, unusual for its inwardness. Two other stories of this period achieve their effect without resort to internal states, relying instead on the use of parallel situations that need no commentary or analysis. "Peasant Wives" is set at a rural inn where Matvey Savvich and his adopted son Kuzka are spending the night. Savvich tells the innkeeper about events in his life that occurred ten years before when he lived with a peasant woman during the absence of her conscript husband. On the husband's return Matvey was relieved that the liaison was over, but the wife, refusing to give him up, poisoned her husband and was sent to Siberia, where she died. Matvey, an irritatingly sanctimonious man, is bringing up her son. The innkeeper's two daughters-in-law listen to this story and react to it unfavorably. Later in the night we learn that the younger one, Varvara, is carrying on with the priest's son and anyone else she can find. Her sin, like that of Matvey's inamorata, is no doubt justified by circumstances, but she too will be found out and destroyed. The bitter lot of peasant women is certainly made evident here, but without special pleading and without the reader's emotions being deeply engaged. The story does end with a painful appeal to emotion in a scene showing Matvey's brutal treatment of his foster son, his legacy from his earlier escapade.

"In Exile" uses the same technique of parallels. The scene is at a ferry landing on a Siberian river. Old Semyon, a man of sixty, who has become inured to the rough life of exile after twenty years, is in conversation with a young Tartar who has recently arrived. Semyon tells the youth a story about still another exile, Vasily Sergeich, a gentleman, who came there fifteen years before, whose wife ran way from him, and whose later years have been made desperate by the illness of his daughter, who is all that he has in the world. The point of the story is that this man has made his life miserable by his unwillingness to adapt to circumstances, with the implication that the Tartar must make such an adaptation if he is to survive. The story ends when Vasily Sergeich summons the ferrymen and tells them that he has heard of a doctor who might cure his daughter, obviously just another of the illusions which he entertains. Old Semyon sees this as one more proof of folly. The Tartar responds to the other man's anguish and suffers with him.

Chekhov's first two attempts at a broader canvas, "The Steppe" and "Lights," belong to a transition period that took place about 1888. His letters attest to his self-consciousness in attempting this new form, for he complains of the first story that "it appears bulky, dull, too crowded with detail," and the second he finds dull and ineffective. His attempt in the latter to include some philosophy is very awkward. This is his most egregious failure because he attempted to do something incompatible with the short story as he understood it and violated his innate aversion to theses in literature. "The Steppe, The Story of a Journey," on the other hand, is a fairly successful attempt, though atypical. It tells of the trip taken by Egorushka, aged nine, from his home to a district town across the steppe where he is to be put in school. When the boy's uncle left him, "He sank helplessly on to the little bench, and with bitter tears greeted the unknown life that was beginning for him now. . . . What would it be like?" This story, of vaguely allegorical cast, is a preview of what life is like. The journey in episodic fashion has led the boy past many typical people and situations, in particular a prison and a cemetery. The symbolic meaning of the journey is implicit in the tale, but the boy's point of view is not violated and the allegory is not pressed. What endears the work to many readers, however, is the freshness and detail of the natural descriptions it contains, since nowhere else does Chekhov let himself go to this extent with a response to nature.

As has been indicated, "Ward No. 6" represents a very special case among Chekhov's works in that it grows immediately out of authorial experience, the visit to Sakhalin. Moreover, of all his works it is the one to which a social purpose may be most safely ascribed. The cross section on which the story rests is carefully worked out. The five inmates of the ward are a grieving workman; a little black man who is a Jew and an imbecile; Ivan Dmitrich Gromov, a gentleman, who has developed a persecution complex; a fat peasant with an acrid, stiffling stench; and an artisan, a former postal employee, who has delusions of grandeur. In addition there is Nikita, the brutal soldier warder. Against this human background we have the major portrait of Dr. Andrei Efimich Ragin, who "loved intelligence and honesty intensely, but . . . had no strength of will nor belief in his right to organize an intelligent and honest life about him." The result is that his morale degenerates and he lets everything slide. He is capable of being fired momentarily by enthusiasm for the great advances of medicine, but then he takes to visiting Ivan Dmitrich, whom he finds more sane than the sane officials and townsmen with whom he must associate. He retires more and more into himself and is finally put into Ward No. 6 by his unscrupulous and ambitious assistant. "So this is real life," he muses, and is frightened. When he tries to get out he is beaten by Nikita and dies of a stroke.

As representation of the conditions of penal confinement this work is less satisfactory and less moving than Dostoevsky's *House of the Dead*. The situation of the inmates of the hospital ward is very special. The intrigue by which Dr. Ragin is himself confined is contrived. In short, these reservations about the realism of the work lead some readers to conclude that it must be a case of special pleading. Under a regime of censorship it is no doubt automatic to raise the literal to the symbolic level. Thus it was easy for Russian readers to say that the prison, and more particularly Ward No. 6, represented contemporary Russia, where human decency was absent and human promise completely stultified. Such a reading is somewhat cavalier, for though it might have been apposite to call Russia a prison, it seems overemphatic to call it a madhouse. In the twentieth century it is unfortunately tempting to read this work as allegorical in terms of the absurd, as a pre-Kafka—perhaps better, a pre-Solzhenitsyn—representation of the human condition. At least such a reading has the advantage of being more general and less satiric. But the careful reader must wonder if either of these readings is justified by the materials presented.

Two other long stories, "Three Years" and "My Life," belong to the last years. Both are moderately optimistic and, contrary to standard critical judgment, neither is basically a work with a thesis, though by reason of their length they do present a number of general ideas. Since Chekhov undertakes development of character over a period of time, he is forced to techniques at which he is not very skilled. He is obliged to use more documentation than in his shorter works and he must devise a series of episodes by which the subsidence of the protagonist into acceptance of his lot can be shown. What we get is a framework that is logically acceptable but lacks the flash of revelation of an inner condition which is characteristic of the best stories. At the center of "Three Years" is the Laptev family, proprietors of a Moscow wholesale business. Alexei Laptev falls in love with Iulia Sergeevna when he visits the town where his sister is dying of cancer. After some hesitation she marries him, but it is not a successful marriage. The sister dies and her children are brought to Moscow, where Iulia has the task of reconciling the grandfather to their existence. A brother suffers from a nervous disorder and dies. The old father becomes blind and increasingly difficult to live with and the business falters. The resolution of these personal, family, and business problems falls on Alexei, who concludes that one has to give up all thoughts of personal happiness. He does put the business back on its feet and his father softens toward members of the family. Iulia tells him that she loves him and at the end Alexei is able to express a tentative hopefulness: "Let us live and we shall see." The effort of this story is to get at the slow erosion of living by means of quickly sketched scenes and situations. What it lacks is full documentation. Even the period of three years that it covers is too short, a kind of truncated temporal framework so as somehow to stay within the boundaries of the short story.

"My Life" has been described as a refutation of Tolstoyan doctrine, or at least as an indication of Chekhov's disenchantment with such ideas. This rather overstates the case. The narrative is one of self-discovery through encountering personal and social obstacles, and it is moderately optimistic in tone. The remarkable thing about the story is the objective and dispassionate manner in which, even though it is a first-person narrative, we follow the experience of a social rebel. Misail is in revolt against his father, a dull and conventional architect, and all his standards. Having lost one job after another, Misail decides to give up middle-class patterns and become a common workman. In the course of his revolt he marries Masha Dolzhikova, the daughter of a rich, self-made man, only to find that love in a cottage does not work out and to have his marriage end in divorce. Misail's sister also is unconventional, in that she has an affair with a married man by whom she becomes pregnant. She later dies giving birth to her child. There is a good deal of discussion of ideas, without conclusion as to what is right or wrong. Although Prokofy says with respect to Misail that "Every class should stick to its own rules. And them as is too proud to understand that will find this life a vale of tears," the narrative neither supports nor denies such conventional wisdom. At the end Misail has developed into a successful workman who feels respect for himself and is accepted by the community. But he is not reconciled with his father, he has lost his wife and sister, and he is uncertain as to what personal happiness is possible for him in the future.

Fortunately Chekhov's career is capped not by these gropings for a new form but by the achievement of the dozen stories that belong to the last years and show the application of his skill to a variety of situations. One of these, "The Helpmate" ("His Wife"), is a simple dramatized portrait of a mercenary and self-indulgent woman caught at a revealing moment. It shows Chekhov's skill at its simple and direct best. Two others, " 'Anna on the Neck' " (1895) and "The Darling" (1899), make use of early comic devices to new and mature effect. The first rests on a pun belonging to the stuffy world of officialdom, but out of that format comes a picture of a woman who marries for money, learns to subdue her husband, but loses her human sympathies in the process. "The Darling" uses the comic device of repetition. Olenka (Olga Semyonovna) is a soft, dependent sort of person whose vitality depends on having someone to love, to be interested in, and to derive being from. The story rapidly recounts her marriage to Kukin, a theater manager, a second marriage to Vasily Andreich Pustovalov, who runs a lumber yard, a liaison with Vladimir Smirnin, an army veterinarian, and a temporary guardianship of Smirnin's ten-year-old boy. In each instance there is a brief indication in dialogue of the platitudes that she draws from the latest object of her affection and offers as her own. The effect is an unexpectedly subtle one. Olenka is not the object of comic depreciation, even though the authorial tone is sometimes arch. Rather, in spite of her lack of independent being, she comes alive as warm and admirable, partly by the repeated testimony of the townspeople but more by her own exhibition of heart. She is not diminished by her obvious limitations, for there is something admirable in her tenacity, and at the end the reader feels that something will continue to turn up from which Olenka may derive life and happiness.

Two other late portraits are worthy of attention. "The Bishop" (1902) is a much more internal study than is usual with Chekhov. The events of Holy Week at which Bishop Peter must officiate run parallel with the onset and development of a case of typhus from which he dies the day before Easter. The story makes use of straight narration, passages of dialogue, and summaries of the bishop's ideas and feelings as he responds to the ritual, to the suppliants and officials with whom he must treat, and to his mother and niece who come to him from another world. The effect is to sum up a noble, kindly and not very assertive personality, but not to pass judgment on him, though the ending with the vignette of a rejoicing Easter Day blotting out the death of this man has considerable ironic impact. Less effective because it is less concentrated is "Betrothed" (1903)—sometimes mistranslated as "The Bride"—which is the last story that Chekhov finished. This story portrays a girl of twenty-three who is restive about the conditions of her life and who does not love the man whom she is about to marry. Under the encouragment of Sasha, a rebel and an artist, she breaks her home ties and convention to go away to the university. When she returns a year later, her mother and grandmother have forgiven her, though they feel themselves to be social outcasts because of the broken marriage. Nadya realizes that her home has changed and that she does not belong there. The events in this story are perhaps trite, but the sad sense of necessity that comes from growing up and pursuing one's own course is wonderfully evoked.

Three of the last stories are generally grouped together as statements of the frustration of those whose lives are blocked by circumstances that they cannot alter. "The Lady with the Dog" (1899) covers a period of several months. An inveterate adulterer, Dmitri Dmitrich Gurov, encounters a much younger woman at Yalta and has an affair with her. When she leaves he assumes that the affair is all over and that he will at most remember her complacently as another conquest. Once back home, he finds that he cannot forget her and in spite of the risk he seeks her out in the provincial town where she lives with her husband. Both discover that they are in love for the first time and that they are doomed to shifts and humiliations in arranging rendezvous which they must conceal from their spouses. In the metaphor of the story "it was as though they were a pair of migratory birds, male and female, caught and forced to live in different cages."

"At Home" (1897) and "The Schoolmistress" ("In the Cart") (1897) are compressed statements of the same theme. In "At Home," Vera Kardina comes home to her country estate in the Donets Basin after a ten-year absence. She responds to the natural beauty of the region at first but soon finds that life there is dull and narrow. Having resisted the idea originally, she decides to marry Dr. Neshchapov as the only way available to her to break the bonds of her situation: " 'He's a fine man,' she says. 'We'll manage somehow.' " Philosophically she concludes that "Music, dreams, wonderful scenery are one thing, but ordinary living is another story altogether. Happiness and truth have nothing to do with ordinary life, that's clear enough." "The Schoolmistress" makes a more despairing statement, for Marya, a teacher in the country, is caught in a rut that is more confining than the ruts which direct the course of the cart in which she is riding. When she encounters Khanov, a local squire, a man whose existence is evidently as lonely and as limited as her own, she dreams for a moment of falling in love with him, just as for a moment at the railroad crossing she thinks she sees her dead mother on a passing train. These flickerings of hope and recollections of joy are balanced by the physical actuality, an unpleasant scene at a dirty inn, a soaking when the cart fords a stream, and we realize that for her there is no escape, though she will continue to buoy herself up with dreams as best she can.

The last two stories that we consider, "Peasants" (1897) and "In the Ravine" (1900), are by far the most substantial cases of social analysis in the entire body of Chekhov's work, and they may well indicate that he would have taken a new direction if he had lived longer. In neither story is the emphasis upon a single individual; rather the aim is to catch the nature of a social milieu, that of a peasant village in the first story, and of a commercial middle-class group in a small town in the other. In each case there is at the beginning a quick establishment of the quality of life in metaphorical terms. When the little girl Sasha returns to the peasant village, she notices a cat and tries to entice her. Her cousin tells her: "She can't hear. Deaf." "Why?" "Oh, someone hit her." This sums up the brutal and brutalizing life of the village. Similarly in "In the Ravine" there is an opening anecdote about the sexton who at a funeral feast ate up all the caviar, which seems, not so obliquely, to indicate that one species eats up another. To a degree both of these stories depend on narrative development, though in the first case it is little more than a framework made up of the return of the Chikildeev family to the village from Moscow, a period of waiting for the husband and father to die, and a return to the city by mother and daughter. However, there is extant a tenth section that begins an account of the life of these two women back in Moscow under conditions as sordid and hopeless as those in the village.

"In the Ravine" has a well-defined narrative development as it follows the ways in which Aksinya, one of the Tzybukin daughters-in-law, gains dominance over other members of the family. This story also contains the most heightened event of all the stories, the scalding death of Lipa's baby by Aksinya, as well as a somewhat incredible piece of intrigue about counterfeit money. By means of bringing several members of the central family on scene, each of these stories provides a limited cross section of the life it is examining. In "Peasants" there is, in addition, a definite effort to present facets of village life through short scenes showing a fire, the arrival of the tax collector, a religious ceremony, and the sexual carryings on of Fyokla. Both of these stories are embryonically novelistic in their scope and variety of material and summon up a much greater body of detail than most of the other works.

This kind of social study, however, is not Chekhov's significant contribution to realism. Rather it is his ability simultaneously to convey an environing physical situation and the accompanying emotional state of his characters. This is Tolstoyan in its insistence on the existence of both elements. In approach it is more external than what is shown by Dostoevsky, but overall it does constitute a direct refutation of French realist emphasis on the external to the exclusion of internal or affective states. This contrast is of great importance, for it helps us to see the direction in which realism had to develop if it was to be faithful to its mandate to tell the truth. E. M. de Vogüé, who wrote *Le Roman Russe* before Chekhov's reputation was established, was later delighted by him, for he did restore the human soul, or at any rate the human capacity for thought and feeling, to the hard clay that the French realists had shown as molded largely by external pressures.

Flaubert and after him Maupassant made great capital of the ironic contrast between the actual physical situation of a character as seen by the external observer and the character's evaluation of that situation. Chekhov asserted that this contrast was in the nature of things and, whereas he was aware of the irony and even emphasized it on occasion, he rarely let it prevail. His characters come down to earth not with a thud, but with a sympathetic acceptance of the disparity between illusion and reality, even with the tacit assumption that illusion is a part of reality and is necessary to it. This is the great leap that Chekhov made from his early contrived stories, a leap that Maupassant was not capable of making, with the result that the latter's stories, deft as they are, are generally stereotyped. In other words, Chekhov shows reality as dual: it contains both the determining circumstances of the material world and a capacity for almost irrelevant response that can mitigate, if not negate, those shaping influences.

Although he insists on the validity and actuality of inner states, Chekhov makes no innovations in ways of presenting them. As much as possible he allows external action or statement to indicate the presence of feelings that arise from, but often go counter to, the external situation, as in "The Darling." He frequently resorts to use of summary stream of consciousness, but never sustains it for long. "The Black Monk" is unique in presenting a hallucinatory experience. More significant is the consistent state of "inwardness" in "The Bishop," where external circumstances form a kind of fading frame for the succession of memories, emotions, and evaluations that pass through the dying prelate's mind.

We must not leave this evaluation of Chekhov's stories without inquiring to what extent, in spite of the air of objectivity and impartiality, he directs the reader's response and evaluation. There are four ways in which Chekhov might be accused of tipping the scales if he had let himself go in those directions. The first is the trivial one of tag names, a device of which he was very fond for his early comic sketches but which does not often mar his mature work. A second possibility is the selection of, and harping on, a particular kind of detail—an exclusive documentation of animality, dirt, cruelty, or stupidity. This Chekhov avoids meticulously, partly because of the necessity for economy in the offering of details. It is the variety of data and of illustrative incident that sets these stories apart from even so accomplished a work as Flaubert's *Un Coeur Simple*. A third way is by irony, particularly ironic contrast, in the manner of Flaubert and Maupassant. A number of Chekhov's most important stories do have at the end a kind of gratuitous insistence on the gap between human expectation and what is actually possible. "Gusev" is the flagrant case, for there the demonstrated indifference of nature to the fate of man is underscored by an ironic use of symbols. The heavens light up in a beautiful display, forming shapes that resemble a triumphal arch, a lion, and a pair of scissors, traditional symbols of man's sense of his power and place in the universe, with a reminder that the fates capriciously cut his lifeline. In general such heavy use of irony is unnecessary. The disparity inherent in experience has already been made clear in the course of the story. As for irony as a deflationary device, Chekhov does not use it. Disparities do not diminish his characters, who, if anything, gain by their recognition of them and their ability to live in spite of them.

A fourth directive device, which is used sporadically, consists of the insertion into the story of a slight symbolic element which is a kind of objective correlative of the situation described. "A Calamity" has a fly buzzing against a windowpane to mark the frustration of the two lovers. Vanka's fate, as we have seen, is summed up by that of the dog Wriggles. The thunderstorm in "The Party" is violent but temporary, suggesting the evaluation to be put on the crisis in Olga Mikhailovna's life. The very progress of the cart in "The Schoolmistress" is enough to show Marya's life in its essentially static condition. Probably the counterfeit money is a commentary on the life of the people in "In the Ravine," though there is also a specific correlate for Aksinya in the reference to a snake. Olenka fat and Olenka lean is a directive formula for "The Darling," though significantly the inference of a parasitic existence is carefully avoided, since that would be an unqualified indictment. On the whole, these symbolic elements, though not always necessary, do not diminish or qualify the realism of the stories in question. They may point up what the story says, but that statement is ready there. It is this particular practice of Chekhov's that has been picked up by practitioners of a type of twentieth-century short story that is poetic rather than realistic.

Chekhov's years of mature craftsmanship in the short story are also the years in which he reached mastery in the drama, leaving an oeuvre that has been a primary influence on the theater for over eighty years. When we consider Chekhov's drama, it is difficult to say whether these works are truly realistic, or indeed whether realistic drama is possible. At any rate Chekhov's plays go further in breaking down the conventions of the nineteenth-century theater and in opening up the way for a new and freer form than do any of the other plays of the time. There is a strict progression of development toward this new form through the five plays from *Ivanov* (1887–89), which is rather unsatisfactory, to *The Cherry Orchard* (1903), the high point of his dramatic creation.

The innovations in the drama that had taken place before Chekhov's work began were largely in the area of subject matter, as can be seen in the efforts of the Goncourts and Zola to translate their novels to the stage and in Zola's pleas in "The Naturalistic Theatre." To bring everyday life onto the stage, to show ordinary people muddling through, to insist that there were other actions for drama than the sexual triangle was in itself a considerable advance, and one that was necessary if the theater was to survive as a vital force. It was in this respect that Ibsen's major realistic plays had their great impact. The subjects of Ibsen's plays were fresh and interesting. Business morality in a typical Norwegian town is examined in *Pillars of Society* and *An Enemy of the People,* with social corruption also being part of the subject of the latter. The subordination of a wife is the subject of *A Doll's House,* and the obscurantism and destructiveness of official codes of morality dominates *Ghosts,* which actually brings the sordid problem of syphilis out into the open, though in terms that are rather pretentious. All four of these plays avoid a central love intrigue; all of them may be said to deal with the rules the middle class lives by and the stultifying, when not destructive, effect of those rules. The plays are solid in their evocation of bourgeois life and thought, accurate in their presentation of a recognizable gallery of bourgeois types speaking a language that is their own, not one drawn out of books. Yet this realistic texture does not disguise the fact that in addition to depicting ordinary life it was also Ibsen's intention to expose it. His realism was ancillary to his moral and social purpose. He held up not only a mirror but a whip.[2]

These are good plays, solidly constructed, and even today they are capable of holding the spectator's interest. Yet it is clear that once the novelty, even the shock value, of their unconventional subjects had been assimilated, the plays had little more to offer in the way of influence, either intellectually or aesthetically. Without diminishing Ibsen, it is possible to argue that Ibsen's plays, and those of Hauptmann, Becque, and to a certain extent Strindberg, brought a life-giving infusion of new material into the drama and made it intellectually contemporary without making significant alterations in dramatic form in the way that Chekhov, certain playwrights of the Irish Renaissance, and the early O'Neill did. It would be dangerous to imply that Chekhov created a new theater that displaced the old; that is going much too far. But he did achieve a form that avoided some of the more constricting formal conventions of the traditional theater, and his plays do have an unusual ability to mirror significant human situations without distorting them.

The world shown in his plays is decidedly more limited and more homogeneous than that of his short stories. All five plays depict middle-class groups of a certain economic standing and, for the most part, of considerable cultivation. *Ivanov* is the most exceptional of the plays, both because the hero is a neurasthenic and because he has departed from the social norm by marrying a Jewess. Tolstoy commented with considerable justice that the literary-artistic milieu of the next play, *The Seagull* (1896), was too special a situation for realistic representation. In other respects, however, these two plays portray the same life on a country estate as *Uncle Vanya* (1897) and *The Cherry Orchard* (1903–04) and take in a limited cross section of neighbors, servants, and dependents, none of whom are in any way unusual. Even *Three Sisters* (1900–01), which is set in a large town populated with army officers, does not go counter to this norm.

The situations presented are also fairly ordinary, again with the partial exceptions noted of *Ivanov* and *The Seagull*. They all generate their action from the predictable stresses of people living together and attempting to resolve the various problems they encounter. Although a good deal has been made of the love triangles in a number of the plays, their energies do not derive primarily from these sexual situations, though again *Ivanov* is more highly charged in that respect than its successors. In the plays money is an important motive force; Ivanov and his uncle have none, in contrast with the vulgar Lebedev family. Professor Serebriakov is forced to live on the Voynitsky estate because of the inadequacy of his pension. Part of the diminution life brings to the Prozorov sisters is their loss of fortune, and *The Cherry Orchard* is dominated by a financial crisis to which the characters refuse to respond. A third dominant source of energy is the broad problem of finding direction in life (*The Seagull* is a special case of this), of distinguishing between dream and what is feasible.

The dramaturgical embodiment of these broad situations constitutes the problem for the writer; if nothing had followed *Ivanov* and *The Seagull*, Chekhov would not be considered a great dramatist, for those two plays do not succeed in disentangling themselves from standard stage practice. Ivanov is definitely the center of the play to which he gives his name. He is one more instance of the so-called superfluous man, a condition that has to be taken on faith since the play makes no effort to show how he has declined to his present situation. In any event he is mired down in self-pitying inertia at the age of thirty-five, and he is incapable of meeting the responsibilities that bear upon him. When, after his wife's death, he is about to marry Sasha and start a new life, for which he is convinced he is not suited, he commits suicide. The implications of this work are more far-ranging than those of the usual well-made play, but it sacrifices both psychological and social truth to logical intrigue and a final shattering effect.

The same charge can be made against *The Seagull*, though the psychological examination is more probing and more sustained. Treplev, the son of a famous actress, is self-consciously presented as a Hamlet figure. A would-be writer with no very clear talent, he is easily discouraged, and at the end of the play he commits suicide—off stage this time, in a scene which is carefully muted. As Chekhov wrote to Suvorin on November 11, 1895: "I began it *forte* and ended it *pianissimo*—contrary to the rules of dramatic art." Acting as a foil to Treplev is Nina, the girl with whom he is in love, who is willing to undergo humiliation and misery for the sake of her career as an actress, thus forcing us to see Treplev in perspective. These first two plays both use a program of fairly concentrated action in the first three acts, followed by an interval of a year or two before the final action so as to permit the development of the implicit psychological forces. In other words, in both of these plays there is a sound sense of cause and effect, with the time interval used as a means of bringing the two modes of action into logical relation.

The last three plays are much more successful dramatically

and show a steady development toward a new dramatic form. All three plays make use of a crisis situation as a means of demonstrating the capacities or incapacities of a considerable range of people. None of these plays features a single character. In fact it is difficult to say that one character in these plays is more important than another, though the bias of a director can readily shift the balance of emphasis.

One of the interesting problems about these plays, and to a lesser degree of the earlier ones, is the question of genre. *Ivanov* and *Three Sisters* are described by the author as dramas; *Uncle Vanya* has as a subtitle "Scenes from Country Life in Four Acts." *The Seagull* and *The Cherry Orchard* are called comedies. A difference of opinion developed between the author and Stanislavsky the producer about the tone of the original productions, and that difference has continued to the present day. In the opinion of most critics the Moscow Art Theater productions of Chekhov's plays have had an unfortunate distorting effect on later productions everywhere. Most theatergoers have seen *The Cherry Orchard* produced in a vein somewhere between dripping sentiment and stark tragedy, and the *Three Sisters* is usually performed as a tragedy of frustration. Yet the evidence of the plays themselves, leaving out of account Chekhov's intentions, does not support such a somber, monochrome interpretation. These plays have to be seen as examples of deliberately mixed genres, a violation of convention that is necessary if a new dramatic form mirroring life is to come into being. This tendency toward mixture is already to be discerned in *Ivanov*. Whereas three acts are largely concerned with the hero's unhappy psychological state, the second act is almost pure drawing room comedy, useful in showing what Ivanov is in revolt against but carried on in such high style that it jars with the rest of the play. Chekhov did not make that mistake again. In the other four plays the serious and comic elements are more carefully balanced; they constitute an accurate picture of the mixed situations in real life. Because of the mixture both actor and spectator vacillate in their response to the situations, as people do in real life.

Uncle Vanya merely parades before us a group of people in a situation they cannot tolerate but which they cannot resolve. The method is one of compression and decompression rather than of any organic change. The Serebriakovs have come to the Voynitsky estate because they need to conserve money. They cannot stand it there, and after a while they leave, hoping to manage somehow in the city. Sonya, Serebriakov's daughter by his first wife, is in love with Dr. Astrov, but he loves Elena, Serebriakov's second wife, who is afraid to cut loose from the security of marriage. Voynitsky hates his mother and his in-laws. At the end he is still burdened with his mother, but at least he and Sonya can resume the quiet of their former routine.

The situation in *The Cherry Orchard* is well known, though sometimes distorted by misguided emphasis. Lubov Ranevskaya, a frivolous woman, has come home after a long period abroad, primarily because she has run out of money. Her brother is equally impecunious and even more frivolous. There is a possibility of salvaging their situation by selling part of the estate for suburban development. They resist this opportunity out of sentiment and inertia, but finally the land is lost through foreclosure and they go their appointed ways, no better off than they were and no more capable of decision or amendment.

A commonplace trope of dramatic action pretty well sums up Chekhov's formula: Life is a series of arrivals and departures invested with a kind of fortuitous importance and excitement, but it is actually pedestrian and without significant effect. In *Three Sisters* we get a variant of this, on the whole a more subtle and interesting statement. The Prozorov family had come to live in the garrison town some eleven years before the play begins. What had been looked on as a temporary posting has become permanent because of the father's death and the limited circumstances in which the four children were forced to grow up. The three sisters have an obsessive desire to get away, to go back to Moscow and begin living. The irony is that they have been living all the time, growing up, adapting to circumstances, and suffering modest ups and downs of fortune. The situation that they look upon as a kind of suspension before living is life, whereas their dream of Moscow, where they will begin to live, is actually nonliving, an unrealizable state. The play is unusual for the time span it covers. Each of the four acts mentions various changes that enable us to measure the passage of time, until at the end we realize that three and a half years have passed and that the sisters will never get to Moscow, which must be seen both as a rejection of dreams, a defeat, and as the achievement of maturity, a triumph. The play demands a fairly large cast of similar people. The members of the military establishment who are the Prozorovs' chief acquaintances are themselves living in suspension because of their vocation, though one of them, Baron Tuzenbach, does break away from military life. When the military leave for another post at the end of the play, it seems as though the end of the world has come, but this is not true for them any more than it is for Irina, whose betrothed has just been killed in a duel. Each of these people has become what he or she is and will go on being what he is until the end of his life—no doubt a disappointing reading of life but not a catastrophic one.

This play has two curious outbreaks of violent action that are disturbing to the conception of normality just adumbrated. There is no particular necessity that Tuzenbach be killed in a duel, and the placing of that event within hours of his marriage to Irina and in the last two or three minutes of the play creates a serious strain on our belief. In particular, it forces on Irina the obligation to underreact in a split second to a change of course, and this jars with the slow process of adjustment that we have witnessed in the rest of the play. The other curious event in the play is the fire that destroys several houses and is the topic of the entire third act. Perhaps this can be seen as a kind of touchstone to show how the various members of the family react to actuality—a common point of reference. There is also an element of intrigue in this play that has thrown some critics off. They see the gradual assumption of control by Natasha, Andrei Prozorov's wife, as the action of a villain. In the first act she is a shy and inexperienced girl. Once married, she begins to dominate her husband and to push the sisters aside. In the third act she abuses her maternal role to get what she wants, and in the fourth act she is triumphant. The world is hers: Olga and Masha have left the house, and Irina is going. Yet this growing power need not be called an evil machination. Rather it is a further example of what happens in the process of time. It also has the important function of giving us the measure of the one person in the play who does not want to go to Moscow.

The significant thing about Chekhov's dramaturgy is that on the whole he avoids the two pitfalls which stood most obviously in the way of realistic drama. He does not make capital of the situation that depends primarily on its novelty or its offense to a restricted idea of decorum, as did many of the realistic drama- tists, and he does not cram realistic subject matter into the conventional dynamic framework of conflict which rises to a climax and resolution, which by their neatness are the antithesis of real-life situations. The motive force of his plays comes entirely from an interplay of temperament and environmental circumstance, producing what David Magarshack has called "indirect action" plays. In a way, Chekhov's plays are anti- drama since they reach no more resolution than what time brings and avoid climax and catastrophe. Certainly as has been indicated, they escape generic classification. Chekhov's plays are not tragic, though they have their moments of sorrow and loss. They are not forthrightly comic, though they capitalize on the mechanical, jack-in-the-box behavior that is the stock in trade of comedy. They even avoid the intense dramatic thrust of that intermediate category called *drame*. They are truly a sampling of characteristic situations undistorted by the usual dramatic pressures, and the spectator can acknowledge with satisfaction that life is like that.

There is, however, one serious weakness in these represen- tations: an unusual lack of vigor in pursuit of definite goals, which is a kind of hallmark of Chekhov's plays. This prevailing pattern of behavior is one of too easy and too ready a capitulation, a kind of aimlessness and spinelessness that does not seem typical of human nature. Other realistic drama shows characters fighting back, carrying on a determined action even though defeat is inevitable. Yet before we subscribe to such an adverse generalization, we must remember that there are vigorous characters in these plays. Natasha and Solyony, and even Olga in *Three Sisters;* Lopakhin in *The Cherry Orchard;* and in *The Seagull* Nina and Treplev's mother, as well as Trigorin, to set off against the failures, the ones who take life lying down. Part of the temptation to succumb to such a false generalization is inherent in the plays. If events are played down and superficial verbal and physical responses give way to those that are more deeply revelatory of essential human nature, we may find it easy to make a false evaluation. We forget that for the most part, and increasingly in the later plays, the Chekhov characters do go on living with some hope and occasional enthusiasm. The difficulty lies in the simultaneity of a long-range and a short-range statement. We cannot seem to entertain them both, yet that is exactly what these plays demand.

When we turn to the general assessment of the philosophical attitudes that underlie Chekhov's works, we are as usual in an area largely of inference. A man of science by training and to a certain degree by professional practice, Chekhov certainly should be expected to have a strong sense of material causality. Two letters written some thirteen years apart support such a supposition. The first, to Suvorin on May 7, 1889, comments with respect to Bourget's *Le Disciple* that he objects to that author's "pretentious crusade against materialism." "Whom is the crusade against, and what is its object? Where is the enemy and what is there dangerous about him? In the first place, the materialistic movement is not a school or a tendency in the narrow journalistic sense; it is not something passing or accidental; it is necessary, inevitable, and beyond the power of man. All that lives on earth is bound to be materialistic. . . . To forbid a man to follow the materialistic line of thought is equivalent to forbidding him to seek truth. Outside matter there is neither knowledge nor experience, and consequently there is no truth." In a letter to S. P. Diaghilev on December 30, 1902, Chekhov asserts that modern culture and current religious trends are at odds, and that truth of the real God is not to be come to "by seeking in Dostoevsky, but by clear knowledge, as one knows twice two are four." Such limited statements are certainly inadequate support for generalization, yet there is nothing in the stories and plays themselves to suggest that we qualify them. Chekhov consistently shows human behavior growing out of material circumstances; even the occasional clinical accounts of nervous states are not presented *in vacuo*. Materiality is everywhere in his works, though we are not smothered by it. Furthermore the ideal is not shown as a separate and opposed entity. The implication throughout is that it is something conceived by man and sought by him, though the chances for achieving it are not great. Frequently, as we have seen, the disparity between what man dreams or infers about his world and the actual situation in which he is permits an ironic thrust, but whereas this irony qualifies human insight and strength, it neither raises nor lowers the ideal from its position as a human creation, an insubstantial but necessary dream.

When we consider causality, we find that Chekhov's position is one of accepting the primacy of the material world without denying the existence or importance of mind. There is no instance where he shows mental events influencing or changing physical events. There is an inevitability and finality about the latter that are inescapable. But the point is that this is not all there is to it. People dream, idealize, and generally respond emotionally, and, from one point of view, illogically. Chekhov does not so much justify this as a means for keeping people going in the face of defeat and despair as he merely attests to the existence of such a component of experience. The protests that he does make on occasion are in the form of the irony at the end of "Gusev," more wry than anguished, as he contemplates the disparity between what men read into the indifferent, external environment as signs and symbols and the crude facts of the material universe, which in this instance provide a near-Darwinian statement of warfare among the species.

As was previously indicated, critics have ascribed many moral, social, and philosophic positions to Chekhov, yet without warrant. We can certainly discern that he was eager for a better life for mankind and that overt instances of cruelty and injustice and even nonfulfillment disturbed him. But it is not to be inferred that he located the ideal outside the human creature; rather it is evident that the ideal is a product of human thought. To the extent that Chekhov saw conditions as they were and presented them bluntly he was not very hopeful. Yet he was not a pessimist, for he recognized an illogical human ability somehow to make the best of things and to find hope even in the midst of despair. He caught the essence of life in a multitude of existences. It is no very great hyperbole to say that his depictions in the short story are as various as life itself.

We cannot help wondering how Chekhov responded to a letter that Gorky wrote him in January 1900, in which Gorky says:

> Do you know what you're doing? You're killing realism. And you'll kill it soon for a long time to come. That form has outlived its time. It's a fact! No one after you can go any further on that path; no one can write so simply about simple things as you can. . . . So there you go, doing away with realism. And I am extremely glad. So be it! And to hell with it![3]

Gorky goes on to say that he wants literature to begin to color life, on the assumption that life will then acquire color. The fact is that Chekhov found color in life, but he did not introduce it from outside. If there is heroism, it resides in the very act of living. If there is excitement, it resides in little things. If there is brilliance, it is in the skill and justice of his depiction. Of all the major practitioners of realism in the nineteenth century Chekhov is the only one who seems not to have been tempted to go beyond it. He did not kill realism, as Gorky hoped, but he certainly made it difficult for those who came after him to excel him. In this evaluation it is Tolstoy who deserves the last word. Writing in *Russia* for July 15, 1904, six weeks after Chekhov's death, he declared: "But this is the main thing. . . . He was unreservedly candid, and that is a great quality; he wrote about what he saw and how he saw it. . . . And because of that unreserved candor he created new, to my mind completely new, forms of writing for the whole world, the like of which I have never met anywhere."[4]

8

Benito Pérez Galdós

Any conception of literary realism that cannot accommodate Galdós should be abandoned as incomplete, for, though elusive and unconventional as a novelist, he gives the impression of seizing reality entire. By his very failure on occasion to adhere to the patterns of realism exactly, he comes close to being the *compleat realist* in the novel that Chekhov is in the short story and the drama.

The world of Galdós is the most extensive of those discussed in this volume, for it springs not only from those novels called "contemporary" but also from the more than fifty historical novels, the *Episodios Nacionales,* on which he was engaged during most of his productive life. Fortunately for the purposes of this study certain of his novels can be singled out as belonging with considerable precision to the realistic period of his writing. This group begins with *La Desheredada* in 1881 and ends with *Misericordia* in 1897. Other novels of contemporary life were written before and after this group and their exclusion helps to define the limits of Galdós's realism. The most important of the earlier works are *Doña Perfecta* (1875) and *La Familia de León Roch* (1878), which, though they show a considerable portion of the materials of everyday life, are basically thesis novels having to do with problems of bigotry and religious mania. These problems are important and they certainly arise from observation of contemporary life, but the novels do not exhibit either the attitudes or the techniques of Galdós the realist. At the other end of the time span the distinction in his novels is less sharp. While the novelist was writing the Torquemada novels and *Misericordia,* he was also writing *Angel Guerra, Tristana, La Loca de la Casa, Nazarín,* and *Halma.* The first of these, written in 1890–91, begins like its immediate predecessors as a close study of a segment of Madrid life, though the protagonist is rather unusual, but it drifts rapidly into an emotional and moral climate that can scarcely be called realistic.

For purposes of our analysis we are left with *La Desheredada, El Amigo Manso, El Doctor Centeno, Tormento, La de Bringas, Lo Prohibido, Fortunata y Jacinta, Miau,* the paired *La Incógnita* and *Realidad,* the four Torquemada novels, which are in effect a single work, and *Misericordia.* We examine these dozen novels to determine the realistic achievement of Galdós, with only casual reference to his other writings as they help to illuminate his ideas or technique.

Physically and temporally the fictional world of these works is Madrid in the last half of the nineteenth century. Of the early novels *La Familia de León Roch* first takes us to Madrid, just as *Angel Guerra,* which begins in Madrid, moves away from the capital to Toledo. In the novels under consideration no major action takes place outside Madrid, which instead draws to itself countless provincials or officials on temporary assignment. Its inhabitants on occasion go for pleasure to Paris, Biarritz, and the watering places of the Cantabrian shore. There is also frequent mention of military and administrative assignments to Cuba and the Philippines, the main purpose of which is to indicate a capacity for financial success or failure on the part of a given character, but the basic action of the novels lies in Madrid. It is an action specifically grounded in the rapidly changing political and social events of the 1860s, 1870s, and 1880s, when it was evident to most observers that the old stability, real or imaginary, was disappearing, and that people, even Spanish people, existed in a world of flux and could have their being only on its terms. This is peculiarly a world of empirical observation; abstractions and absolutes have no place in it.

The range of the Madrid world is presented with remarkable completeness, providing a social panorama that is at least as extensive as that of Zola and which gives the impression of being more faithfully studied than his. The highest levels of society are pretty much cut off—court, government, army, and higher clergy are merely stationary background. But the rest of society is there, to the very lowest depths of the mendicant and shelterless poor. As Ricardo Gullón has pointed out,[1] Galdós largely ignores the way in which people make a living, preferring to emphasize their behavior outside working hours, although we do get a glimpse of Juan Bou's workshop in *La Desheredada* and of the pharmacist's establishment in *Fortunata y Jacinta*. Financial manipulation has its place in this depiction, but there is little of Zola's or Balzac's interest in contemporary industrial and commercial process as a force in a developing society. A Galdós character often has made money in the past—Bueno de Guzmán in *Lo Prohibido* has spent many years in Cádiz amassing a fortune before he comes to Madrid and the dissolute Juanito Santa Cruz lives on money provided by his tradesman father, who is in retirement.

If these novels are noteworthy for their lack of vocational detail, they out-Balzac Balzac in their emphasis on money as a primary fact of social existence. It is in these works that we really come face to face with man as consumer. How he earns his living is subordinate to how much he has to spend, to the shifts and straits to which he is reduced in order to make do with the money he has. Nearly all these novels are dominated by money problems; the characters are illuminated by their attitudes and behavior in respect to money. This is the key to Isidora Rufete in *La Desheredada* rather than her illusion of noble birth. What undoes her is that money runs through her fingers. She has to have what she sees in the shop windows;

she worries about the quality of her shoes; she takes a cab when her poverty makes it imperative that she walk. She falls into the arms of a lover because she despairs of getting money in any other way, and he, a particularly unprepossessing specimen of the *genus Pez,* is equally characterized by his inability to manage money. In *Miau,* a much later novel, there is a full-scale picture of living on nothing a year as the result of Villaamil's losing his government post and the avidity of the women in his family for show and pleasure. Finally in *Misericordia* we sink to the very depths of destitution, to the world of beggars and of the genteel poor, whose existence depends on another form of begging.

No quick summary can do justice to the part that money plays in these novels, to the minute, galling, despairing efforts to make ends meet, to juggle debts, to stave off disaster by improvisation. *Reales, pesetas, duros*—we are constantly totaling them up in our minds, wondering with the fictional characters where the next meal is coming from. In her frantic manipulations, Benina in *Misericordia* is merely the culminating exhibit in the series, the final demonstration of desperation for money. It is the immediacy of this anguish that is important. It is the lack of any other lubricant than money to make society move that is impressed upon us. There is a minimum of abstraction here. Although there are frequent references to the action of the stock exchange, the chaotic condition of the national debt, and the uncertainties of the financial future, these characteristics of the fluctuating, insecure modern society are brought down to earth in terms of personal finance.

From this excursion into the place of money in the Galdós world we return to the segment of the population that is most deprived of it, the very poor, with whom the novelist is truly in his element and in whom his talent for sympathetic portraiture shines forth. He appropriates the slums of the older part of Madrid and re-creates their grim decay with a substantiality equaled by none of his contemporaries. By an accident of history and of terrain this older section hangs on the southern slope of Madrid, the streets angling steeply down to the river, to the gas works, the railroad yards, the slaughterhouse—to the nauseous, ugly offices of a great city. Social movement begins in that section—and often ends there—and there is always the implicit suggestion that it is what is most real, whereas the Paseos, the Retiro, the fairer *barrios* to the north and east are somehow lacking in vitality. The slums incubate suffering and want, but they also have a teeming, never-failing liveliness. Symptomatic of this is the quickly sketched figure of Celipín Centeno, a floater from the provinces who leads a precarious existence in the slums and who at the beginning of *El Doctor Centeno* is seen coming up the path to the Observatory from the depths around the Atocha Station, starving yet obscurely drawn to knowledge and, as it turns out, to food.

Better still, Chapter 6, "Hombres!," of *La Desheredada* gives a detailed picture of children of the slums and of what we now call juvenile delinquency. Since the narrative voice does not scruple to comment, we are told in answer to the question: "Where had all these people come from?" that "They were the discord of the future, a growth on the body of future Spain, and they would have a considerable statistical part to play in the years to come if they were not rid of measles, smallpox, fevers, and rachitic bones. They were the joy and life of the *barrio*, the hope and burden of their parents, deserters rather than alumni of the schools, a stock from which perhaps some useful men would come, but certainly vagabonds and criminals. . . . Bad food and worse clothing reduced them to a sorry level." This comment is hardly necessary, for we see the unhappy slum-dwellers at play, witness the fight, the sudden knife stroke by which "Pecado" kills another of the ragged urchins, and follow him on his desperate flight. *Fortunata y Jacinta* brings us some unforgettable scenes of the poor. Early in the novel Jacinta visits "the fourth estate" on her deluded search for Fortunata's son by Juanito. We see the old town, and particularly the *rastro*, under the guidance of Doña Guillermina, whose apt comment is that to penetrate that world one must have both "caridad y estomago," that is, compassion and guts. In the last of the

Torquemada novels Don Francisco returns to his haunts of earlier days; his meal in a typical inn is one of the high points of Galdós's evocation of the old city.

This predilection for the lower depths of the capital should not cause us to lose sight of the fact that the novelist is a connoisseur of Madrid life as a whole. He is at home on the Paseo de la Castellana or in the Retiro, in the new middle-class residences to the north, and in the aristocratic palaces, including the Palacio Real. Nearly every novel has some unique and striking scene of city life: the disorderly bohemian element in *El Doctor Centeno;* the institution of the wet nurse in *El Amigo Manso;* the labyrinth of the royal palace in *La de Bringas;* three separate and contrasting interiors in *Lo Prohibido;* the lottery, the café, and the Convent of the Micaelas in *Fortunata y Jacinta;* the theater and government offices in *Miau;* a testimonial banquet and the ostentatious Palacio de Gravelinas in *Torquemada en el Purgatorio.* These are not set pieces but flow naturally out of the events of the novels. Galdós on occasion may linger longer than necessary over such scenes, but it is clear that he values them for their own sake as parts of the reality he has undertaken to show in its entirety.

Although he is a historical novelist of stature, Galdós in these works makes no effort to incorporate the figures at the top of the social structure, the actual governors of the state. He does not go even as far as Zola in this respect, but those upper-class figures that do populate his world have a reality equal to that of his lower-class figures, which is not the case with Zola. The evocation of the *genus Pez* is highly stylized but the members of that bureaucratic fraternity are well drawn, as are the various aristocrats and bureaucrats of middling level. The novels teem with these characters, and they are by no means carbon copies of each other. We have only to consider how different from each other are the three members of the fallen Aguila family in the Torquemada series or the differences between the sisters in *Lo Prohibido.* One of the most varied galleries of all is the officials who figure in *Miau,* the novel in which Galdós takes his most prolonged look at the world of lower officialdom.

For the most part Galdós avoids the world of the eccentric and the exotic, with the notable exceptions of Isabel Godoy, Alejandro Miquis' aunt, who is straight out of Dickens, and the blind beggar Almudena in *Misericordia* (although he is reportedly drawn from real life). Less egregious but still troublesome is the priest Polo, Amparo Emperador's inamorato, for whom the mistake is one of treatment. He is well enough individualized at first (though he does bear some resemblance to the prebendary in Leopoldo Alas's *La Regenta*), but he degenerates into the romantic stereotype of the spoiled priest in his relationship with Amparo. Mauricia in *Fortunata y Jacinta* is another questionable exhibit, largely because she is given more attention than her usefulness in the novel warrants. Even if she does work as a foil to Fortunata by showing the toughness that is natural to women of the people, her deathbed agonies are too detailed and too harrowing. On the whole, these figures and others like them are only minor lapses on Galdós's part. The world presented is very much of a piece; the eye of the narrator-observer never strays for long from the average human being of the milieu under study. It is this fact that makes it possible to draw a reasonably acceptable line between the Madrid novels and Galdós's earlier and later works, such as *Angel Guerra*, where the emphasis has shifted to the exceptional case.

Another way to check the normality of Galdós's depictions is to ask what happens to his characters, to what extent the pattern of their existence conforms to that of ordinary existence. *How* the author conducts an action is considered later; the *what* of the actions is properly examined here. At first glance he comes off badly in this respect. The fallen woman is a stereotype that is best avoided. The fallen woman who claims to be the heiress of a noble house and who is denied her rights by egotistical pride of race is straight out of cheap fiction. Nonetheless this basic intrigue of *La Desheredada* is made to serve a conception that in itself is perfectly valid, if a little obvious. The novel is not studying Isidora Rufete in the first instance, but is concerned with the effects of a faulty understanding of life and a false relation to it, citing Isidora's case as evidence. It certainly errs in the choice of materials for this demonstration because they are much too high-flown and romantic to engage our belief. However, Isidora's claim to noble birth is a self-generated illusion and her downfall comes from her refusal to live in the real world. Viewed in this way, the novel becomes more acceptable, especially since there is the parallel case of Mariano, her brother, who is the victim of another set of illusions, and the contrasting figure of Augusto Miquis, who counsels seeing the world as it is and coming to terms with it. *Tormento* also uses stereotyped action but manages to end on a matter-of-fact note. The passional domination of Don Pedro Polo over Amparo, his "tormento," is left in the obscure and sinister realm of diabolic power. This contradicts everything the novel shows about Amparo, not to mention the generally realistic milieu portrayed, and it surprises the reader as much as it does Caballero, Amparo's suitor. However, the novel does work the problem out legitimately. If Amparo cannot marry Caballero she can be his mistress and they can live happily in Bordeaux, if not in Madrid. In short, a fall from virtue is neither glossed over nor punished. Sentimentality is neatly deflated by a commonsense ending, though for a moment it threatens to prevail when Amparo attempts suicide.

It is important to see Galdós as a novelist who in taking human experience as his subject matter and an external dramatic representation as his method never reduces his characters to the status of puppets. There is feeling, there is turbulence, and there is inconsistency within them. The Galdós characters act on no mathematical principle of logic. They contradict themselves, and they lash out savagely at others and at the heavens. There is a felt, if not always visible, freightage of emotive life, which is part and parcel of the whole man, an indispensable ingredient of reality as it is presented by this novelist, whose works, contemporary with those of Zola, eschew the mechanical demonstration of the latter and incline in the direction of Chekhov, whose works he did not yet know.

Like other spontaneous realists Galdós owed his world to observation. Madrid was his literary province as well as the arena of his own life. He was a journalist and politician as well as a writer. He fused a sense of past and present history with a feeling for contemporary phenomena. No writer ever exhibited a stronger sense of place; no writer has been more curious about the various existences around him, and none, it would appear, has had a surer eye and ear for details of behavior and speech. There is no evidence that he labored to fill capacious notebooks, but there is every indication that his mind was such a notebook, overflowing with materials drawn from observation ready to spill upon the page and form the substance of his novels.[2]

As a technician, Galdós has been the despair of conventional critics, some of whom have gone so far as to say that he did not write novels. Such reservations resolve themselves satisfactorily if we see him, in the works under consideration, as avoiding fixed forms in the interest of a verisimilitude that conventions of the novel do much to negate. This looseness of form is characteristic of all his realistic works; he never writes by formula. He commits follies we may wish undone, but they are in the interest of life and vividness, not the result of adherence to sterile and constricting rules. In general, his body of work always strains toward the dramatic as the most direct and faithful path to realism. From this point of view it is reasonable to look upon the *novelas contemporáneas* as a single sprawling work given over to the depiction of life in Madrid during a period of about thirty years. The novelist dips into this stream at will, or, better, he concentrates now on one section, now on another, of the figured tapestry that undulates before him. His novels have a cohesiveness that is more convincing than that provided by the analytical structure of the Rougon-Macquart or by the forced unity of *La Comédie Humaine*. Sometimes the novels flow into each other. *El Doctor Centeno* has a subsidiary interest in Don Pedro Polo and Amparo Emperador. *Tormento* brings them to the foreground, with Amparo as protagonist in an action involving the de Bringas family. Then in *La de Bringas* that family becomes the protagonist, while Amparo recedes to the background and her sister Refugio, "la del diente menos" ("the one with the missing tooth"), steps forward. Although this particular grouping does not go beyond this latter novel, Refugio does turn up again as the mistress of Juan Pablo Rubín in *Fortunata y Jacinta*. Another major character complex is provided by the Torquemada novels, in which, although the main characters are new, there is an intermediate attachment to *Fortunata y Jacinta* through the death of Doña Lupe. Even Isidora Rufete turns up here as one of Torquemada's clients from an earlier day.

Even more important for the unity of these works is the host of background figures who function in most of them or link at least some of them together. An excellent example is Dr. Augusto Miquis, who appears in six of the novels under discussion plus *Angel Guerra* and *Tristana*. We see him as a young medical student with Isidora, and he appears as a famous doctor later on. We become acquainted with his brother Alejandro in *El Doctor Centeno* and his brother Constantino in *Lo Prohibido*. They are all somewhat whimsically given roots in El Toboso, which is in La Mancha—Quijote country. Even more ubiquitous is the Pez family. They are introduced, somewhat awkwardly, in an ironic sermon on the *genus Pez* early in *La Desheredada*, where they are exhibited as an unscrupulous, egotistical, office-holding breed. (Tolstoy offers much the same kind of exhibit with the Kuragin family in *War and Peace*, but without the elaborate disquisition.) The head of the family appears in nine novels but has an important role only in *La de Bringas*. Some ten members of the family appear fleetingly here and there, but only the eldest son, Joaquín is individualized.

Every novel has a few characters who carry over from or go forward to other novels, so that an impression of continuity and cohesiveness is conveyed. This rarely seems artificial, though the reader is likely to be taken aback when in *Misericordia*

Benina is confused by the slumdwellers with the energetically charitable Doña Guillermina from *Fortunata y Jacinta*. In general, because their roles are minor and their personalities are not intrusive, these background figures give the impression that this Madrid and these people exist, that the reader may run into them on the street at any time. They help also to enhance the authenticity of the major figures, who are often completely new. If the latter have been instrumental in helping a Pez on the road to a sinecure or have borrowed money from Torquemada or have been attended in illness by Dr. Miquis or have appeared at a social gathering with any of fifty background figures, this fact serves immediately as a passport to authentic existence.

Reinforcing this sense of continuity and verisimilitude are two other devices, use of precise topographical detail and the presence of precise chronological reference, particularly with respect to historical events. The streets and buildings of the capital are described in exact detail. The perambulations of the characters can be followed on a city plan. There is a genuine relish in the evocation of the stones and bricks of the old town, with a somewhat more casual summoning up of the middle-class districts. Galdós surpasses the achievement of Jules Romains in parts of *Les Hommes de Bonne Volonté*; he is equaled only by James Joyce in *Ulysses*. If the building described is no longer standing, he tells us so, indicating that it was pulled down at such and such a time and describing what has been erected in its place. Even the vacant lots where Villaamil and Federico Viera die take on character. City landmarks like the Segovia viaduct or the various churches and monasteries have personality.

Similarly, if less insistently, we are always in historical time. The events of *El Doctor Centeno* begin precisely on February 10, 1864, for the young hero has just witnessed the funeral procession of Calvo Asensio. *Tormento* takes place in 1867, and *La de Bringas* takes place in 1868, for it was in February of that year that Don Francisco secured his new position and moved his family to the Royal Palace. *Lo Prohibido* begins in 1880 with a carefully dated account of Bueno de Guzmán's previous life in Cádiz. Torquemada buys a house in the Calle de San Blas "in the year of the revolution." Weather is carefully identified, such as the excessively cold winter of a given year. Such instances are legion but they are not excessive. The reader comes to expect them as an unobtrusive tie with the world of fact.

Some discrimination is necessary when we consider how a historical event becomes a referent of more than background utility. Whereas Galdós as a historical novelist in the *Episodios Nacionales* arranges the fabric of events and personalities with the purpose of illuminating history, he has a different aim in the *novelas contemporáneas,* in which the actual events of the disturbed era of dynastic instability are a given but are not themselves subject to examination or dramatization. However, they do on occasion serve as a correlative for the experience of the fictional characters. This is not a consistent practice, but it is very effective when it is employed. In *La Desheredada* a connection is made between the violence of the boys playing at bullfighting in the slums and the instability of political institutions: "Tired of playing at bull-fighting, we are now playing at civil war." The short-lived rule of Amadeo of Savoy comes to an end as Isidora is forced to relinquish her illusions about her noble origin, and she dramatizes her plight by thinking of herself as an abdicating queen. In *La de Bringas* the household revolution that occurs when Doña Rosalía escapes the iron-willed financial control of her husband is paralleled by the actual revolution which drives Queen Isabel from her throne and brings the de Bringas' security to an end. In *Fortunata y Jacinta* there is considerable use of this device. Early in the novel Estupiñá's life is recounted in terms of the political events that he has witnessed. The abdication of Amadeo and the public events of 1874 (including even quotations on the stock exchange) form the backdrop for Fortunata's change of fortune. Later on, the restoration of Alfonso XII has its parallel in two other "restorations," that of Juanito Santa Cruz to family respectability and that of Fortunata to the bed and board of her husband.

These historical parallels contribute to the reader's sense of the fluidity and mobility of contemporary society, which are the constant preoccupation of these works. When we consider the use of other techniques to this end, we are immediately struck by the fact that Galdós is something of a dissident with respect to the realist doctrine of narrator-withdrawal and impersonality. Throughout the novels there is obviously a degree of awkwardness and uncertainty about where to stand in relation to events. In the first group of historical novels with which he made his debut as a novelist Galdós was content to use a first-person narrator who, sometimes by a considerable stretching of probability, was present at all the important happenings of the Napoleonic wars or, when credibility would have been strained too far, received eyewitness reports from others. In three of the contemporary novels Galdós likewise employs the first-person narrator of distinctive personality. In *El Amigo Manso* the title character, a professor of philosophy, gives an account of his unsuccessful involvement in life. The theme is highly particularized; the appeal is primarily to sentiment and not to social observation; the technique breaks down into fantasy at the end when Manso comments on the present state of things from his vantage point beyond the grave. Similarly in *Lo Prohibido*, which is also somewhat specialized in its depiction of the successive illicit affairs of the narrator-protagonist, Bueno de Guzmán, by nature a prudent and reflective man, is able to view events in an impersonal way as he puts them down for the record when his health and fortune have been undermined and he is waiting for death. In a third case, *La Incógnita*, we also have a first-person narrative, this time with the use of the epistolary form, which because it is withdrawn and analytical distances events.

These, however, are all special cases. The usual narrative stance is a compromise, and a fairly individual one. By predilection Galdós stops short of impersonal, omniscient narration.[3] Instead he uses an impersonal and unspecified first person, thus investing the novels with a degree of warmth and quasi-personality but at the same time ensuring some objectivity of approach. In this way we get a sort of guarantee of the accuracy of the events recounted. This is particularly the case in *La de*

Bringas and in *Fortunata y Jacinta.* In the former we are
introduced to the palace labyrinth directly by the narrator, who
speaks of "The first time that Don Manuel Pez and I went to
visit de Bringas in his new domicile," and continues with a
running description of getting lost in the maze of corridors and
stairways. The novel thereafter proceeds in the normal third-
person fashion, with occasional reminders of the narrator's
existence by interpolations such as "For my part, I confess . . ."
or "In our day the marvelous exists just as it did in the past, only
angels have changed their name and appearance and never
come in by the keyhole." At the end of the novel, however, we
come back to the narrator as a distinct person when he indicates
that after the revolution it was he who was designated custodian
of the palace, thus bringing him into close contact with the de
Bringas family again and rounding off the narrative on a
personal note.

Fortunata y Jacinta begins with a description of Juanito
Santa Cruz: "The earliest information I have about the person
who bears this name was given me by Jacinto María Villalon-
ga." When Estupiñá appears, we are told: "When I personally
became acquainted with this worthy son of Madrid, he was
already nearing 70." Once the novel is under way there is only
an occasional reminder of the presence of this narrator, as, for
example: "Jacinta has told me that one night she became so
upset. . . ." Sometimes these interruptions are very self-
conscious, as when, introducing the hallucinations of Mauricia
la Dura, the narrator says: "It is very burdensome for the
historian to find himself obliged to mention many details and
circumstances which are completely puerile." There are also
intrusions of social commentary strictly from the standpoint of
an impersonal observer but attributable to the first-person
narrator. In fact, there may be justification for such practice:
such comments are less obtrusive if they emanate from a
known, if shadowy, personality. This approach is characteristic
also of the four Torquemada novels. In the opening section the
first-person narrator is identified as a novelist who has given
other accounts of Madrid life. Except for some tiresome

authorial byplay in *Torquemada en el Purgatorio,* the narrator withdraws increasingly as the work develops, and he vanishes entirely in the last part.

From this description it is clear that Galdós does not make a fetish of authorial withdrawal but that he does on the whole move toward the position taken by other realists. The net effect of this impersonal first person is to reduce distance as well as to attest to facts. The latter is unimportant, for by Galdós's day such efforts to guarantee truth were decidedly old-fashioned. But the reduction of distance is important; it does much to remove the sense of human insignificance and ugliness about which many readers of realistic works complain. Moreover, commentary, if held to a level of objective observation of social data and process, can be tolerated except when it is self-conscious or mannered, as in the sermon on the *genus Pez* at the beginning of *La Desheredada.*

As was suggested earlier, Galdós had a strong predilection for dramatic presentation, which carried him away from the novel to the play in his later years. This is partly the result of the fact that he had an unusually accurate ear for varieties of speech at all levels of society. It is a curious experience to go back to *La Familia de León Roch* or forward to *Angel Guerra* after an immersion in the realistic novels and discover that the speech in these other works rings false, especially in the former, which is stiff and literary in many of the dialogue scenes. It is evident that Galdós delights in the speech of his realistic characters and that this speech, while avoiding obscenity and profanity, has rich variety. Not only does he make use of the stock devices of malapropism, popular mispronunciation, and overuse of pretentious locutions, but he has a fine ear for dialectal variation when there is occasion to use it. Many of his finest effects depend entirely on language, usually on contrasts of speech indicating contrasts of social level, as between Torquemada and Cruz del Aguila and others of her birth and education, or between young Centeno and the group of young men whom he encounters in the bohemian world of Alejandro Miquis.

This interest and ability lead naturally to the use of dialogue scene, which is the very stuff of which the novels are made. Some of the novels open with such scenes. *La Desheredada* begins with the monologue of Rufete, develops a hospital scene by means of descriptive detail, and upon the entrance of Isidora comes back to dialogue for a single long action covering some thirty pages. In *El Doctor Centeno* there is first a description of the starving boy's climb up to the Observatory, enlivened with a kind of interior monologue. This is followed by a passage almost entirely in dialogue with Miquis and the others, then by several pages of description ending in more dialogue. The sequence of initial presentations in *La de Bringas* is very subtle. First there is a bit of symbolic description of the ridiculous miniature tomb made by Don Francisco for his patron, Don Manuel Pez, followed by a dialogue scene in which he shows his masterpiece, and finally an expository passage. *Misericordia* begins with the unforgettable scene of the beggars at the doors of San Sebastián, but this is more descriptive than dramatic. Actually one of the best opening scenes is in *Angel Guerra,* in which the protagonist seeks asylum with Dulcenombre. Although they contain many spirited scenes, the longer novels are perhaps the least sustained in dramatic presentation. *Fortunata y Jacinta* contains a high proportion of straight narrative. The Torquemada novels vary. The first is expository and the second begins dramatically with the death of Doña Lupe, then gives up scenic treatment for a while, but returns to it in the middle. The last two of these novels depend largely on narrative interrupted by big scenes.

The specific pattern of the novels is less important and less impressive than their overall suggestion of dramatic treatment. Except for a few instances of overly dense exposition there is nothing to impede the fluid, dramatic movement. Since Galdós's arrangement of chapter divisions offers little guidance, we tend to remember the novels in terms of scenic blocks. In part this is the result of the vivid historical and topographical detail, but it is also the result of the tendency to present actions economically in dramatic form. There are a number of occasions where the novels suddenly give up novelistic form entirely and use the format of the play. (This is without regard for *Realidad, La Loca de la Casa,* and other late works that are presented as plays.) Galdós in his preface to *El Abuelo* discusses this procedure, explaining that he wishes to give "the greatest scope possible, on this occasion, to the dialogue process and to restrict description and narrative forms to a minimum." As he points out:

> The dialogue system, already adopted in *Realidad,* permits a quick and substantive presentation of characters. These are born, given body, and, we may say, enabled to imitate living beings most readily when they manifest their moral quality in their own words and thereby, as in real life, provide us with the more or less high and sharp relief of their actions. In general terms, the author's words when he narrates or describes do not have as great effectiveness or give as direct an impression of spiritual truth. By means of the mysterious virtue of dialogue it seems that we can see and hear the actions and the actors without extraneous interference, and we can more readily forget the hidden artist who offers us an ingenious imitation of Nature. Although the artist can be more or less concealed, he never disappears entirely, nor do the makers of a picture succeed completely in concealing him, however skillfully composed the pictures may be. Authorial impersonality, prescribed today by some as an artistic system, is no more than an empty emblem on literary banners which, if they wave triumphantly, do so only because of the vigorous personality of the captains who upraise them in their hands.

This kind of presentation is clearly experimental and it is offered sparingly. What is more usual is that scenes can frequently be seen to be organized as if for the stage. Scenes of popular life are often of this nature, for example, the scene between Isidora and La Sanguijuelera as they discuss a trip to the pawnshop, or the wet nurse scene in *El Amigo Manso.* There are many outstanding scenes: the visit of Rosalía de Bringas to Refugio, who plays with her mercilessly before she lends the money Rosalía must have, and the confrontation between Fortunata and Jacinta, though this is marred by a conventional eavesdropping trick. Yet overall it is not the individual scenes, brilliant as they may be, which give dramatic tone to the novels. It is the proportion of dialogue, the ease and fluidity with which narration merges into patches of dramatic speech. Whatever Galdós's uneasiness about the legitimacy of the authorial voice, he is not self-conscious about moving back and forth from summary narrative to direct presentation, usually accompanied by a minimum of expository material. The scenic intensity of these novels makes one think of *War and Peace,* except that Galdós presents fewer people at a time and does not create the mosaic that is the Tolstoy scene. Since there is also less obvious forward propulsion in these Spanish novels, they depend for their vitality on the simultaneous rendering of what the bystander sees and hears. In effect, what we have here is a new free form capable of great versatility and almost free of artificiality and contrivance.

When we ask ourselves how these novels as wholes are put together, what characteristic structures are to be found in them, the answer is that they are surprisingly unstructured, that in their tendency toward free improvisation, toward avoidance of formal plot patterns, they are almost not novels at all. This is another reason why the novels ending with *León Roch* and beginning with *Angel Guerra* have been left out of this discussion. They are structured, they do develop, and they are resolved. Whatever sampling from the stream of life occurs in them, the materials so gathered are forcibly shaped.

El Amigo Manso, Lo Prohibido, and *La Incógnita,* the three novels with a specific first-person narrator, are by this fact subject to a degree of shaping that is exceptional in the contemporary novels. In the first two of these novels a termination is imposed by the death of the narrator, and the substance of the novel is what he has learned from his involvement in a series of events, in both cases counter to his previous experience. In the third work the substance is what the narrator has observed of a mysterious situation and his failure adequately to assess it. In other words, the presence of this kind of narrator almost inevitably leads to a conclusion, a judgment. (As we have seen, Tolstoy's *Family Happiness* is a parallel case, for Masha is writing after the fact and what she recalls is structured by what she now understands. This kind of novel may avoid explicit judgment by recourse to irony, as in Robert Herrick's *Memoirs of an American Citizen*, in which the narrator-protagonist recounts actions that to him seem logical and virtuous and is unable to understand the opprobrium with which they are received.) Granting the necessity of some sort of judgment in these three Galdós novels, the conclusion nonetheless seems less important than the experience on which it is based. Manso's loss of Irene to the younger man is a matter of no great moment, and if the novel is a psychological study it falls of its own weight, or lack of it. Rather it is best understood as exhibiting a segment of Madrid life from a certain limited viewpoint, the very limitations of which illuminate more sharply than an objective view would do. As in all of Galdós's novels there is social movement and transformation here, with which the static position of Manso is incompetent to deal. He can tutor Manolo Peña and give him intellectual nurture and social gloss, but he cannot turn him into a philosopher, a fact that is underlined by the contrasting speeches of mentor and disciple at the charity fête.

Much the same judgment is to be made of *Lo Prohibido*, which is an examination of middle-class mores from the standpoint of a libertine. Bueno de Guzmán is an intriguing personality. By hard work and commercial probity he has put himself in a position where he can indulge his unprincipled sexuality in the easygoing society of Madrid. Not only is he an adulterer but his chosen targets are his three cousins—forbidden fruit from both a social and a moral point of view. In a way this is Zola's *La Curée* translated to Spain and presented in a less hectic and therefore more convincing form. The mainspring of the action is not passion, but money: money by means of which Bueno de Guzmán can suborn, and money with which his victims, Eloisa in particular, can debauch themselves. It is proper enough that as the narrator becomes more and more sexually besotted he should lose his financial judgment and undermine the reputation he has built up. It is ironic that he should leave what remains of his fortune to the child of Camila, the one who has been proof against his golden lures.

As we might expect, *La Desheredada* is the most conceptually organized of the novels and the most undermined by traditional romantic elements. In its subject, the gap between illusion and reality, it makes one think of *Madame Bovary*, which Flaubert handled with greater psychological truth but with less richness in the evocation of the constricting circumstances of everyday life. Something of the same difficulty is present in *Tormento*, the basic pattern of which is a simple contrast between Amparo Emperador and her sister Refugio, with a further contrast with Rosalía de Bringas, in a world in which *things* are important. Refugio has no illusions. Since nobody respects the poor working girl, she has no intention of wearing herself out at the sewing machine when there are quicker and more rewarding paths to luxury. Rosalía de Bringas wants luxury on a level of respectability and has no idea of the price that must be paid for it. Amparo is a decent, modest girl, uncomplaining about her servitude in the de Bringas household and tiresomely conventional in her insistence that Refugio follow her path. Into this group of women comes Don Agustín Caballero, who has made a fortune in Mexico and now seeks a conventional life of wealth and domestic responsibility in Spain. His wealth further addles Rosalía, and his admiration for Amparo and his proposal of marriage are taken by the worldly as evidence that she has spread a careful net and has landed a big fish, whereas the simple fact is that the proposal is a recognition of her virtue. She cannot bring herself to reveal her past to Caballero, who naturally hears of it from others and repudiates her. Since he loves her too much to give her up, he carries her off to Bordeaux as his mistress, where they live happily ever after in sin to the envy and indignation of Rosalía. There can be no quarrel with the conclusion: This is the way of the world. However, the working out of the plot owes too much to contrivance and stereotype.

On the whole, the other novels escape such a charge. They eddy and flow about the reader in such a way as to suggest that they are miscellaneous fragments of life that the author observes. They impose themselves by their vividness and variety rather than by their novelistic neatness. They are differentiated from each other chiefly by the social milieu on which they focus, even as they merge together to make up the totality of life in Madrid in the Isabeline and Alfonsine period.

In *Fortunata y Jacinta,* however, there is a kind of symmetry that is rare in Galdós, probably necessitated by the very broad scope of the novel. Although the implications of the title are misleading—Fortunata is more important and more closely studied than Jacinta—there is a continual relationship between the two in the contrast of mistress and wife and in the compulsion of the latter to adopt the child of her husband and his inamorata, an effort at which she fails in the beginning of the novel and at which she succeeds at the end. There is a forward movement in the successive encounters of the two women, or rather in the expectation of a meeting between them. But beyond this minimal shaping the novel sprawls to such an extent that it is no doubt out of balance. It grows by accretion of personalities. Because Maximiliano Rubín falls in love with Fortunata we become acquainted with his two brothers, neither of whom is strictly relevant to the course of the novel, and with his aunt, Doña Lupe, "la de los pavos" ("the turkey woman"), who is one of Galdós's finest creations. Fortunata's stay in the Convento de las Micaelas brings her into contact with Doña Guillermina, who is also attached to the Santa Cruz group. Fortunata's flight from her husband brings her into relationship with Don Evaristo Feijoo; her later flight before the birth of her child takes her to the slums and still another group of memorable people.

The four Torquemada novels are another instance of this accretive process. The first, *Torquemada en la Hoguera,* is a brief sketch, almost Maupassantian in its irony. The other three have continuity of event and social observation. They are built on a contrast between the Aguila family, true aristocrats, and the rich but self-made peer that Torquemada becomes. Once the mechanism of making Torquemada over is set in motion, the novel goes where it will in the interest of an accurate and varied depiction of contemporary life. This, rather than the frequently praised *Fortunata y Jacinta,* is probably Galdós's finest work, precisely because it is unprogrammatic, even wayward, in its sampling of Madrid life.

The other two novels in the group, *Miau* and *Misericordia,* also present the novelist at his creative best, although in quite different ways. *Miau* is more concentrated on a single figure than the other novels and gives a considerable portrait of the unhappy Villaamil, who has lost his official employment only a few months before he would have been eligible for retirement on a pension and whose vain efforts lead him to bitterness and suicide. These events seem to make up the novel, and yet one begins to wonder if that is really so. The grandson, Luis Cadalso; the wife, the sister-in-law, and the daughter, whose catlike faces lead to the sobriquet, *las Miaus;* and Victor, the worthless and scheming son-in-law—are all in themselves interesting and enduring creations. Yet their roles are pretty much confined to what they contribute as background to the central figure and the tone of the work is of a rare uniformity, a symphony of increasing discord ending in despair. As for *Misericordia,* Benina, the servant whose devotion leads her to become a beggar in order to support her querulous mistress, is the central figure, but she shares the stage with the army of illusionists whom she serves.

The reader's overall impression is that these Madrid novels constitute a single amorphous work which the reader can enter at any of the vantage points offered by the beginning of a novel, without prejudice to his understanding of the whole. There is no evidence of program here, deliberate or spurious—as in the case of Balzac. One feels that there is an abundance and an endless reservoir of material that would permit the author to go on indefinitely, offering more examples of this life. If there is an art of the cross section here, it is not deliberate or at all sustained. But the total effect is one of a cross section in which all elements of contemporary society are exhibited with the exception of the clergy, whose presence in the novels is less than it is in the society being examined. The memorable characters in these works are drawn from all ages and conditions; the child, Luisito Cadalso; the adolescent, Celipín Centeno; young men like Manola Peña, Rafael del Aguila, and Alejandro Miquis; young women like Fortunata, Jacinta, Amparo, and Refugio; people in middle life like Francisco and Rosalía de Bringas; old people in great number, to mention only José de Relimpio, Ramón Villaamil, Guillermina Pacheco, Doña Lupe, and Benina. With these people in mind we dare not say that Galdós's forte is the depiction of middle-class society or of proletarian society, for he is at home with both and moves with ease from one to the other.

What is most striking about this gallery of portraits, this array of lives lived in detailed down-to-earth terms, is their psychological vitality. Feeling, the affective accompaniment of visible action, has a prominent place in their depiction, producing an aura of human sympathy for which the author has been justly acclaimed. This is not unlike what Tolstoy achieved, but the means are different. Tolstoy's authorial withdrawal is more consistently maintained; he brings warmth and sympathy in spite of distance. In Galdós's novels point of view is a main determinant of this effect. We must speculate that one reason he could not bring himself to use the truly impersonal third-person point of view is that he wanted to put his readers as close as possible to persons and events. Certainly this was the case in the *Episodios Nacionales,* which by their immediacy qualified at once as popular textbooks of history. In the novels of contemporary life, in which the third person is predominant, the attitude of the ubiquitous but unspecified narrators is consistently one of interest in human destinies, of sympathy for human folly and failure, and of recognition of weakness or evil without any temptation to castigate it or even underline it. We are never really told that Juanito Santa Cruz is vicious; except for his relationship with Fortunata his extramarital adventures are kept in shadow. When castigation comes, it comes from the mouth of Jacinta, and we feel almost a sneaking sympathy for the guilty man who has been found out. It would be improper to say that the narrator's attitude is one of skepticism—it is too warm for that—but it surely is not one of sentimentality or illusion.

As has been already indicated, the admission of mental and emotional life as necessary constituents of human portrayal contributes to the warmth of the picture. This is not to deny that the prevailing approach is external; we see actions, we listen to dialogue, and we are informed of external circumstances and events. But we are not usually confined to these. One of the great scenes in *La Desheredada,* in which technique is as yet uncertain, is that of "Pecado," Isidora's brother, playing in the slums with other underprivileged boys. Their play turns to altercation, and "Pecado" knifes a companion in an outburst of anger. But the narrative does not stop there; the event is capped by insight into the boy's emotions. We do not merely have a picture of a young animal at bay—this is not Jeanlin of *Germinal*—but we also learn that "Pecado," even in his fright and hunger, knows that he has done wrong and regrets his action. We do not enter directly into his mind, but a balance is maintained in our view of him. Somewhat similar is the effort to show Isidora's feelings after the passage of some years of disordered social and moral existence, where a chapter of declamatory rhetorical questions ends with the comment: "Whether this be the voice of Isidora's conscience or the indiscreet questioning of the author, what was written is true." Another form of thought summary is found in the correlation between Isidora's feelings about having to give up her claim on Aransis lineage and her identification with the abdicating queen. A more contrived instance of the same kind in *Fortunata y Jacinta* is Ido's mania about his wife's infidelity—though his suspicions are completely absurd—which acts as a means of indicating what Jacinta must feel about Juanito's behavior and what Maximiliano evidently does feel about Fortunata's.

Many characters clearly share in the quality explicitly ascribed to Maximiliano of living "two existences: that of daily bread and that of chimeras." This is true of Jacinta when she convinces herself that she has found Juanito's child, and it is almost continuously true of Fortunata. It is a perfect description of the state of Isidora Rufete, who ceases to exist when this duality becomes impossible, or so she thinks. It is applicable to Villaamil in his compulsive pursuit of bureaucratic justice, and to his daughter Abelarda, who is charmed into amorous intoxication by her unscrupulous brother-in-law. It is the permanent state of Almudena, although in his case the duality is almost erased by his capacity for dreams and self-delusion that loses sight of "daily bread." This is true also of other characters in *Misericordia,* where the shadowy life of make-believe is what sustains them until the forced resolution of the denouement. The case of Torquemada is particularly revealing in this respect. He never ceases to be the down-to-earth man of the people who has grappled with actuality on its own terms and mastered it insofar as it is possible to do so. Yet, in his social transformation, in his acquisition of great wealth, in his receiving of honors and adulation, he too lives a life of illusion. There are times when he is so caught up in it that we fear he is being made into a dupe, but then we discover that it is part of the role he is playing to appear to be a dupe while maintaining a healthy perspective and turning the tables on his would-be manipulators. This is in contrast with the brother-in-law, Rafael del Aguila, for whom chimeras get in the way of his daily bread and whose blindness must be seen to have symbolic relevance, as it undoubtedly does also in the case of Almudena.

Since the life of the mind and of the emotions was credited with such importance, the novelist was bound to attempt a variety of ways to reproduce it. The opening scene of *La Desheredada* briefly reproduces the dying Rufete's ravings, which are described as "headlong and diffuse," but which are actually logical in organization. The whole of Chapter 11 of that novel is an interior monologue by Isidora after her visit to the Aransis palace, presented without any introductory framework. Her monologue is a summary of her thoughts during a sleepless night rather than a transcript of a block of continuous thought, but it contains the essential discontinuity of ideas of the interior monologue without providing the associative links. Whatever its crudity of execution, it is an effective externalization of her inner state. Something like this occurs in one of the pseudo-dramatic scenes between Isidora and Joaquín Pez, in which Pez *solo* utters a soliloquy; then a bit later while he sleeps, Isidora muses over her life and wardrobe in another near interior monologue. *La de Bringas* offers a similar range of techniques: Rosalía's thoughts about Pez (Chapter 17) are well formulated and logical, whereas her thoughts about him as she falls asleep (Chapter 19) are summarized, as indicated by the past tense and third person. Later on, after she has given herself to him, there is a paragraph of interior monologue followed by one of summary consciousness (Chapter 44). The intensity of *Miau* is mirrored internally in the case of Victor Cadalso during a sleepless night: "And in a short time, his eyes closed, his brow furrowed, and in the manner of some somnambulists he mentally reproduced the situations which he could not put out of his mind." There follows an intense, spasmodic, but not really disorganized monologue. Abelarda Villaamil also has a reverie, which the narrator characterizes as "an endless and disordered monologue," that comes much closer to the interior monologue in its use of the associative process.

Certainly Galdós has a considerable range in reproducing mental states. He uses directed exposition introduced by "he thought," "he felt," and the like; there is summary of consciousness indicated by the past tense and third person; there are the conventional soliloquy and aside; there is interior monologue, or something close to it; and there is fantasy, such as Luis Cadalso's conversations with God. The latter is one of the extravagances that have brought Galdós's realism into question, since it falls into the category of invention, not observation. In general, in spite of the intensity of the inner experience of some of the characters, these attempts to represent inwardness are minimal in quantity. Such passages are rarely long, being rather emphatic points in the generally dramatic external representation. They certainly do not suggest that what goes on in the mind takes precedence over what is external. Galdós is not an innovator in this area, but neither does he shear off the mental states of his characters in favor of a strictly behavioristic depiction. He keeps what is basically an external type of novel in balance with a sufficient recognition of internal elements.

The freedom that Galdós allows himself in the way of intrusive commentary produces some interesting observations on literary and social topics. Since his cast of mind is strictly empirical and not theoretical, philosophical statements are less frequent and less revealing of his intellectual position. The literary commentary is useful because it shows an awareness of the tenets and purposes of realism and the amusement that romantic extravagance provokes. Toward the end of *La Desheredada* in a dialogue passage between Isidora and Joaquín the latter says: "Novelists have brought a multitude of erroneous ideas into the world. They falsify life and should therefore all be sent to jail." At the end of *El Doctor Centeno* there is a spirited and highly stylized dialogue between the young protagonist and one Ido, a writer of fiction, which makes fun of the shallowness and pretensions of nonrealistic fiction. This is picked up again in Chapter 10 of *Tormento,* where Refugio comments on the gap between popular plots about orphans and the actual circumstances of herself and her sister. The most interesting comment of this kind is made in *Torquemada en Purgatorio* by Fidela, who considers even novels of the naturalistic type to be figurative and conventional, to be made up of things hypothetical, lying, and fantastic, so that "Between the novels which most sought the truth and the truth of life itself, Fidela always saw an abyss." She confessed to a preference for memoirs, accounts of what happened to the one who wrote them, even when they were heavy and full of stupidity like those of Chateaubriand.

Several of the first-person narrators have opinions about what novels should contain. Manso declares: "Idylls from balcony to balcony do not enter into my program, nor is what I am recounting anything more than a very ordinary instance of life. . . ." Bueno de Guzmán points out that he is not a hero but "the product of my age and race, and in fatal harmony with the milieu in which I live. . . ." He assures his readers that there is nothing set down by him which is not scrupulously in accord with fact: "I did not wish to contravene the rules that I laid down for myself from the beginning, and I have fully recorded my prosaic adventures in Madrid. . . ." The epistolary narrator of *La Incógnita* gives assurance that he will not try to dress up the nudity of reality, adding in Chapter 14 that "I faithfully observe, make corrections where necessary, put in and leave out what reality forces me to . . . and I pursue objective truth, sacrificing the subjective, which is usually a false idol created by our minds so that they may adore themselves in effigy." In all fairness, since this novel in its search for truth comes off less well than its counterpart, *Realidad,* we must acknowledge a somewhat contradictory remark made by Augusta in the latter: ". . . I am commonly inclined to admit the extraordinary, because in that way it seems to me I am better able to interpret reality, which is a great inventor, an artist always fecund and original."

These remarks should not be taken too seriously, but they do indicate awareness of the realistic current in literature toward the end of the century. There are, however, a few statements carrying Galdós's personal authority. He early observed in an article that "we Spaniards are not good observers, and on that account we lack the principal virtue necessary for the creation of the modern novel . . . we are unbridled idealists and take more pleasure in imagination than observation. . . ."

In a 1901 essay on Leopoldo Alas, he met the problem of naturalism head on, insisting that it was nothing but "the repatriation of an old idea," though "radically disfigured," and concluding that it was not the dangerous phenomenon which conservative criticism had made of it:

> When it was seen that there was neither danger nor system, nor indeed novelty, but that we had had the essential elements of naturalism at home since remote times, and that the ancients and moderns already knew the sovereign law of adjusting the fictions of art to the reality of Nature and the Soul, representing things and persons, characters and places as God has made them. The only novelty was in the exaltation of the principle, and in a certain depreciation of the imaginative resources of an expansive and fanciful psychology."[4]

The most significant statement that Galdós made on the subject of realism is somewhat oblique since it involves social ideas as well. Picking up the topic of his 1870 article, "Observaciones sobre la Novela Contemporánea en España," in which he had urged that the novel concern itself with urban life and the middle class, Galdós offered a discussion of contemporary society as novelistic material in his long deferred speech of installation in the Royal Academy of the Language, which took place in 1896.[5] Primarily this speech is a plea directed at his ultraconservative colleagues to be hospitable to the new materials of literature and to accept the inevitability of social change that underlies them. In effect, he says that the day of classicism is over, its taste for generic types being replaced by accurate observation and depiction of the individual: "With the breakdown of categories masks fall at one blow and faces appear in their true purity. Types are lost, but man is better revealed to us, and Art is directed solely to giving to imaginary beings a life that is more human than social." This tactful depreciation of classical models and gentle advocacy of the new observed individual materials adequately sum up what in fact Galdós did in his contemporary novels and indicates the source of his particular artistic interest—the changing forms of the society around him.

These changes are the very substance of Galdós's depiction of Spanish life, and the incidental commentary occurring in the novels is scarcely necessary. In Chapter 6 of *Fortunata y Jacinta* the narrator digresses to comment on the new society:

> It is curious to observe how our ego, unfortunate in respect to other ideas, offers us a happy confusion of classes, or, better, the concord and reconciliation of all of them. In this, our country has an advantage over others, where decision is still pending in their grave historical suits for equality. Here the problem has been resolved simply and peacefully, thanks to the democratic cast of mind of the Spanish and the lack of vigor in those of noble pretensions. A great national weakness, a mania for official employment, also has its part in this great conquest. . . . Insensibly, with the aid of the bureaucracy, of poverty, and of the academic education that all Spaniards receive, all classes have been penetrating each other, and their members go from one to the other, weaving a thick fabric which ties and contains the national body.

The salient fictional example of the breaking down of class barriers is Torquemada, who underwent a transformation that could only take place "in this second half of the nineteenth century, which has almost made a religion of the decorous materiality of existence."

It seems clear that Galdós is a determinist, and that material causality plays a major role in his understanding of events. Sometimes his characters give voice to what can be called philosophical ideas, which though not properly ascribable to Galdós, are not out of harmony with his beliefs. Amparo, reflecting on the events through which she has lived in *Tormento,* concludes that "we do not make our lives, but it is life that makes us. . . ." Several of the characters pick up the popular Darwinian metaphor. To Isidora is ascribed the phrase, "the struggle for existence, law of laws," which is echoed in *El*

Doctor Centeno by Cienfuegos' advice to Celipín, "Chico, the struggle for existence is the most cruel of laws." This conception extends beyond material struggle. Amparo and Refugio are badly treated by Rosalía de Bringas, who by reason of her limited intelligence and perverse moral upbringing, in spite of her varnish of urbanity, gives evidence that "the struggle for existence is here more rude than elsewhere. . . ."

Remarks such as these are only a straw in the wind, at best giving only a hint of philosophical tonality to these works. As we range through the contemporary novels, however, we are struck by the consistency with which Galdós shows men and women adapting and surviving, or failing to adapt and being destroyed. Once we accept two background premises, that the material forces of existence are ineluctable and that change is the law of life, we can see how all of the novels and, more exactly, all of the characters who are presented in depth in the novels are case studies from which we may derive a general conclusion about the nature of experience. This fact becomes the key to Galdós's plots, which are characteristically studies in social transformation, or its failure. This is why Galdós's plots rarely are neatly tied up; by definition a character is capable of continuous change, unless, of course, the action is carried on until his death. This is why both the physical background of the city and the fluctuations of social-historical events have a primary place in these narratives. They are facts of life that both echo and impel the transformations of human beings. This is why, on the whole, the novels are not ironical. The ironist implies or emphasizes a violation of natural order and expectation. Galdós accepts change, and accepts it without the superior air of the man who somehow rides above it.

As might be expected, the novels vary considerably in the amount of transformation shown, but its presence (or absence) is implicit in all of them. On the one hand, there is a gallery of personalities more or less bound by rigid attitudes and conceptions; they misunderstand the conditions of their existence and they grossly miscalculate the strategy necessary for survival.

Bueno de Guzmán, for example, embraces two stereotypes, that of the prudent English man of affairs and that of the libertine. Both stereotypes collapse under the impact of experience, and he is left without a viable basis for existence. His three adversaries, Eloisa, María Juana, and Camila, vary in their vitality and adaptability; it is Camila and her husband, the rough-hewn Constantino Miquis, who exemplify true human promise. The succeeding novels are full of examples of this capacity for transformation. The boy Centeno keeps going by his goodness of heart as well as by his guttersnipe wit. Amparo and Refugio Emperador, Agustín Caballero, even Rosalía de Bringas and Milagros de Tellería, all refuse to be contained in conventional forms.

The best demonstration of all, because it is the most extended, occurs in *Fortunata y Jacinta* and in the Torquemada series. Constant ability to adapt is what gives unforgettable life to Fortunata, who actually undergoes a symbolic rebirth by means of her five-month immersion in the Convent of the Micaelas. Born of the people, she is obsessed by a desire somehow to be recognized as the equal of the well-born and chaste Jacinta, succeeding vicariously through the agency of her second child. Doña Guillermina is a wonderful example of transformation, one of the most memorable in all of Galdós's works. Not only is she herself a fluid character, but through her energy she transforms those around her, and in the material world she literally makes bricks without straw. We must also not overlook the three Rubín brothers. Who would expect Juan Pablo to become governor of a province, even a third-rate one? Who would dare prophesy that the sickly Maximiliano (impotent, says Gullón) would aspire to Fortunata and would survive the lacerating experience of being her husband?

The great, the cumulative, demonstration is the figure of Francisco de Torquemada, in whose being this conception is given the most complete development, though we must not forget Benina in *Misericordia*, who is a kind of foil for him in her selflessness and steadfastness growing out of her ability to "plant herself firmly in reality." Torquemada figures in the background of many of the early novels as a usurer, a vulgar spider who catches the impecunious in his web and acts as the grand marshal of a host of moneylenders like Doña Lupe. It is her dying wish that Torquemada undertake to succor the Aguila family, nobles who have sunk to the point of destitution. Cruz, the dynamic member of the family, finds him not unmalleable, seeing in him the principle of energy lacking in her own brother, and leads and coerces him until he becomes a man of great affairs, a senator, and a nobleman. He is completely assimilated to the pattern of magnificence, though he is never taken in by the external trappings of his success or the spurious values to which he seems to assimilate. (When in a moment of intellectual insecurity he asks his sister-in-law what realism is, he wisely does not stay for an answer.) Cruz's brother Rafael, who is caught in the vise of caste and rigid social and moral conceptions, prefers suicide to dishonor, but just before his death he admits to Torquemada that all of his beliefs have been mistaken, and he praises his brother-in-law for his ability to adapt to the new social forms. Torquemada is supremely conscious of the *reality of things,* and he quizzically utters his own epitaph to a group of friends: "I have a great inclination for the real, for the true, I am realism par excellence!"

These novels of Galdós are thus *realism par excellence,* though it is difficult to determine what sets them apart from those of other writers in other countries. There may well be something in the repeated insistence of the Spanish that they did not need to import realism because they had always had it, that it was part of their heritage since the *Quijote.* But there is more to it than that. Perhaps it is a quality of relaxation present in these works we have been discussing. The novels do not strain toward demonstration; they take the gap between illusion and reality in stride; they are not eager to shock, to condemn, or even to make fun of human imperfection. Above all, in their geniality they convey the warmth of life even in the most grim and painful circumstances. Galdós is no pessimist; that is plain.

Though the historical background on which these works rest is chaotic, even premonitory of social dissolution, the characters live under no darker shadow than comes from the storm clouds of any time and place. They experience suffering, death, crime, and folly. Social and personal imperfections are glaring enough, since this is a world inhabited by human beings. But these weaknesses are balanced by energy, gusto, humor, compassion, and even sustaining illusion, which give proportion and perspective to the universal experience of living. There is unexpectedness and incongruity in the life shown, just as there is in the manner of showing—something echoed even by the cadences and patterns of the speech itself. Galdós acknowledges the dark forces that constrict and deform human destiny but he vividly proves that they have only a partial dominion. For him rigid doctrines of literary realism and of deterministic philosophy are only partial truths, which must be ignored if they get in the way of a full and truthful representation of what it is to be a human being.

Galdós completes the roll of the realistic giants of the nineteenth century. He and the six others whom we have been discussing do not constitute the full range of European realism during that century, but they are its chief shapers and their works are representative of the variety and abundance of the mode. A full spectrum of nineteenth-century realists would include at least Eça de Queirós, Giovanni Verga, Maxim Gorky, Henrik Ibsen, August Strindberg, and Gerhardt Hauptmann, not to mention writers in English such as William Dean Howells, George Moore, and Arnold Bennett, and at the beginning of the twentieth century, Somerset Maugham and Theodore Dreiser, though each of these later figures derives to some extent from the European masters. The collective body of their writing is both astonishingly homogeneous and predictably various. As Horace Gregory has commented: "The realistic novel, as we have known it, is of protean shapes; it is of many tongues and of many varieties, depths and colors. . . . The mask that realism wears is international and yet the hidden limitations of the realistic novel are regional. The best and most far-reaching examples of its art depend upon an intimate awareness to a particular environment; the particulars of human behavior present their immediate problems to the author and reader alike, for both must feel the external truth of what is being said and done."[6]

The works of the seven writers under discussion illuminate the main interests and accomplishments of realism and give a sufficient indication of the difficulties that lay in the way of representing reality with fidelity and minimal distortion. In these writers we see the emphasis on contemporary life in its average activities and the avoidance of the special case, be it exotic or pathological. There are assuredly subjects that they did not turn to, or that they glanced at only in passing, but the force of their general preemption of the public domain was such as to open the door to all subject matter. Their example is primarily one of external representation, but not entirely. Even leaving out of account the fecund but not altogether realistic influence of Dostoevsky, the realists moved toward a recognition of the importance of inner states, of an interplay between social fact and individual feeling, as is particularly evident in the works of Chekhov and Galdós. On the whole, this group of writers established the idea of authorial withdrawal, even when they violated it in various subtle ways. The self-subsistence of their work has become a prime doctrine, one that has influenced works which are not in their basic orientation what we would call realistic. There is an aesthetic challenge in letting a work speak for itself without the mediation of the author; there may even be a certain authorial satisfaction in subordination to things.

On the whole, these writers moved toward a dramatic scenic presentation as the logical outcome of such subordination. They attempted to avoid trite and conventional plots, or any plots at all. Though none of them went so far as to present a slice of life without beginning or end, unless it be Chekhov in a few of his stories, there was an increasing awareness that neatly tied-up actions fall short of the realist ideal. These authors were very much aware of the loaded nature of literary analogues and largely avoided them. When they used myth and symbol, we are inclined to say that they fell short of, or went beyond, realism. They used traditional metaphor sparingly, but they did create what we might call a Darwinian body of metaphor that they considered apposite to the reduced stature of man, and thereby they may have tipped the scales away from objectivity. With them language became an instrument that was to be as little evident, and therefore as little distorting as possible, not something to be played with for virtuoso effects.

From the many casual or formal critical remarks of these authors cited earlier, it is clear that they were very much aware that there was a literary movement called realism and that they participated in it. They were, for the most part, conscious of each other's example, even when they denied its validity or violently repudiated it. With the partial exception of Dostoevsky, they support the statement of Jaime Domenech that realism "presupposes a subordination of creative activity of the artist to the images and data of the external world."[7] Theirs is, ideally, the role of impartial witness, of neutral spectator. Whereas traditional critics, notably Sir Philip Sidney in *The Defense of Poesie,* consider the use of nature to be a means to art, the realists, we might say, seek to use art as a way to the reproduction of nature. In other words, traditional art permitted a judicious infusion of the data of actuality in order to give body and a degree of verisimilitude to the work of art without seeking accurate representation as an end in itself. The realists were committed to such accuracy of representation as their primary goal, but, despite charges of naïveté that have been made against them, they were subtle enough to recognize that a degree of art—an inconspicuous but nonetheless pervasive presence—was necessary if they were to produce the illusion they sought. Theirs was a new, if imperfectly articulated, aesthetic, defining a basically new literary mode. It engaged the attention, if not the complete allegiance, of two or three generations of the most forceful and original writers in Europe. Fortunately it did not succeed in establishing itself with the exclusivity that it asserted polemically to be necessary for man and art alike.

A swing away from realism was both predictable and healthful. In the terms that Zola employed in a conversation with Edmond de Goncourt in the summer of 1870, there was nothing left for the young to do in the area worked over by their elders. For the sake of their own self-respect as creative beings, they had to set off in new directions. This was largely the point of the answers received by Jules Huret, the enterprising journalist who in 1890 took the pulse of French literary opinion about naturalism, asking two questions: Is naturalism dead? and What will come after it? Except for Paul Alexis's famous telegram: "Naturalism not dead. Letter follows." there was a fair agreement that the movement was over and no agreement whatever as to what new paths would or should be followed.

Edmond de Goncourt agreed that the movement would be dead by 1900—of natural causes, not by poisoning from its own products. But he found the examples of a new literature that was then current to be trivial and not to be compared with the monumental works of his generation. Zola agreed without rancor that the demise of naturalism was possible: "The future will belong to those who will get hold of the soul of modern society, who, freeing themselves from theories that are too rigorous, will allow a more logical, a more compassionate acceptance of life. I believe in a broader and more complex depiction of truth, in a wider opening upon humanity, in a kind of classicism of naturalism."[8] J.-K. Huysmans, who had already deserted the movement, expressed the general dissatisfaction with the most point: "Everything has been done, everything there was to do in the way of the new and typical in the genre. Oh, I am well aware that it could go on to the end of time: it would be possible to take the seven deadly sins and their derivatives one by one, all the professions listed in *Bottin* [the

French business directory], all the diseases found in the hospital! Masturbation has already been treated; Belgium has given us the novel on syphilis. Yes, I think that in the domain of pure observation we may very well stop there!" Disdaining the adultery of the neighborhood grocery woman and the corner wine merchant as a subject, Huysmans expresses a desire to seek out "rare and enormous exceptions."[9]

By the end of the nineteenth century most writers had begun to resent the self-denying ordinances on which realism is based. They wanted to be *seers* as well as *makers*. They wanted to be known for their unique vision. They wanted to a considerable extent to do what Flaubert had forbidden: they wanted to *write themselves*. They wanted to engage in fantasy on the one hand, and they wanted to be heard as defenders or attackers in the actual world on the other. Perhaps what they found most galling was to be confined to the dull precincts of reportorial language. They wanted to exercise verbal ingenuity, to engage in verbal pyrotechnics, and to commit themselves to the personal signature of an individual style. They wanted, in short, to be seen and to be heard, to have identity as artists, not to be conduits through which, somehow, the stuff of novels flowed.

It does not seem that recognition of the limits of realism constitutes an indictment of the mode itself. All ways of writing have their limitations; all fall into stereotyped statement and method after a time and need to be replaced. Healthy as was the influence of the realists in bringing the literature of their time back into touch with material and psychological actuality, their complete and permanent domination would have been a disaster. Nonetheless, when the current self-absorbed exploration of private states begins to pall at the end of the twentieth century, in its turn having fallen into stereotype and unintelligibility, the great realists of the nineteenth century will still be there in their imposing veracity to remind us of a public world and being. Their relevance today is greater than their detractors are willing to admit. This relevance rests, to be sure, on certain assumptions that not everyone is willing to accept, on a basic constancy of human nature and human experience, on the presence of order beneath phenomenal chaos, and on the accessibility of that order by means of orderly processes of analysis. As Zola foresaw, these works are imposing by their mass, by their inclusiveness, and by their assurance that what they show is indeed the way things are.

Notes

CHAPTER 1: Precursors

[1] George J. Becker, *Documents of Modern Literary Realism* (Princeton, N.J.: Princeton University Press, 1963).

[2] Karl Bleibtreu, *Revolution der Literatur* (Leipzig: 1886) p. 30.

[3] See Becker, *Documents,* p. 201.

[4] E. M. de Vogüé, *Le Roman Russe* (Paris: 1886); see Becker, *Documents,* pp. 315–16.

[5] Mary Colum, *From These Roots* (New York: Scribner, 1937), p. 223.

[6] Gamaliel Bradford, "Mid-Nineteenth Century Realism," *Reader* 8 (September 1906): 452.

[7] Charles F. Richardson, "The Moral Purpose of the Later American Novel," *Andover Review* 3 (April 1885): 315.

[8] Joseph Warren Beach, *American Fiction 1920–1940* (New York: Macmillan, 1941), p. 4.

[9] W. L. Courtney, *Old Saws and Modern Instances* (London: Chapman and Hall, 1919), p. 189.

[10] E. Preston Dargan and Bernard Weinberg, *The Evolution of Balzac's Comédie Humaine* (Chicago: University of Chicago Press, 1942), p. 89.

[11] Edgar H. Lehrman, *Turgenev's Letters* (New York: Knopf, 1961), p. 286.

[12] *Ibid.,* p. 281.

[13] Ibid., p. 352.

[14] Ibid., p. 300.

CHAPTER 2: Gustave Flaubert

[1] Compare the comment of Alison Fairlie (*Flaubert: Madame Bovary* [London: Edward Arnold Ltd., 1962], p. 11) that "Before Flaubert, both Balzac and Stendhal had turned to the rich triviality of contemporary life. But their central characters are still outstanding individuals, whether in intelli-

gence, sensitivity, villainy or sheer force of resistance, and they usually lead eventful lives, forging their way upwards with relentless persistence or meeting a downfall paradoxically satisfying in the very intensity of its drama. Flaubert allows us no such outlet."

[2] These remarks appeared in an article in *Le Moniteur* for December 22, 1862. They are reprinted in Flaubert, *Oeuvres,* Bibliothèque de la Pléiade vol. 1 (Paris: Gallimard, 1951), p. 737.

[3] Ibid., p. 1031.

[4] Ibid., p. 1037.

CHAPTER 3: The Goncourts

[1] Pierre Sabatier, *Germinie Lacerteux des Goncourt,* in Les Grands Evénements Littéraires series (Paris: SFELT, 1948), p. 19.

[2] Compare a letter of Chekhov to D. V. Grigorovich in 1887: "I remember, two or three years ago, reading a French story (I do not remember the author's name; the title, I think, is 'Chérie') in which the author, while describing a minister's daughter and probably without being aware of it, gave a true clinical picture of hysteria."

[3] See Dr. Jean Durand, *L'Observation et la Documentation Médicale dans les Romans des Goncourt* (Bordeaux: 1921).

[4] Sabatier, *Germinie Lacerteux,*
pp. 27–28.

[5] Ibid., p. 7.

[6] Ibid., p. 89.

[7] Quoted in ibid., pp. 120–21.

[8] Robert Ricatte, *La Genèse de "La Fille Elisa"* (Paris: Presses Universitaires de France, 1960).

[9] William Busnach, founder of the Athénée Theater, adapted Zola's novels for the stage.

[10] Sabatier, *Germinie Lacerteux,* pp. 321–22.

[11] Paul Bourget, *Nouveaux Essais de Psychologie Contemporaine* (Paris: 1886), p. 137. We must bear in mind that this entire volume is an oblique attack on Zola and his school and that praise of the Goncourts and Turgenev, for example, is one way of depreciating Zola.

CHAPTER 4: Emile Zola

[1] Gabriel Reuillard, "Zola Assassiné?," *Le Monde,* June 1,
1954; p. 8.

[2] Armand Lamoux, "Emile Zola,

280

Père du Roman Américain Moderne," *Carrefour*, October 10, 1952.

³ Emile Zola, *Correspondance (1858–1871)*. Volume 48 of *Les Oeuvres Complètes d'Emile Zola*, (Paris: Edition Eugène Fasquelle), pp. 248–57.

⁴ Ricardo Baeza, *Centenario de Emile Zola (1840–1902)* (Buenos Aires: 1940), p. 33.

⁵ See Ambrose Macrobe, *La Flore Pornographique, Glossaire de l'Ecole Naturaliste Ex-*

trait des Oeuvres de M. Emile Zola et de ses Disciples (Paris: Doubleelzevir, 1883).

⁶ J.-K. Huysmans, "Emile Zola and L'Assommoir," 1876; see George J. Becker, *Documents of Modern Literary Realism* (Princeton, N.J.: Princeton University Press, 1963), pp. 232–33.

⁷ Emile Zola, *Correspondance (1872–1902)*, pp. 633–34. (Volume 49 of *Les Oeuvres Complètes*, Edition Fasquelle.)

CHAPTER 5: Leo Tolstoy

¹ See the introduction to *La Guerre et La Paix*, Bibliothèque de la Pléiade (Paris: Gallimard, 1952), p. xviii. In his essay, "A Few Words regarding War and Peace," in that volume, pp. 1611–12, Tolstoy notes that some readers have complained that the nature of the times was insufficiently shown. He retorts that what they are looking for is the horrors of serfdom, the sequestration of women, the beating of grown-up sons, and popular uprisings. "But these traits which live in our imagination I do not consider faithful, and I have not thought it necessary to represent them. In studying letters, memoirs, traditions, I have not found all these hor-

rors to be any greater than those I can encounter now, as in any era."

² E. M. de Vogüé, *Le Roman Russe*, (Paris: Plon, 1886), p. 285: "This book marks a date in literature: the definitive break of Russian poetics with Byronism and romanticism in the very heart of their citadel. ..."

³ Percy Lubbock, *The Craft of Fiction* (New York: Scribner, 1921), pp. 40ff.

⁴ E. M. de Vogüé, *Le Roman Russe*, p. 315, protests that no reader would voluntarily undergo the fruitless fatigue of wading through the second epilogue and complains that Tolstoy feels obliged to offer abstract reasoning about ideas

that his characters convey much more clearly to our eyes and ears by their actions and speech.

5 One of the significant things about the Anna-Vronsky liaison is that it attempts to reproduce the forms of marriage without the sense of family responsibility that is the spirit of true marriage.

6 In *The Critic* 36 (April 1900): 355–56, a reviewer stated of this novel: "The descriptions are Zolaesque in their faithfulness. The difference is that Zola writes for the sake of the description, Tolstoy writes to reform. His book is a tract. We walk through mud, but the mud does not cling."

7 Maxim Gorky, *Reminiscences of Tolstoy, Chekhov, and Andreyev* (New York: Huebsch, 1920), p. 62.

CHAPTER 6: Fyodor Dostoevsky

1 J. Van der Eng, in *Dostoevskij Romancier,* (The Hague: Mouton & Co., 1957), pp. 44–45, cites the phrases by which critics have tried to cope with this difference: "réalisme mystique," "symbolisme réaliste," "réalisme transcendental ou symbolique," "réalisme d'un épileptique," "réalisme démoniaque," "réalisme fantastique," "réalisme du dernier dégré," "réalisme allégorique," "réalisme psychologique."

2 Years later, speaking in his own person in "The Peasant Marei," Dostoevsky comments: "Perhaps it will be noticed that even to this day [1876] I have scarcely once spoken in print of my life in prison. *The House of the Dead* I wrote fifteen years ago in the character of an imaginary person. . . ."

3 Ralph E. Matlaw, *The Brothers Karamazov Novelistic Technique* (The Hague: Mouton & Co., 1957), p. 5.

4 Sigmund Freud, "Modern Evidence: Dostoevsky and Parricide," *Partisan Review* 12 (Fall 1945): 530–44.

5 In the notebooks to *Crime and Punishment* there is an entry indicating the novelist's intention to have Svidrigailov talk at length to Raskolnikov about his life of debauchery, stopping at nothing and taking sensual pleasure in the telling. Then the novelist catches himself up with the observation that it is "impossible to recount that."

CHAPTER 7: Anton Chekhov

[1] All excerpts from Chekhov's letters are taken from Louis S. Friedland, ed., *Letters on the Short Story, the Drama, and Other Literary Topics*, (New York: Benjamin Blom, 1964).
[2] On one occasion, apropos of Ibsen's *The Wild Duck*, Chekhov declared: "Look here, Ibsen does not know life. In life it does not happen like that." See S. S. Koteliansky, ed., *Anton Tchekov Literary and*

Theatrical Reminiscences (New York: Benjamin Blom, 1965), p. 161.
[3] Maxim Gorky, *Reminiscences of Tolstoy, Chekhov, and Andreyev* (New York: Huebsch, 1920), pp. 97–99.
[4] Quoted in I. C. Chertok and Jean Gardner, eds., *Late Blooming Flowers and Other Stories* (New York: McGraw Hill, 1964), p. xx.

CHAPTER 8: Benito Pérez Galdós

[1] Ricardo Gullón, *Galdós, Novelista Moderno* (Madrid: Taurus, 1960).
[2] However, we should not ignore a statement made by Galdós in the special preface to the 1913 edition of *Misericordia*, reprinted in W. H. Shoemaker, ed., *Los Prólogos de Galdós* (Champaign: University of Illinois Press, 1962), p. 108. In this he recalls that years earlier he had visited the Whitechapel and Minories slums of London and that in preparing to write *Misericordia* he had spent months in direct observation of the miserable slums in the southern part of Madrid.
[3] Gullón, *Galdós*, p. 139, quotes an interesting comment by Galdós on the position of the nar-

rator: "He who composes a piece and gives it poetic life, in the novel and in the theatre, is always present; present in lyrical outbursts, present in passionate or analytical narration; present in the theatre itself. His imagination is the indispensable agent by means of which imagined beings that imitate the palpitancy of life can enter into the artistic mold." This should be compared with the remarks in the introduction to *El Abuelo*.
[4] "Leopoldo Alas," *Obras Completas*, vol. 6 (Madrid: Aguilar, 1961), 1447–48.
[5] For the text of this speech see George J. Becker, *Documents of Modern Literary Realism* (Princeton, N.J.: Princeton Uni-

versity Press, 1963), pp. 148–
53.

6 Horace Gregory, "George
Moore and Regionalism in Re-
alistic Fiction," *The Dying
Gladiator and Other Essays*
(New York: Grove Press,
1961), p. 127.

7 *Las Formas del Ideal Artístico*
(Madrid: J. M. Yagües, 1932),
p. 55.

8 Jules Hureb, *Enquête sur L'Evolution Littéraire* (Paris: Charpentier, 1891), p. 173.

9 Ibid., pp. 177–79.

Bibliographical Note

A. General: The following are the most useful general treatments of modern literary realism:

Auerbach, Erich. *Mimesis, the Representation of Reality in Western Literature.* Princeton, N.J.: Princeton University Press, 1953.

Becker, George J. *Documents of Modern Literary Realism.* Princeton, N.J.: Princeton University Press, 1963.

———. *Realism in Modern Literature.* New York: Ungar, 1980.

Bonet, Carmelo M. *El Realismo Literario.* Buenos Aires: Editorial Nova, 1958.

Bornecque, J.H., and Pierre Cogny. *Réalisme et Naturalisme. L'Histoire, la Doctrine, les Oeuvres.* Paris: Hachette, 1958.

Brinkmann, Richard. *Wirklichkeit und Illusion: Studien über Gehalt und Grenzen des Begriffs Realismus für die Erzählende Dichtung des Neunzehnten Jahrhunderts.* Tübingen: Niemeyer, 1957.

Colum, Mary. *From These Roots.* New York: Scribner, 1937.

Levin, Harry. *The Gates of Horn.* New York: Oxford University Press, 1963.

McDowall, Arthur. *Realism: A Study in Art and Thought.* London: Constable, 1918.

Snow, C. P. *The Realists: Eight Portraits.* New York: Scribner, 1978.

B. Nineteenth-Century Authors:

For the authors examined in this volume accessibility of their works and adequacy of translation are the primary considerations. It seems best not to list works of criticism, since they tend to ignore realistic elements in favor of what is peripheral to, or beyond, realism.

1. Balzac:
   La Comédie Humaine, in ten volumes, Bibliothèque de la Pléiade. Paris: Gallimard, 1950–56.
   The Comédie Humaine. Edited by George Saintsbury, in forty volumes. London: J. M. Dent & Co., 1895–98.

2. Stendhal:
   Oeuvres, in three volumes, Bibliothèque de la Pléiade. Paris: Gallimard, 1956.
   The Works of Stendhal, in six volumes. Translated by C. E. Scott Moncrieff. New York: Boni & Liveright, 1925–28.

3. Gogol:
   Sobranie Sochinenii, in six volumes. Moscow: 1950.
   The Works of Nikolay Gogol, in six volumes. Translated by Constance Garnett. London: Chatto & Windus, 1922–28.

4. Turgenev:
   Sobranie Sochinenii, in eleven volumes, Moscow: 1949.
   The Novels of Ivan Turgenev, in seventeen volumes. Translated by Constance Garnett. London: Heinemann, 1919–23.

5. Flaubert:
   Oeuvres, in two volumes, Bibliothèque de la Pléiade. Paris: Gallimard, 1951–52. There is no English edition of the works. The Eleanor Marx-Aveling translation of *Madame Bovary* has been superseded by that of Francis Steegmuller. New York: Modern Library, 1957.
   Correspondance, in nine volumes. Paris: Conard, 1926–33. In English there is *Selected Letters.* Translated and edited by Francis Steegmuller. New York: Farrar, Straus, 1954. This volume has now been superseded by Steegmuller's *The Letters of Gustave Flaubert, 1830–1857.* New York: Belknap, 1980. See also *Documents of Modern Literary Realism* for passages from the letters dealing with realism, pp. 90–96.

6. Edmond and Jules de Goncourt:
   There is no edition of their novels in French. The following are available in English: *Germinie,* New York: Greenwood, 1969;

Elisa, New York: H. Fertig, 1975; *Sister Philomène*, Fertig, 1975; *La Faustin*, Fertig, 1976.

The integral text of the *Journal* in twenty-two volumes, Paris: Fasquelle and Flammarion, 1956–58, supersedes the nine-volume edition published by Edmond de Goncourt in his lifetime and reissued by the Académie Goncourt as the "definitive" edition.

7. Zola:

> *Oeuvres Complètes. Texte de l'Edition Eugène Fasquelle, Notes et Commentaires de Maurice LeBlond*, in fifty volumes. Paris: 1927–29.
>
> *Les Rougon-Macquart*, in five volumes, Bibliothèque de la Pléiade. Paris: Gallimard, 1960.
>
> There is no English edition of Zola's complete works. Many of the individual Rougon-Macquart novels are available in translation.

8. Tolstoy:

> *Polnoe Sobranie Sochinenii*, in ninety volumes, Moscow: 1928–58.
>
> The three-volume edition in the Bibliothèque de la Pléiade (Paris: Gallimard, 1951, 1952, 1960) contains *War and Peace, Anna Karenina*, and *Resurrection* as well as the major short works of fiction.
>
> *Tolstoy Centenary Edition*, in twenty-one volumes. Translated by Louise and Aylmer Maude. London: Oxford University Press for the Tolstoy Society, 1929.
>
> *The Library Edition* of the novels of Leo Tolstoy, in six volumes. Translated by Constance Garnett. London: Heinemann, 1901–04. This translation has been used for the Modern Library editions of *War and Peace* and *Anna Karenina*.
>
> *The Short Novels of Tolstoy*, edited by Philip Rahv (New York: Dial, 1946) uses the Maude translation.

9. Dostoevsky:

> *Sobranie Sochinenii*, in ten volumes, Moscow: 1956–58.
>
> The five-volume edition in the Bibliothèque de la Pléiade (Paris: Gallimard, 1950–56) contains material from the notebooks for the major novels as well as the five novels themselves.

The Novels of Dostoevsky, in twelve volumes. Translated by Constance Garnett. London: Macmillan, new edition, 1949–50. This translation is used for the Modern Library editions of the major novels and also for *The Short Novels of Dostoevsky.* New York: Dial, 1945.

The Diary of a Writer, in two volumes. Translated by Boris Brasol. New York: Octagon, 1973.

Chekhov:

Polnoe Sobranie Sochinenii i Pisem, in twenty volumes. Moscow: 1944–51.

The Tales of Chekhov, in thirteen volumes. Translated by Constance Garnett. London: Macmillan, 1916–23.

Friedland, Louis S., ed. *Letters on the Short Story, the Drama, and Other Literary Topics.* New York: Benjamin Blom, 1964.

Hingley, Ronald. *The Oxford Chekhov,* in nine volumes. London: Oxford University Press, 1964–78.

The Portable Chekhov. Translated by Avrahm Yarmolinsky. New York: Viking, 1947.

Yarmolinsky, Avrahm. *Letters of Anton Chekhov.* London: Cape, 1974.

In general, the titles of the stories listed in this chapter are those given them by Constance Garnett. Where a second title appears in parenthesis, that is the one used by Yarmolinsky in his popular collection.

Galdós:

Obras Completas, in six volumes. Madrid: Aguilar, 1958–63.

There has been no edition in English. The only novels available in translation from the *novelas contemporáneas* group are *The Disinherited Lady (La Desheredada),* New York: Exposition Press, 1957; *Misericordia,* New York: Dryden Press, 1946; *The Spendthrifts (La de Bringas),* New York: Farrar, Straus, 1952; *Torment (Tormento),* New York: Farrar, Straus, 1953.

Index